K

GOD'S TIME FRAME:

...ssence

of Prophecy

by

Rev. Harry D. Powell

OLD RUGGED CROSS PRESS

God's Time Frame: The Essence of Prophecy
Copyright © 1993, Rev. Harry D. Powell

ISBN - 1-882270-13-4

Library of Congress Cataloging in publication
93-85495

Editor: Old Rugged Cross Press,
1160 Alpharetta Street, Suite H
Roswell, GA 30075

———————————————

To all who have so constantly encouraged me in
this writing, and especially to my dear wife, Norma,
I dedicate this work. I trust that it will in truth
be for the glory and honor of our blessed
Lord and Saviour, Jesus Christ

———————————————

Table of Contents

LIST OF WORD STUDIES

Wilson, Williams, *Old Testament Word Studies*, (Kregel Publications, Grand Rapids, MI 49501)

Thayer, Joseph H., *Greek – English Lexicon of the New Testament*, (Zondervan Corporation, Grand Rapids, MI 49506)

Bullinger, Ethelbert W., *A Critical Lexicon and Concordance to the English and Greek New Testament*, (Zondervan Corporation, Grand Rapids, MI 49506)

Vine, W. E., *Vine's Expository Dictionary of New Testament Words*, (MacDonald Publishing Company, McLean, VA 22101)

LIST OF FIGURES

LIST OF CHARTS

ACKNOWLEDGMENTS

I wish to express my great thankfulness to the MONTAUK AVENUE BAPTIST CHURCH of New London, Connecticut, where I serve as Pastor, for the privilege that they have graciously granted me — to continue my writing with the use of the Church office and equipment. Their love and encouragement are so very greatly appreciated. May the Lord richly reward you all.

Also, I herewith express my great appreciation for the help and counsel given to me by my friend and fellow author, Mrs. Joanne Karpacs, who so painstakingly read and edited my manuscript. She has been a very real encouragement, and I praise the Lord for her patient, practical help. I am grateful to my son, Harry III, for his help with the artwork of Nebuchadnezzar's Dream. And, thanks to my brother, David, for his help in the final draft of my manuscript. Each of us give all the glory to the Lord.

PREFACE

Upon the completion of my schooling, my wife and I joined the South America Mission for mission work in South America. It was at the Mission Headquarters that we were introduced to the General Director, Dr. Joseph Davis. He introduced us to his book, *The Climax of the Bible.*

This book set my sails for the years that followed in my careful examination of the prophetic truth. Because, as a student for my ministerial preparation, I began to search the Scriptures. I found things in prophetic teaching that simply did not appear to be truly compatible with the Scriptures themselves.

This present work, therefore, is the outcome of the past thirty-five years of study and teaching the prophetic Scriptures. I have read many authors and views; have seen numerous contradictions; and found real confusion expressed by various writers on the subject.

There has been much said and written concerning Bible prophecy. Indeed, any number of books are available at Christian bookstores on this subject. However, it does not take long, as one browses through them, to see that the waters of Bible prophecy are quite muddied. There is such a diversity of understanding and of opinions expressed on this subject, that it seems an oddity in itself. Certainly, prophecy is God speaking to us concerning His plan and purpose. He is sharing with us that which he is doing and purposes to do. He wants us to know! He wants to encourage us and to forewarn us to be constrained to holy living through our knowledge of His purpose.

Somewhere along the line, apparently, His message is not getting through with the same clarity that was intended when given by our Lord. We need to realize anew that: (1) God always means what He says, and (2) that God always says what He means. Let us learn to simply take God at His word and to stop putting words into His mouth. My desire in the writing of this book is not to add to the muddy water, but to filter out some of those things which are not strictly Scriptural and, thus, to clear up our prophetic vision.

It is important at the outset to know that we can have no correct knowledge of Spiritual truth except through faith, and faith is simply and sincerely to believe God. To just believe what God has said, that is faith! Many people believe in God, but few there be who *believe*

God, truly believing what He has said.

This study will proceed through several prophetic portions of the Scriptures to get a clear, concise view of the glorious story that God is sharing with mankind, and in which you and I are the actors. As we go step by step, and our understanding confirms each prophetic Scriptural truth; we will continually build our understanding until the structure begins to take its beautiful shape in God's perfect symmetry. I am sure that Christians will thrill at the perfect harmony of these prophetic pictures.

Do not play hopscotch with God's Word, jumping over words that are given to us full of meaning. Each word is a part of the puzzle and each has its own place in the entire picture. It is painted with the prophetic paint brush held in the Master's hand. Though, like the pieces of any puzzle, these must not be forced into position, for then the picture is ruined. If force is needed, it is the wrong place. So let us not twist and carve and shape prophetic truth to our liking. Not try to make it fit into our mold. View the picture of prehistory just as God gives it to us, and know by faith that it will be confirmed as an historical event at the time of its fulfillment.

Now, lest this seems to appear overly dogmatic, consider this wise saying: "No prophecy of the Scriptures can be fully understood except in the light of its fulfillment." It is a simple truth that God does not give us all of the answers to all of our questions. He is not interested in satisfying our curiosity, but in establishing our faith. One of my favorite verses, upon which I constantly rely, is:

> *The secret things belong unto the Lord our God: but those things which are revealed belong unto us and to our children forever, that we may do all the words of this law.*
> (Deuteronomy 29:29.)

I trust that the following pages will be a blessing, and that the truth contained herein will enable the sincere Christians to have a practical, working knowledge of prophecy in these last days. All of the Scripture quoted in this work is from the authorized *King James Bible*. The words and phrases in capitals are my own emphasis, helping the reader identify quickly and easily the focus of truth.

I have been encouraged by a good number of Christians to share this study. Because of this encouragement, and my own sense of the necessity for clarity on these wonderful truths in this dark hour, I have endeavored to help the reader see clearly the realities that are related to God's prophetic time-frame! All of these things are about to be fulfilled. Your own understanding of these truths will greatly help you to stand strong against the evil of this hour.

Look up. Jesus is coming! But, oh the events that will fill these final hours. Will your faith weaken and fail, or will you be strengthened? Will you be of help, or in need of help? Will you be discouraged, despondent and confused; or will you rejoice with full confidence as the great events unfold and we hear the sound of the Trump of God?

What a magnificent day to be alive and living for Christ our Lord. It is my prayer and hope that this work will be a great help and encouragement to you in these days of darkness before the Day dawns.

ONE
Laying The
Foundation

This introductory chapter is of vital importance. Before serious study of the prophetic Scriptures can begin, a person must lay a solid foundation for the structure he will build with his Bible convictions. Like any construction, and so here, this foundation will largely determine whether the finished understanding can stand, and withstand, the storms of challenge that come from within the Church; as well as the corrosion of unbelief from the acid-rain of the godless, scoffing world.

So, before one builds a house of eschatology he must be sure that the foundation is well laid; that it is of the best materials and meets the strict demands of the building inspector — the Lord Himself. The foundation must not be built upon whim, reason, tradition, logic or custom. It certainly cannot be built upon man, upon what men may have said and taught, nor upon man's opinion. The only sure foundation to build convictions upon is the Lord, God, and His eternal WORD.

BIBLICAL AUTHORITY

As this basic truth is examined, consider first the term PROPHET.

It was prophets who were the men used by God to give us His Holy Word. Turning to the book of Exodus, the Lord clearly gives His view of what a prophet is and how the term should be understood. First look at Exodus 4:10-16:

> *And Moses said unto the Lord, O my Lord, I am not eloquent, neither heretofore, nor since thou hast spoken unto thy servant: but I am slow of speech, and of a slow tongue.*
>
> *And the Lord said unto him, Who hath made man's mouth? Or who maketh the dumb or deaf, or the seeing, or the blind? Have not I, the Lord?*
>
> *Now therefore go, and I WILL BE WITH THY MOUTH, AND TEACH THEE WHAT THOU SHALT SAY.*
>
> *And he said, O my Lord, send, I pray thee, by the hand of him whom thou wilt send. And the anger of the Lord was kindled against Moses, and he said, Is not Aaron the Levite thy brother? I know that he can speak well. And also, behold, he cometh forth to meet thee . . .*
>
> *And thou shalt speak unto him and PUT WORDS IN HIS MOUTH: AND I WILL BE WITH THY MOUTH, AND WITH HIS MOUTH, and will teach you what ye shall do.*
>
> *AND HE SHALL BE THY SPOKESMAN unto the people: And he shall be, even he shall be to thee in stead of a mouth, and thou shalt be to him instead of God.*

Notice that some of this quote is in capital letters. This method of emphasis is used so that the essence of what God was saying can easily and quickly be seen. An individual should clearly understand the term PROPHET within this context that God Himself gives.

First, please notice that over against Moses' objection to God's call upon his life, God had to remind him that He was the Creator of man, and the origin of all of man's abilities. That He, God, could and would control Moses' mouth. See, it was not Moses' mouth that was the problem; it was his heart! When God said that He would be with Moses' mouth, and that He would teach him what he should say, God is introducing the truth of:

REVELATION

Revelation is the fact of divine truth communicated by God directly to a man. Revelation is God's objective truth. This truth has its existence completely independent of the mind and emotions of man. It is truth or reality outside of and beyond human experience. Since revelation is this objective truth of God communicated by God directly to a man, man received it just as God gives it: truth for truth, word for word, and line upon line. It is truth unmixed with error. It is Truth in its purest form.

Next, God says that He will go even further. Moses was to then give this revelation to Aaron, his brother. God promised that He would be with Moses' mouth as truth was given by him to his brother. Thereby controlling the transfer of revealed truth from Moses to Aaron. Here God introduces the principle or doctrine of:

INSPIRATION

Inspiration is not the same as revelation, but it is closely related to it. Inspiration is when that same divine, objective truth, which has been received by revelation, is now communicated to another; be it written or spoken, in the same purity with which it was received from God. This is accomplished by the super-imposed influence and power of the Holy Spirit of God.

Inspiration is the communication of revelation, and is absolutely error free, under the providential guidance of Sovereign God. Then there is one step further of which God assures Moses and mankind.

The message of revelation had to get to the people for whom it was intended in the will of God. It was now to be Aaron's job to give that message to the people. Therefore, God told Moses that He, God would be with Aaron's mouth as well. This was to ensure that the words which Aaron spoke, in his communication of the revealed message, would be the very words of God as received by Moses from God Himself.

Thus, the people were to be assured that it was the very WORD OF GOD given to them. This last step was just as important as the first two, REVELATION and INSPIRATION. This last step in the process of the communication of God's divine, objective truth is the fact of:

PRESERVATION

Preservation is the work and promise of God that His truth would not fail, ever. It is because of this truth of preservation that today one can trust the Bible. It is because of the truth of preservation that the Bible is called and known to be THE WORD OF GOD.

The Bible is God's REVEALED truth, INSPIRED in its written form, and PRESERVED for you and me by God's own providential care and oversight. Consequently, thousands of years later, everyone can, with total confidence, trust this Holy Book as the infallible, inerrant Word of God. It is fully authoritative, as though God were Himself talking with us personally.

Without the doctrine of PRESERVATION, the truths of INSPIRATION and REVELATION fall to the ground as worthless relics of ancient history. The Bible would be untrustworthy and irrelevant to us in our day. It would leave us without a faithful guide in the spiritual darkness of this age of evil. It would leave us without hope. God speaks to us today through what He spoke to His prophets, having preserved that Word for us in our generation. So now look at the word:

PROPHET

Look at the connection between the text just examined in this search for understanding and the text of Exodus 7:1-12, where the term PROPHET is found.

> *And the Lord said unto Moses, See, I have made thee a god to Pharaoh: and AARON THY BROTHER SHALL BE THY PROPHET.*

> *Thou shalt speak all that I command thee: and Aaron thy brother shall speak unto Pharaoh, that he send the children of Israel out of his land.*

Here again we see God speaking to Moses (REVELATION), and Moses speaking to Aaron (INSPIRATION), and now Aaron speaks to Pharaoh (PRESERVATION). It was God's message. Yes, it was. Pure and straight. It was the WORD OF GOD.

Notice in this text that Aaron was called the prophet of Moses by God. He was to speak for Moses. He was Moses' mouthpiece. Aaron was not God's prophet, for he received not his message from God. He received the message of God from Moses. He was Moses' prophet. Here is seen the SCRIPTURAL understanding of the term PROPHET:

1. A Prophet of God is one who receives a revelation directly from God by the means of God's choice, be it a vision, a dream, or audibly.

2. A Prophet of God is one who communicates that above mentioned REVELATION by the means of INSPIRATION, as God's spokesman and under God's superimposed control.

This is the only Biblical meaning of the term PROPHET, and it should be your understanding as well. It should become one of your CONVICTIONS. A Prophet may have been a preacher, but a preacher is not a prophet. Be very careful of adding anything to God's description of His prophets. This will help to keep you free from deception by the many false prophets of this day.

Now concerning God's prophet, remember that he stands in God's stead as God's spokesman. He stands or speaks in the place of God as he relays the message. Clearly, it is the prophet speaking, but it is the Word of God which is being spoken; for he is speaking instead of God, and under God's control.

It might be good, here, to reread and compare the two Scriptures just looked at (Exodus 4:10–16 and Exodus 7:1–2). To let God refresh the understanding of, and enable the mind to grip the truth being given. The conclusion, consequently, is that because the prophet speaks in the place of God and under God's superimposed control, what he says is the very WORD OF GOD and carries with it:

DIVINE AUTHORITY

For an example of this truth, look at another text of Scripture:

For this cause also thank we God without ceasing,
because when ye received the Word of man, but as in
truth, the Word of God which ye heard of us, ye received

> *it not as the WORD OF GOD, which ineffectually worketh also in you that believe.*   (I Thessalonians 2:13.)

Is it not clear in this text that Paul, as a prophet of God, fully recognized that his message to the people of Thessalonica was the very Word of God? It is equally true that the Christians there received it also as the Word of God. It was not the vain word of mere man. He commended the believers there in that they received, by faith, the message as from God Himself.

We also see that the Holy Spirit, in Acts 17:10–12, witnesses to the "nobility" of the Berean Christians because they, in recognition of the divine authority of the Holy Scriptures (the writings of the Prophets), used them as a standard, or canon, by which to determine the truthfulness of Paul's message. They knew that God could not deny Himself by contradicting Himself.

It would be wonderful if Christians today could be as "noble" as these were. Realize that the only way to correctly measure the truthfulness and reliability of teaching today is by making a very careful study of Scripture. Learn to compare all teaching to the CANON of the Word of God. Far too many Christians simply accept what is taught; and their standard of truth is their trust in the speaker, or scholarship, or tradition, or even personal preference and opinion.

It is a fact that most Christians are unskilled in the Scriptures. Many have not even read the Bible through one time. They are unable to use the Bible to test the teachings they hear. It is not that one must have a formal Bible education in a school of higher learning, but one MUST be an earnest, honest, diligent student of the Word. The Holy Spirit is our Teacher and:

> . . . *he shall teach you all things* . . . (John 14:26)
>
> . . . *he will guide you into all truth* . . . (John 16:13)
>
> *He that believeth on the Son of God hath the witness in himself* . . . (I John 5:10)

The Holy Spirit will not only teach us the Scriptures, but He will teach us how to use the Scriptures. This learning comes through practice. There is no instant shortcut to Bible knowledge.

What is the importance of this teaching of the authority of the Scriptures? Simply put, it means that what God says, what God has revealed to His prophets, is TRUE— count on it. If God said that such and such will be, then it will be. It will, in fact, be just as God has said.

As a dear friend of mine, Martin Bosco, has wisely said, "I know how it is all going to turn out, because I have read the last chapter in the Book." Praise God for faith like that. Believing in the authority of the prophetic Scriptures gives encouragement in the darkness of the hour, the present period of history. Because, Scripture tells how it is all going to turn out. Believers can be on the victory side.

Many people are terrified thinking about World War III with its nuclear exchange, and that it will mean *the end of the world*. You do not need to fear that! How can one be so sure? Read the last chapter of The Book. We ought to be very thankful for the authority of Scripture, and this includes the prophetic Scriptures, because it assures us that God is in control. He knows the end from the beginning, and one thing is certain, God is never going to be taken by surprise. He is in control!

SIGNS

We are not left to guess about His authority and the authenticity of this divine message because, together with the message, God always gave proof that it was from Him. He did not, nor does He now, ask His people to believe in blind faith. Notice, if you will:

And thou shalt take this rod in thine hand, wherewith
thou shalt do SIGNS. (Exodus 4:17.)

This rod was Moses' staff, which, under God's order, he had cast to the ground. It had become a snake; see verses 2-5. Then God told him to pick it up by the tail. When he did, it became a rod again. This rod was, from that time on, the rod of God. It was used by Moses as God directed to perform the SIGNS. Supernatural wonders or miracles that would prove to the people that, indeed, God Himself was with them; speaking and working through His prophet Moses. These miracles authenticated both the message and the messenger as being from God. This same Bible principle is again seen and confirmed for us:

And it shall come to pass, if they will not believe thee,
neither harken to the VOICE of the first sign, that they will

believe the VOICE of the latter sign. (Exodus 4:8.)

You will notice that these signs SPEAK! They say something! What is it they say? They say to the people, "Stop, listen! GOD IS SPEAKING!" Nicodemus recognized this scriptural principle when he said:

> *. . . we know that thou art a teacher come from God: for no man can do these miracles that thou doest, except GOD BE WITH HIM.* (John 3:2.)

Again this truth is to be seen and confirmed in the New Testament:

> *And they went forth, and preached everywhere, the Lord working with them, and CONFIRMING THE WORD WITH SIGNS FOLLOWING . . .* (Mark 16:20.)

Here we see the messengers sent forth with the message. In their going forth, they were accompanied by God Himself. He confirmed the message they gave through the marvelous workings of His miraculous power. God worked in and through these men as they spoke and performed His will; but it was clearly the POWER OF GOD CONFIRMING HIS WORD. This Biblical principle is reiterated for us with very grave warnings:

> *How shall we escape, if we neglect so great salvation; [THIS IS THE MESSAGE] which at the first began to be spoken by the Lord, and was CONFIRMED unto us by them that heard Him. [THESE ARE HIS MESSENGERS]*
>
> *GOD ALSO BEARING THEM WITNESS, BOTH WITH SIGNS AND WONDERS, and with diverse MIRACLES, and GIFTS of the Holy Spirit ACCORDING TO HIS OWN WILL?* (Hebrews 2:3-4.)

This is a very important statement. Please notice with care the thoughts that I bring out in the verses by means of the capitals. The entire statement is a QUESTION, and demands a thoughtful answer. It indicates the dire consequences of neglecting the authority and the authenticity of the message of salvation. It was delivered to us by His messengers, and confirmed by divine power as He worked real miracles as proof.

The essence of the answer to the above question is understood to be that there is no escape. We are FULLY ACCOUNTABLE to God for the message that He has given, in His grace and by His love, through His prophets. To neglect it is to reject it, and to reject it is to reject His grace and love. It is to die in our sin, believe it or not!

Finally, concerning the authenticity of the Word of God, we read:

> And many other *SIGNS* truly did *JESUS* in the presence of his disciples, which are not written in this book:
>
> *BUT THESE ARE WRITTEN THAT YE MIGHT BELIEVE* that Jesus is the Christ . . . and that believing ye might have life through his name. (John 20:30–31.)

All of the miracles which Jesus did were done and recorded to authenticate His person, His mission and His message.

With this truth so clearly set forth in the Scriptures, we, today, who truly love the Lord and honor His Word, need a clear understanding about the so-called religious "miracles" that are reported in many religious circles. We must not be deceived by them. God does not continue to authenticate His Word, once given, to each succeeding generation. The miracles of the scriptural account were performed by God working through His prophets, or through His Son who is the chief spokesman for the Father.

There are no prophets today. We know this to be true (conviction) simply because no one is permitted to add to His REVELATION. This is so because there is no REVELATION being given, and God places a dreadful curse upon all who would claim to have received a revelation from Him. See Revelation 22:18.

Since the close of, or the termination of given Scripture (the Inspired recording of Revelation), and the death of the last prophet, John, no revelation has been given by God to be received by man. With no revelation being given, there simply is no need for the confirmatory signs and sign gifts. On the contrary, we are exhorted to believe the message once delivered and already confirmed.

In contrast to this, you will remember that the Bible does speak of lying miracles: these are miracles performed in the last days through Satanic power for the purpose of deception. Now, the only way not to be deceived by these lying miracles is to believe and be grounded in the WORD OF GOD, authenticated and ". . . once delivered unto the saints." (Jude 3.)

DIVINE INSPIRATION

As we take a closer look at the truth of INSPIRATION, it is not for the purpose of covering the same ground again, but to examine the implications of that truth. True Believers believe in the verbal–plenary inspiration of the Word of God. The "verbal" part has to do with the fact that every single word of Scripture is inspired. God chose the exact words that He wanted to express, the exact thoughts and truths being revealed. This truth puts extreme value on every and each word in the Bible. This truth is expressed in the following verse:

> *And the Lord said unto Moses, Write thou these words: for after the tenor of these words I have made a covenant with thee* . . . (Exodus 34:27.)

According to William Wilson in his *Old Testament Word Studies*, the word "tenor" there means "speech, without a mediator or interpreter." It means that God meant just what He was saying, as was indicated by the select words He used and the clear meaning of those words.

God does not use idle words. Every word is important, and every word must be regarded and guarded with a holy reverence. They must not be changed or discarded, twisted as to meaning, or relegated to the place of unimportant. A book of word studies is an important tool to every student of the Word of God, only because every word is important. (See "List of Word Studies" following "Contents.") Many times the meaning of a single word will be the key to significant understanding. The reader should take to heart what the Lord says:

> *The WORDS of the Lord are PURE WORDS: as silver tried in a furnace of earth, purified SEVEN TIMES.*
>
> *Thou shalt KEEP THEM, O Lord, thou shalt PRESERVE THEM FROM THIS GENERATION FOREVER.* (Psalm 12: 6–7.)

What a wonderful truth that is. First, notice the use of the plural "words," indicating that the individual words Are purified and preserved. It is not just their collective whole that is pure and preserved, but the individual words themselves. All of them! It is not just the Bible that is PURE, but every word in the Bible is PURE and PRESERVED.

They are pure, without mixture of error. They are purified "seven times," that is, to PERFECTION.

This should help us to see the importance of EACH WORD of Scripture, and to accept God's personal promise to keep or preserve them for us, even to our generation. If God puts such importance upon His Word, should not we do the same? Let us not tamper with the Scriptures. It may be best if you do not use a "Bible" that has been tampered with by so-called or self-appointed scholars.

We should rise up in holy terror and indignation against those who toy with the Truth for profit. Who in the world has the right to correct God? God has promised to preserve His Word for YOU. Believe it. Accept it. Study and protect it.

> *Thy word is very pure; therefore thy servant loveth it.*
> *(Psalms 119: 140.)*

> *Every word of God is PURE; He is a shield unto them that put their trust in him.*

> *Add thou not unto his words, lest he reprove thee and thou be found a liar.* (Proverbs 30:5–6.)

That sounds rather strong, doesn't it? Yet, that is the Word of God. He is not only warning us; He is assuring us of confidence in His Word. It is worthy of our trust. The "add" in this verse is not just adding more words, certainly that is included, but it has to do with adding to the meaning, or changing the intent of what God is saying.

This is a practice that is very common today. People will often say that God did not really mean what He said, or the way it reads. They want to put THEIR words into His mouth, to make His thoughts conform to their thoughts. This kind of thinking is wrong and it is sinful. It is the expression of unbelief.

This practice will be judged by God in the day when the books are opened, and men, both great and small, stand before God. Our Saviour, Jesus Christ, speaks of this truth of the importance of the WORDS of God when He said:

> *. . . It is written, Man shall not live by bread alone, but by*
> *every word that proceedeth out of the mouth of God.*
> *(Matthew 4:4.)*

Therefore, fellow believer, when you hear a teacher or preacher making fast and loose with the words of the Scripture, be alerted at once that something is wrong. Every teaching of that teacher should be questioned, for he is on shaky ground. Don't believe everything you hear; believe God and His Holy Word. Remember that biblical faith is BELIEVING GOD. Faith is to take God at His Word.

We have seen that "verbal" means every word individually. Now look at the word "plenary" and find that it means every word in their collective whole. The WHOLE Bible is inspired; all of Scripture is the Word of God. As some would say, "from cover to cover," it is all true because it comes from God.

This word also means that there is no word from God for us now apart from, or not included in the Scripture. There is no Word of God outside of the Scriptures. God is not continuing to speak to man through direct revelation to prophets today. There is no new REVELATION from God, not since the INSPIRED prophets wrote.

However, it is true that what they wrote is preserved for us by the supernatural, providential care of our all powerful, loving Lord. We have the Bible, God's Holy Word, complete and unaltered.

Those works which fundamentally attack the preservation of God's Word by discrediting and changing many parts of the Bible; causing people to doubt God's Holy Word, ought to themselves be discarded. It may be bold to say so, but faith in the integrity of the Word of God is a shield and a guard against compromise and infidelity. In this regard, Revelation 22:18-19 are extremely important verses, and it is of no little import that they are found in the closing words of all of REVELATION.

INTEGRATION

The heart of the word "integration" is the meaning "whole," a complete, unified whole. It is like the weaving of a piece of cloth, interwoven or "integrated." This is a picture of Scripture. One of the most marvelous features of Scripture and the truth of inspiration is: the Word of God, in its entirety, is of divine origin.

The Holy Spirit is the true Author; it is a totally integrated book. It is, indeed, a unified whole. The significance of this is that it is completely interrelated. It is ONE BOOK, and not a bunch of unrelated thoughts of men jumbled together in one mass. With this in mind, look at the following verses:

Knowing this first, that NO prophecy of the Scripture is of any PRIVATE interpretation.

For the prophecy came not in old time by the will of man: but holy men of God spake as they were moved by the Holy Ghost. (II Peter 1:20-21.)

There are several beautiful truths here:

(1.) Prophecy, which is REVELATION, or the manifestation of God to His prophet, who was God's spokesman. This PROPHECY has been communicated to us by INSPIRATION under the guiding control of the Holy Spirit in the writings of Scripture.

(2.) It came, all of it, from the mind of God, and not from men as is here clearly stated.

(3.) Prophecy cannot be understood "privately" by man apart from the Author, the Spirit of God. Men, therefore, have no right whatsoever to put their own interpretation upon Scripture.

(4.) In conjunction with this last point, no single Scripture can be taken alone and out of context to be interpreted apart from the harmony of the rest of Scripture.

(5.) It is God's Book, one integrated whole. He "wrote" it, and He must teach it. We must prove every understanding, or teaching, by the Bible itself alone in its total harmonious unity of truth, just as the Berean Believers did in Acts 17:11.

(6.) Human wisdom, intelligence and ability cannot equip man, or suffice to understand and correctly interpret Scripture. Scholarship alone, apart from the ministry of the Holy Spirit, cannot rightly divide the Word of God.

(7.) Whenever, even as Christians, we implement our own wisdom, ideas, opinions or tradition, and cause it, through human pride, to violate and nullify divine truth, we at once divert into error.

A very important Scripture dealing with this truth is the contents of the second chapter of I Corinthians. The entire chapter speaks concerning this subject, but now we will look at just a few of the verses.

But as it is written, Eye hath not seen, nor ear heard, NEITHER HAVE ENTERED INTO THE HEART OF MAN, the things which God hath prepared for them that love him.

[NOTICE THAT IT IS CLEARLY BEYOND US.]

But God hath REVEALED THEM UNTO US BY HIS SPIRIT:

> *for the Spirit searcheth all things, yea the deep things of God.*
>
> *For what man knoweth the things of a man, save the spirit of man which is in him? Even so THE THINGS OF GOD KNOWETH NO MAN but the Spirit of God.*
>
> *Now we have received, not the spirit of the world, but the Spirit which is of God, THAT WE MIGHT KNOW the things that are freely GIVEN TO US OF GOD.*
>
> *Which things also we speak, not in the words which man's wisdom teacheth, but WHICH THE HOLY GHOST TEACHETH; comparing spiritual things with spiritual.*
> (I Corinthians 2:9–13.)

Here we see that spiritual truth must be compared, or examined, in the light of other spiritual truth. You see, what God is telling us is that the Bible interprets itself. The "natural man," that is, the man not saved and not having the Spirit of God (Romans 8:9) cannot and does not receive the things given to us by the Spirit of God. They are not given to him, the unsaved, because he cannot understand or appreciate them. The Scripture says that they are SPIRITUALLY DISCERNED!

Very clearly, spiritual truth is seen to be known only by the aid or illumination of the Holy Spirit. The Spirit of God uses the wholly integrated, the complete unity of the Scriptures in teaching us. This truth is important for us as Christians in our study of prophecy. God's truth is taught by His Spirit from the whole of Scripture. We must be very careful to listen to the Holy Spirit. We must let Him guide us in our study and research of the Scriptures in our pursuit of TRUTH. It is always well to remember:

> *Ye shall NOT ADD unto the word which I command you, neither shall ye DIMINISH ought from it, that ye may keep the commandment of the Lord your God which I command you.* (Deuteronomy 4:2.)

Here the thought goes beyond the idea of adding words. It includes the adding to or diminishing from the MEANING or INTENT or TENOR of the words and thoughts expressed. See Exodus 34:27. Taking away from God's Word is commonly done by belittling what

God has said, or by changing it to suit our fancy. We need to learn to take God literally. He means just what He says. You can believe God.

As a concluding thought on this subject, may I take you to one of my favorite Scriptures. It is one of those profound statements made by the Apostle Paul with wisdom that comes only from the Holy Spirit.

> *Now therefore, ye are no more strangers and foreigners, but FELLOW–CITIZENS with the saints, and of the HOUSEHOLD OF GOD.*
>
> *And are built upon the FOUNDATION of the apostles and prophets, JESUS CHRIST HIMSELF BEING THE CHIEF CORNER STONE. (Ephesians 2:19–20.)*

What tremendous truth. It is upon a foundation that you build a structure. The apostles are the prophets of the New Testament era. They, united with the prophets of old, are God's spokesmen. Together they have laid the foundation for our faith. This FOUNDA-TION is the Word of God, and the chief cornerstone of that foundation, the focus of all prophecy, is Jesus Christ our Lord.

We must clearly understand that our foundation must not ever be MEN or church tradition, custom or our scholars, and certainly not our opinion. The only foundation that will last and give you lasting and sure convictions is the Word of the Living God. Please, always remember this truth. You will find that tradition or custom without scriptural support is used. At times they are used as a foundation, even in fundamental circles, among Christians. This is especially true when it comes to prophecy.

THE DIVINE PROGRAM REVEALED

Can we really believe that there is a plan and a program designed for the ages? Can it be that all of life and history is in reality foreknown and supervised by a supernatural Being? Yes, if you believe the Bible, you can believe just that.

It is a many fold program. It is a very intricate and comprehensive plan. It is, as someone has truly said, "HIS – STORY." It involves God's infinite love, His creative powers, His glory and His goodness. It involves redemption, forgiveness and heaven. For this we thank the Lord. It involves YOU, and it involves me, too. It is a beautiful and wonderful plan, and as David said, "Such knowledge is too wonderful for me, it is high, I cannot attain unto it."

Perhaps one of the most wonderful things about this marvelous plan of the ages is that God has actually taken us into His confidence. He has shared His thoughts and purposes and "secrets" with us. He wants it all to be encouraging to us, to give HOPE in the darkness, and to fill us with joy and expectancy. Surely, it will make us love Him more. Oh, what a wonderful Lord and Saviour we serve.

GOD'S SOVEREIGNTY

God reveals to us not only that there is a plan, but that it is His plan. He is in control of that plan. He is fully able to accomplish His plan. It will be, just as He has said it would be.

Now, that is being a little dogmatic, isn't it? Well, God has a tendency to be dogmatic. After all, He is the one who knows what's going on. God speaks very emphatically, and it behooves us to listen when He speaks. This is because God is SOVEREIGN. He does what He will. We can be very thankful that, in His sovereignty, he is also love and infinite goodness. God is also HOLY and RIGHTEOUS and JUST.

His sovereignty involves His ability to carry out His own Divine will. He is capable, and in His capability He is also "all knowing" or omniscient. He is all wise. So in understanding God and His character, we must always remember that He is both OMNIPOTENT AND OMNISCIENT. He is GOD! Our Lord is also everywhere present, or OMNIPRESENT, so as to carry out His will in His own time and way. This is all seen in the Word of His REVELATION of Himself to Daniel the prophet:

> *This matter is by the decree of the watchers, and the*
> *demand by the word of the holy ones: to the intent that*
> *the living may KNOW that the MOST HIGH RULETH in the*
> *kingdom of men, and giveth it to whomsoever HE WILL,*
> *and setteth up over it to the basest of men.*
>
> *And all the inhabitants of the earth are reputed as*
> *nothing: and HE DOETH ACCORDING TO HIS WILL in the*

*army of heaven, and among the inhabitants of the earth:
and NONE CAN STAY HIS HAND, OR SAY UNTO HIM,
WHAT DOEST THOU? (Daniel 4:17 & 35.)*

The emphases, of course, with the capitals, are mine; but, oh, what a picture of our majestic, magnificent Lord. I'll tell you something: I will gladly serve Him, and willingly yield to such a sovereign master. The fact is that I'd be a fool not to do so. I am sure that we can all see what His sovereignty entails. It really is a matter of faith. Will we believe this witness of the prophet?

If we do not accept the fact of God's sovereignty, then the only other option open to us is to confess that there is no God at all. Then we must be willing to accept all of the frightful, hopeless complications to which this would lead.

God is in charge. It is not America, or our President, or England, or a Hitler. It is not Russia, or a Khomeini, or a Pope. It is OUR BLESSED LORD. He is in control of our universe. He holds the whole world in His hand.

Though the world of sinful men join forces with all of the satanic rulers of darkness and stand in rank rebellion against the Lord of Glory, He will still accomplish His eternal purpose. Satan can never win the victory. How can we be so sure of this? Well, just read the last chapter of the Bible and you will see what is going to happen. The Serpent is forever silenced. As King David said:

*The SECRET OF THE LORD is with them that fear him,
and he will SHEW them his covenant. (Psalm 25:14.)*

HOW BLESSED! How sweet the goodness of the Lord is. How gracious He is to those who love Him. Yet, of this same merciful Lord, David wrote again:

*Let all the earth FEAR the LORD: let all the inhabitants of
the world stand in AWE of Him.*

*For He spake, and it was done; He commanded, and it
stood fast.*

*The Lord bringeth the counsel of the heathen to nought:
he maketh the devices of the people of none effect.*

*The counsel of the Lord standeth forever, the thought of
His heart, to all generations.*

BLESSED is the nation whose God is the Lord; and the

> PEOPLE *whom He hath chosen for His own inheritance.*
> *(Psalm 33:8–12.)*

The glory of His majesty — Let it grip your soul. Isaiah, the prophet, speaks as a spokesman for God and says these memorable words:

> *Look unto me, and be ye SAVED, all the ends of the earth:*
> *FOR I AM GOD, AND THERE IS NONE ELSE.*

> *I have sworn by myself, the word is gone out of my*
> *mouth in righteousness, and shall not return, that UNTO*
> *ME EVERY KNEE SHALL BOW, EVERY TONGUE SHALL*
> *SWEAR.* (Isaiah 45:22–23.)

That is SOVEREIGNTY. The day of accountability will come. All rebellion will be put down. The revolt of every sinful heart will be silenced before Him with whom we have to do.

The "swear" of this verse, of course, is not cursing, but a confessing. It is the admission of and the yielding to His absolute sovereignty. It is unconditional surrender to, and acknowledgment of CHRIST AS LORD, as recorded by Paul the apostle:

> *. . . every tongue should confess that Jesus Christ is Lord,*
> *to the glory of God the Father.* (Philippians 2:11.)

Men may scoff now as he, in the exercise of His grace, waits; and thus gives to each of us the ultimate opportunity to confess His love and redeeming Blood. But, as sure as that day came when God closed the door to the Ark of Noah, even so will He one day close the door of His grace and the door of heaven.

It will forever be TOO LATE.

Don't ever think that because He holds back His wrath now, and He does not now let His judgment fall, that He cannot or will not do so. It is called: "THE GREAT DAY OF THE WRATH OF GOD ALMIGHTY." Let us again hear the mighty, emphatic voice of our sovereign Creator:

> *Remember the former things of old: for I AM GOD, and*
> *there is none else; I AM GOD, and there is NONE LIKE ME,*

Declaring the end from the beginning, and from ancient times the things that are not yet done, saying, MY COUNSEL SHALL STAND, and I WILL DO ALL MY PLEASURE:

Calling a ravenous bird from the east, the man that executeth my counsel from a far country: Yea, I HAVE SPOKEN IT, I WILL ALSO BRING IT TO PASS; I HAVE PURPOSED IT, I WILL ALSO DO IT. (Isaiah 46: 9–11.)

Such words need not be explained. They are clear. The ear of faith will hear and bow and say, "Amen." The heart that believes will simply say with Paul, "Lord, what wilt Thou have me to do?" The scoffer will scoff, and the unbeliever may continue in his infidelity and unbelief. There is only one thing for sure, however, and that is:

As sure as there is a sun in the sky,
　　There is a sovereign God up on high.
As sure as the moon shines in the night,
　　Just as sure in Scripture we see His light.
If there is no water in the vast blue ocean,
　　If no sand on the long seashore,
Then there is nothing to look forward to;
　　There is no HOPE anymore!
If there is no love at all in my life,
　　And life is all a bad dream;
If there is no gurgle to be heard
　　In the waters of the clear mountain stream,
If there is no Calvary as in the Bible,
　　No Saviour's blood for sinners shed,
Then indeed there is no sovereign God,
　　And we are all, now, and forever, DEAD!

H. Powell

GOD'S SECRETS

If we are convinced, have gained the assurance of Biblical conviction, that there is a sovereign God in control of the progress of history: we can find a truly great source of joy in finally realizing that our loving Lord, our heavenly Father, wants to share His SECRETS with those of us who sincerely love Him. In the Bible we find that God considered Abraham to be in a special relationship, calling him "a friend of God." While talking with Abraham, His friend, concerning the destruction of Sodom, God said:

> *Shall I hide from Abraham the thing which I do?* (Genesis 18:17.)

The rest of that chapter is the conversation between God and His friend, Abraham, as they talked about what God planned to do in Sodom. Abraham's nephew, Lot, lived in Sodom, and God would not judge and destroy the city without first talking to His special friend. What a gracious Lord.

He was not obliged to have that beautifully tender conversation, sharing the hurt of His loving heart so full of an infinite love for a people whose rebellion and sin had led them into a perverted immorality that cried out for judgment before His absolute holiness. God was not obliged to do it, but He did because Abraham was His FRIEND.

Nor is that incident unique in God's relation with His children. It is the natural expression of His love, and the consideration he has toward those who love Him. It is His prophet, Amos, who tells us:

> *Surely the Lord God will do NOTHING, but He revealeth His SECRET unto his servants the prophets.* (Amos 3:7.)

The emphasis in capitals is, again, mine, as throughout this study, to awaken the mind to vital truth. Beyond all doubt, God is telling us that He wills to share His secret plans with His prophets; and they, being His spokesmen, were to communicate that REVEALED SECRET to His believing children.

This very truth is the core of the conversation that the Lord had with His disciples shortly before His crucifixion and exit from this world. John the apostle records the words of our Saviour:

> *Henceforth I call you not servants; for the servant knoweth not what his lord doeth: but I have called you FRIENDS; for ALL THINGS that I have heard of my Father I HAVE MADE KNOWN UNTO YOU.* (John 15:15.)

It is true that one of the distinguishing characteristics of true friendship is the ability to and the pleasure of sharing the "secrets" of our lives. We do not share these things with just anyone, and especially not with strangers. We only have such confident sharing among true friends, those we know we can trust.

From this we learn that, even as Abraham was called a friend of God, so are we. Christ's words to His disciples apply equally to each of us, if indeed we are His disciples. We must, however, consider the fact that Christ limits this friendship by saying:

Ye are my friend, IF YE DO whatsoever I command you.
(John 15:14.)

Yes, our Lord is DISCRIMINATING between Christians. He is telling us that we have no claim to that privileged group, if we are not willing to walk with Him in obedience to His command. He is telling us that not every Christian is taken into His confidence as a "friend." The reason, of course, is the attitude of heart that we must have toward Him and His LORDSHIP in our lives. We find in the gospel account of Jesus, and this closeness of friendship, that there were those "believers" with whom He simply did not confide:

Now when he was in Jerusalem at the Passover, in the feast day, MANY BELIEVED in his name, when they saw the miracles which he did.

But Jesus DID NOT COMMIT HIMSELF UNTO THEM, because he knew all men,

And needed not that any should testify of man; for he KNEW WHAT WAS IN MAN. (John 2:23–25.)

Beyond question, God's SECRETS are only for those whose hearts are right before Christ — The individuals who bow before Him in humble obedience to all His holy will, then walk with Him in the sweetness of fellowship and the beauty of holiness.

Jesus knows your REAL heart attitude towards Him. Maybe you believe to a point, but have never truly made the commitment to crown Him LORD of your life. Why not? Take the step of faith. Make that decision. Commit your life fully to Him and become a "friend" of the Saviour. Promise Him obedience, and then be obedient to His will and Word.

To do so we can all, simply and sincerely, pray:

"Oh Lord, forgive me for my self-will and disobedience. Lord Jesus, I do believe that you shed your precious blood to redeem my soul. I know that I am your child, and I thank you for saving me. Now, Lord, before Thee I bow and surrender my heart and life to Thee. I truly want you, alone, to be the Lord of my life. I now and henceforth forever, offer my body to be a living sacrifice to do your will; guided by the power of the Holy Spirit whose temple I am. Thank you, Lord for taking control of my life. This I pray and ask in Jesus' name. Amen."

Now, begin to live and to walk in the truth of that commitment, and as a FRIEND of the Lord our God.

Read James 4:4, and remember that HE KNOWS what is in the heart of man.

The pure FACT that God reveals His SECRETS is clearly set forth in Scripture. The revelation of God's secrets is always for the accomplishment of His will and purpose. It is NEVER done just to satisfy our curiosity, or so that we can go around, as a child would do, saying: "I've got the secret." We all used to do that just to get the other kids mad or jealous at us. God is not like that, nor is the Christian whose heart is right with God.

God's secrets are revealed for us so that we can share them, preaching and teaching and warning of impending danger. The purpose is to bring others to FAITH in Christ. Also, so that we ourselves will love the Lord to a greater degree and want to walk with Him in an ever greater purity of life.

CONSIDER JOSEPH

We all know the dramatic story of Joseph in Genesis. God had now brought him to the point of usefulness through much suffering. The Lord then shared His SECRETS with Joseph. Then, as God's spokesman, Joseph said:

And Joseph said unto Pharaoh, The dream of Pharaoh is one: GOD HATH SHEWED PHARAOH WHAT HE IS ABOUT TO DO.

. . . What God is about to do He sheweth unto Pharaoh.

And for that the dream was doubled unto Pharaoh twice;
it is because the thing is established by God, and GOD
WILL SHORTLY BRING IT TO PASS. (Genesis 41:25, 28 &
32.)

What a revelation. Pharaoh had dreamed two dreams. However, the SECRET was not given to Pharaoh. The SECRET was given only to God's FRIEND, Joseph. Joseph then, as God's spokesman, told Pharaoh just exactly what God was going to do.

The dream concerned seven years of plenty and seven years of famine in Egypt. You will notice that it was with absolute certainty that God would bring it to pass. The purpose of the whole affair was to be God's providential care of the children of Israel, Joseph's own family at that time in history. God was going to take care of His own, and He was going to use this heathen King to do it. Here we see God ruling as SOVEREIGN in nature and in politics to accomplish His divine plan and purpose. You will remember that it happened in the exact manner that God had told Joseph it would.

CONSIDER DANIEL

In the life of Daniel we have a very similar occurrence. The prophet, God's spokesman, is Daniel, and the King now is Nebuchadnezzar of Babylon. This is many years later and in another part of the world, but God is still sovereign and Ruler of the world. He does not change. Again, the King had a dream. He forgot his dream but felt an urgency to know what the dream was and what it meant. Daniel was given the SECRET.

Daniel is called before the King, and being careful to take no glory or credit for himself, he told the King that he was the servant of Jehovah, God, the God of Israel, and the glory belonged to Him. Then Daniel, the FRIEND of GOD, tells the King:

. . . there is a God in heaven that REVEALETH SECRETS,
and maketh known to King Nebuchadnezzar, WHAT
SHALL BE IN THE LATTER DAYS . . . (Daniel 2:28.)

Joseph's "secret" was of the present and immediate future, while Daniel's "secret" was of the present and far distant future, THE LATTER DAYS. Time is no barrier to God. He knows the end from the beginning. But, listen, did you get what Daniel said?

GOD IN HEAVEN REVEALS HIS SECRETS!

Believe it. It is so. You can not only believe that He does, but you can "bank" on it. You can "bet your life" on the fact that the "secret" thing will come to pass. God's very name is at stake. He will not fail. He is SOVEREIGN. In our study of the prophetic Scriptures we must always bear in mind this glorious truth, this clear statement of fact, because some of His "secrets" are almost unbelievable.

God does tell us what is going to happen; WHAT HE IS GOING TO DO. It will happen just as He has said it would. BELIEVE IT.

In order to confirm this wonderful truth, this blessed reality of GOD IN ACTION, let us look at another verse:

For, lo, He that formeth the mountains, and createth the wind, and declareth unto man WHAT IS HIS THOUGHT, that maketh the morning darkness, and treadeth upon the high places of the earth, The Lord, the God of hosts is his name. (Amos 4:13.)

Oh, please, let God take you into His confidence. According to the HEBREW used in this verse, we understand that the term "HIS THOUGHTS" are GOD'S THOUGHTS which He declares unto man. Matthew Henry has this to say on this verse:

"He makes known his counsel by his servants the prophets to the children of men, the thoughts of His justice against impenitent sinners, and the thought of good he thinks towards those that repent. He can also make known, for he perfectly knows, the thoughts that are in men's heart; he understands afar off, and in the day of conviction will set the evil thoughts among the other sins of sinners in order before them."

We must always remind ourselves that the purpose for us in REVELATION is never to satisfy the mind or heart with knowledge. It is to satisfy the mind and heart with God, and to help us serve our Lord in a greater capacity. This is expressed in what Daniel said:

I came near unto one of them that stood by, and asked him the TRUTH of all this . . . (Daniel 7:16.)

Also in our Lord's high priestly prayer He prayed:

Sanctify them through the TRUTH: THY WORD IS TRUTH. (John 17:17.)

Thus, we understand that the truth of God's Word is to sanctify us. He separates us from sin and error unto Himself. Then enables us to bear faithful witness in this godless world to what He is going to do, as well as what He has already done. Let us give Him all the glory and praise, and let sinful men everywhere see that WE BELIEVE GOD, that it shall be even as He has said. Let us let men know that we are God's "friends." See I John 2:15–17.

THE LADDER OF TRUTH

Gaining a spiritual understanding is like climbing a ladder. Too many people look at the Bible and say, "I can't understand it." They give up before they get started. Even preachers will sometimes say that it is "hard to understand." The fact of the matter is that we cannot understand it, not all at once. That is what most folks want, INSTANT UNDERSTANDING. Like we have instant coffee, or instant pudding, people want instant understanding. They whine and complain because they do not get it.

Most Christians have not even read the Bible through ONE TIME, and they think, somehow, that they have been left out. Understanding does not come in ready-mix packages, ever. Even in the secular world, to have an understanding or a workable knowledge on any given subject such as a language, or a science, or music, or whatever it may be, one has to STUDY. He has to DIG. One has to learn day-by-day and class-by-class, one day at a time. This is even more true of Bible knowledge. See figure 1.

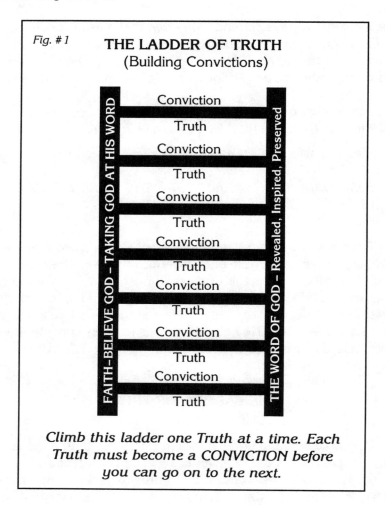

Fig. # 1

THE LADDER OF TRUTH
(Building Convictions)

Climb this ladder one Truth at a time. Each Truth must become a CONVICTION before you can go on to the next.

As you look at this figure, you will see that one side of the ladder of truth is called FAITH. The other side is the WORD OF GOD. These sides go together; you cannot have a ladder of truth without BOTH of these. The connecting rungs of the ladder are the individual TRUTHS that you will encounter, and each of which you must conquer and stand upon. This is done one at a time. You must stand upon each truth before going on. All are important. You must be able to stand with both feet solidly placed on each rung of the ladder, each truth of God, letting it become part of your FOUNDATION.

Go too fast and you will slip and fall, as so many before you have experienced. You have "conquered" a "rung of truth" when that truth is transformed into a PERSONAL CONVICTION. Many people are persuaded of a given truth, but it is not their conviction. The difference is that a persuasion is somebody else's conviction that we are carrying, or else it is not a TRUTH at all. Such a load soon becomes burdensome and will be dropped sooner or later.

A CONVICTION is when one has been persuaded by God Himself, through His Word, of a particular TRUTH by the convicting power of the Holy Spirit. Once this happens that CONVICTION becomes yours. You will never part with it. It becomes part of you and is molded into your character and personality, and your character and personality are molded by it (Romans 12:2). You begin to live within its context. That, my friend, is BIBLE CONVICTION, and it is something that far too few Christians have. Build yours.

Many Christians are persuaded about many things, but they have almost no convictions about anything. This is demonstrated by the fact that they can prove almost nothing by Scripture.

As you are able to stand firmly upon a rung of truth on this very real ladder, you can then go on to the next "rung," and then to the next one, etc. Finally, WOW! WHAT A SIGHT. Your heart thrills with the spiritual view God gives to YOU. Your insight grows, growing ever brighter and clearer as you climb higher, always higher.

Surely you can see that if you stand on the ground and just say, "I can't," and never start climbing, you will NEVER get there. You will never understand without climbing. You cannot do it on your own, and there are dangers, too, but the Holy Spirit is there to help you.

I remember when my boys were little. I was using a ladder one day to do some work on the house. Jonathan wanted to climb the ladder like Daddy. He was so small, but I was there and taught him how to climb the ladder. It was real work for him, but he did it. I did not lift him from rung to rung. He did it. You can, however, be sure that I was there, right behind him, watching his every move. When he was unsteady, I steadied him. When his little foot tended to slip, I was there to secure him. I did not make him do it; he wanted to do it, and he wanted to do it by himself. What a spiritual lesson. My little son climbed the ladder. He could have said, "I can't," and he would have missed the thrill of it all. He trusted me; he knew that I was there.

Faith is imperative in climbing our ladder, for it is said:

Without FAITH it is impossible to please him. (Hebrews 11:6.)

Please, always remember that FAITH = BELIEVING GOD. Yes,

this is the essence of the meaning of BIBLE FAITH. It is simply to take God at His WORD. If we will not take God at His Word, we will NEVER be able to climb this ladder. We might just as well give up right now and condemn ourselves to the darkness of doubt and unbelief, if we WILL not *believe God*.

Faith is an act of the WILL. I WILL believe. I DO believe ALL that God has said. It is true that salvation is a necessary part of faith. Without this basic experience of FAITH we lack the presence of the HOLY SPIRIT, who is alone our Teacher as Christ said:

> *Even the Spirit of truth; whom the world cannot receive, because it seeth him not, neither knoweth him; for he dwelleth with you, and shall be IN YOU.*

> *But the Comforter, which is the Holy Ghost, whom the Father will send in my name, HE SHALL TEACH YOU ALL THINGS* . . . (John 14:17, 26.)

A person, without the aid of the Holy Spirit, can study the Scriptures and gain some degree of academic knowledge on a purely human level. But, without the special instruction of God's Holy Spirit, one can never gain a SPIRITUAL understanding of divine truth. You might recall this:

> . . . *it is given unto you to know the mysteries of the kingdom of heaven, but to them IT IS NOT GIVEN.* (Matthew 13:11.)

In order to emphasize this truth concerning the Spirit's special ministry to believers, Jesus said:

> *Howbeit when he, the Spirit of truth, is come, HE WILL GUIDE YOU INTO ALL TRUTH: for he shall not speak of himself, but whatsoever he shall hear, that shall he speak; and HE WILL SHEW YOU THINGS TO COME.* (John 16:13.)

Will you notice that Jesus refers to the Holy Spirit as THE SPIRIT OF TRUTH. This is because TRUTH is SPIRIT revealed. Going back to Joseph for a moment, we find him responding to Pharaoh's servants in prison:

*And they said unto him, We have dreamed a dream, and
there is no interpreter of it. And Joseph said unto them,
DO NOT INTERPRETATIONS BELONG UNTO GOD? . . .*
(Genesis 40:8.)

Joseph himself did not know the interpretation, but HE KNEW
GOD. Truth is God revealed,

God the Holy Spirit. Without Him we simply are left in the DARK,
and we cannot, thus, climb the ladder of truth. Never look to MAN.
Never look to the Church. Look up. Look to the Lord. Bow before HIM,
and with His Book before you ask Him to show you the TRUTH. HE
WILL. He wants to.

I must say that to profess salvation is not enough either; one
must possess the Holy Spirit and be possessed of Him. As you yield
to the Holy Spirit and give Him charge of your life, the result will be
not fanaticism, but true spirituality. Paul the great apostle prayed this
prayer for the Believers in the Church at Ephesus:

*That the God of our Lord Jesus Christ, the Father of glory,
may give unto you the spirit of wisdom and revelation in
the knowledge of him:*

*The eyes of your UNDERSTANDING BEING
ENLIGHTENED; that ye may KNOW what is the hope of
his calling, and the riches of the glory of his inheritance in
the saints,*

*And what is the exceeding greatness of his power to us-
ward who believe . . .* (Ephesians 1:17-19.)

My prayer is the same for you, be you a student or a working
adult, a man or a woman, a layman or a preacher, a missionary or
an evangelist. My prayer is that you will let God the Holy Spirit be your
teacher as you read and study the truth that I share with you in this
study about the Word of God.

UNDERSTANDING WITHHELD

It is a biblical truth that understanding of a truth can be, and sometimes is, withheld until its appointed or appropriate time because God is in control. This is quite vividly portrayed in the experience of the two who walked the Emmaus road on the afternoon that our Saviour arose from the grave. As they walked along, the resurrected Lord came and joined them in their journey. He talked with them, and walked with them until the daylight began to fail. The day was far spent and it was drawing on toward evening, but THESE TWO DID NOT RECOGNIZE JESUS. They did not recognize His face or even His voice. WHY? Well, simply, such was the WILL of the Saviour according to His own declared purpose, as clearly stated in:

> . . . *Jesus himself drew near, and went with them. BUT THEIR EYES WERE HOLDEN THAT THEY SHOULD NOT KNOW HIM.* (Luke 24:15–16.)

How marvelous is our Lord, and how infinite His power. He had a purpose, and in His own time he opened their eyes:

> *And it came to pass, as he sat at meat with them, and he took bread, and blessed it, and brake, and gave to them.*
>
> *And THEIR EYES WERE OPENED, AND THEY KNEW HIM; and he vanished out of their sight.* (Luke 24:30–31.)

This is no GHOST STORY. Instead, it is a vivid example of the truth that understanding is not automatic. It is subject to the will of God. Our sovereign Lord is in control of even our comprehension of spiritual reality, both as to content and TIMING. Again, in order to underscore this Biblical truth, we return to Daniel and view his per-onal experience as one of God's own spokesmen:

> *And the vision of the evening and the morning which was told is true: wherefore SHUT UP THE VISION; for it shall be for many days . . . and I was astonished at the vision, but NONE UNDERSTOOD IT. (Daniel 8:26–27.)*

Not even Daniel understood the vision, but understanding was revealed by God and given when, according to His own will, the time had come. This is even more surely stated:

> *But thou, O Daniel, SHUT UP THE WORDS and SEAL THE*

*BOOK, even TO THE TIME OF THE END: Many shall run
to, and fro, and KNOWLEDGE SHALL BE INCREASED.*

*And he said, Go thy way, Daniel: for the words are
CLOSED UP and SEALED TILL THE TIME OF THE END.*
(Daniel 12:4 & 9.)

Daniel had asked about these things and the Lord told him
"NO." It was not to be known and understood till the end of time, when
God would then bring enlightenment and knowledge, or understanding, concerning this prophecy. Many would endeavor to uncover the
secrets of God. However, understanding would only fully come as
God increased knowledge as to His sovereign purpose, and in His
sovereign will. He would, in time, open men's spiritual eyes to
comprehend. This is one of the reasons why there has been such
confusion in the doctrine of eschatology.

Men will often times give an answer, or a teaching, based upon
"scholarship," without the enlightenment of the Holy Spirit. When our
answers to the questions of prophecy to any degree violate the
internal evidence and unity of the integrated whole of the Word of
God, we will invariably come up with wrong conclusions. Our answers
may sound plausible, but if they are not in complete accord with the
Word of God, they are nothing more than OUR answers.

The time of the end is upon us. We should now look for and
expect the Spirit of God to make these "secrets" plain to us. As we
go through our study, do not focus your attention upon MAN or upon
what men may have said.

Look to the Spirit of God for clear comprehension. If you come
across something that is new to you, or perhaps different from that
which you are accustomed to hearing, please do not close your
mind's eye to it. Open your mind, your heart, and your Bible. Expect
understanding as you climb higher and higher up the ladder of truth.

Do not go faster than you can build your convictions. Remember, if your convictions are not based solidly upon the Word of God,
then they are not BIBLE convictions at all. You will probably find that
they are nothing more than the opinions of someone else. If so, they
should come under the heading of "tradition" or "customs of
understanding," by which you have been persuaded without personal Biblical research.

In more than thirty-five years in the Gospel ministry, I have found
that the hardest people to teach are CHRISTIANS. People who have
known the Lord Jesus for many years. Those that think they need not

be taught anything more. This is certainly true of many pastors — as in the old cliche, "They are in love with their own opinions."

The Believers in South America, where we served the Lord for many years, taught me a very real truth when they said, "The hardest door to open is the door of a closed mind." As sons of the Living God, we should never come to that place where we think that we cannot learn more of God's wonderful "secrets."

DIRECTION

In this, our study of the prophetic Scriptures, we will look first at the book of DANIEL, for it is basic to prophetic understanding. This then will be followed by:

- ♱ Ezekiel 36 – 39
- ♱ II Thessalonians 2:1 – 12
- ♱ I Thessalonians 4:13 – 5:11
- ♱ I Corinthians 15:50 – 52
- ♱ Matthew 24 (along with Mark 13, Luke 17 & 21)
- ♱ REVELATION will bring this study's conclusion.

This may seem like a lot at first. Just remember, God has a lot to share with us. It may seem heavy, but with the aid of the Holy Spirit I know you will be able to climb the ladder of truth. You will even surprise yourself, I am sure. Prophecy will come ALIVE for you as never before. Some of the many important questions we will seek to find answers for in the Word of God are:

1. The 70th Week of Daniel: The What, When, How and the Who of it?
2. What is meant by "The times of the Gentiles"?
   A. When does it begin?
   B. When does it end?
      C. What is its purpose?
   3. What is the "Tribulation Period"?
      A. How long does it last?
   4. What is "The Great Tribulation"?
      A. What is its relation to the "Tribulation"?
      B. Why is it so called?

C. Who and what does it involve?
5. The significance of the "last trump"?
    A. When does it occur?
    B. What happens when it is blown?
6. Will Israel be invaded?
    A. By whom and when?
    B. What will be the outcome?
7. What is meant by the RAPTURE?
    A. Why is there to be a rapture?
    B. Who does it involve?
    C. What about the WHEN of the Rapture?
8. When does the Resurrection occur?
    A. What is meant by the "First Resurrection"?
    B. Will there be a second?
9. What can we know about the Antichrist?
    A. His identity?
    B. His appearance and his revelation.
    C. The TIME of his rule.
10. What is the "Abomination of Desolation"?
    A. When does it occur?
    B. Why is it significant?
11. When does the battle of Armageddon occur?
    A. How will it end?
12. Will there be a Third World War?
13. Will there be a nuclear war?
14. What is the "Kingdom age"?
    A. Will it be a LITERAL Kingdom?
    B. If so, how long will it last?
    C. What will it be like?
    D. Who will it involve?
15. When does the last judgment occur?
    A. What is the difference between the TWO judgments?
16. What does the Bible say about the "Bride of Christ"?
17. WHAT ABOUT AMERICA? Is America in the prophecy?

I would remind you that answers to these and ALL questions must be supported by the internal unity of the Word of God, as well as the verses that directly deal with the subject at hand. Just because a thing is taught by good Bible teachers does not make it correct. A Teacher may be persuaded by TRADITION and CUSTOM and the pressure to conform to POPULAR understanding.

The BIBLE is our ONLY sure foundation. The Bible must be

understood by WHAT IT SAYS. For some details, we may have to wait until they are fulfilled to be able to see them in their Scriptural reference. When we see Jesus, we will get the FULL answer to all of our questions. It is well to remember that in our prophetic studies we are delving into those great SECRETS our Lord so wants to share with us. They are for YOU, believer.

UNDERSTANDING TERMS

A basic understanding of the following common terms used in the subject "The Last Things" will be a great help to you in your comprehension of the viewpoints of others. It will also assist you in knowing where some depart from clear Scriptural teaching, and where they need help in order to get BACK ON THE FOUNDATION.

PREMILLENIALISM

PREMILLENIAL understanding is based upon a LITERAL understanding of the Word of God. We know that the Lord does use many types of symbols and figures of speech, as well as parables, throughout the Scriptural account. However, the general record of Scripture is given and is to be understood in a literal fashion, in the same manner of our communication.

We all use illustrations and examples to clarify and explain, in our attempts to put our messages across understandably. The Premillenial view is that Christ will return to the earth in His glory and in His glorified body — that He will establish His earthly KINGDOM. It will be a LITERAL Kingdom with Christ Himself ruling from Jerusalem. His Rule will be a righteous rule, and He will rule with a "rod of iron." The length of this Rule will be a LITERAL One Thousand Years.

Premillenialists believe, as the Bible literally teaches, that the whole world will hear the Gospel message. But it will not be received by the masses. Therefore, the judgment of God will be poured out upon the unbelieving, Christ rejecting, world like it was in the days of Noah.

This time it will not be of flood waters, but Divine judgments which will afflict man as he has never been afflicted. Its purpose is not eradication, but punishment, and will be so severe as to have no parallel in history, either before or after. It is called THE GREAT TRIBULATION and is sometimes referred to simply as THE TRIBU-LATION PERIOD. It will be at the close of this JUDGMENT that Christ will come in His Glory to establish His Kingdom.

This present work is PREMILLENIAL in its scope. See Revelation 19 – 20.

POSTMILLENIALISM

Postmillenial teaching rejects the literal understanding of the Bible. It teaches that there will be NO LITERAL KINGDOM OF CHRIST, *no 1000 year reign of our Lord upon the Earth.*

Postmillenial teaching would have us believe that the world WILL eventually accept the Gospel message and turn to Christ. People will become better and better as humanity is prepared to receive Christ upon His return. Basic to this teaching is that there is no place for ISRAEL as a nation, today, in Bible prophecy. God had finished with national Israel. This teaching is very Philosophic and humanistic in its view; rather than BIBLICAL, having moved off the FOUNDATION. Postmillenialism is seen by this Pastor as simply UNSCRIPTURAL.

AMILLENIALISM

Amillenialism is an understanding that outright rejects clear, literal, scriptural teaching. Its thesis depends upon an analogical and allegorical interpretation of Scripture. It rejects all literal understand-ing of biblical statements and teaches that everything must be understood SYMBOLICALLY. Therefore, there will be NO FUTURE REIGN OF CHRIST UPON THE EARTH AT ALL. This teaching views Christ as reigning NOW. His Reign is His Church. This has been basic Roman Catholic doctrine from the beginning.

It, too, is anti-Semitic because it gives no place for national Israel in the plan of God. No fancy word or seemingly knowledgeable speeches can cover the fact that AMILLENIALISM is fanciful, imaginative and un-Biblical. It should be systematically rejected by ALL who love the Word of God.

PRETRIBULATIONALISM

Pretribulationalism teaching puts the stress on the PRE, prior to, the TRIBULATION of the wrath of God. This teaching stresses the Biblical truth that God has promised to remove His Church BEFORE His wrath falls. Christ will come to receive His Church (as in I Thessalonians 4:13–18), removing it from the "hour" which is to come upon this Christ rejecting world of unbelievers who, in rejecting Christ, have opened their arms to the Antichrist.

This PASTOR is absolutely convinced, after better than 35 years of Bible study, that the Church of Jesus Christ WILL BE RAPTURED BEFORE THE TRIBULATION PERIOD. The Church will not go into, or through, any part of that period of divine judgment — the pouring out of the wrath of God. The Church will be "caught up" BEFORE THAT JUDGMENT STARTS.

In this study we will weigh carefully the words of Scripture so as to gain a clear, Biblical understanding of this great truth. It is precisely here that many are misled, due to un-Biblical teaching. If you are a believer, you need not fear the WRATH of the Lamb. But you should be prepared, in your heart and mind, through Bible study, for the events immediately ahead of us. This is a glorious time to be ALIVE FOR CHRIST!

POSTTRIBULATIONALISM

Posttribulationalism places the stress upon the prefix POST and teaches that the Church WILL GO THROUGH THE TRIBULATION PERIOD. This is in direct contradiction to the specific promise of our loving Saviour. They teach that Believers will be kept by the power of God during that time of the outpouring of His divine wrath upon the godless world of unbelievers.

This teaching holds that the RAPTURE will occur at the close of, or AFTER, that period of judgment. The teaching of the rapture is minimized in this view because it loses its Biblical significance. Christ, at that time, does not come to take up His Church but to establish His kingdom. A careful, honest study of the Word of God will reveal the un-Biblical stand of this teaching.

The terms *Pretribulationalism* and *Posttribulationalism*, in their view of the KINGDOM AGE, are both *PREMILLENIAL* in their understanding. Their differences lie in their placement of the RAPTURE of the Church relative to THE TRIBULATION PERIOD.

THE TIMES OF THE GENTILES

This TIME PERIOD is the grand, revealed program of our Sovereign Lord for the period of Gentile rule and supremacy among world powers. Its specific purpose is for the dealing with, and chastisement of, unbelieving NATIONAL ISRAEL. It is that time in which world power and leadership is divinely committed into the hands of Gentile nations; and the ancient people of God, the Children of Israel, undergo divine discipline because of their sinful rebellious pride and unbelief.

Its purpose is to BREAK THAT PRIDE and bring Israel to repentance and submission to the sovereign will of God. To bring Her to faith in His WORD and the assurance of REDEMPTION and RIGHTEOUSNESS through the promised SEED, the MESSIAH, JESUS CHRIST.

During this long period, many important things take place which make up the scope of Bible prophecy. This time of Gentile rule will end ONLY upon the return of KING JESUS to take His REIGN and His glorious KINGDOM. This is OUR TIME, and it is fast drawing to a dramatic close.

May a diligent study of these prophecies and the reading of this work help you to be prepared for the very traumatic events JUST AHEAD. You are reading about some of them even now in your newspapers.

Look next at what God said, through Daniel, about these times.

TWO

Learning From Daniel

With a solid foundation on the objective Truths of the Living, Sovereign Lord, and determined never to leave this Foundation, we can now go forward and begin to climb our "ladder of truth." You are encouraged, in your climb upward, to constantly refresh your memory of the realities shown in Chapter I of this study. People tend to forget, and in forgetting they tend to stray. Keep your eyes steadfastly upon our Sovereign Lord; remember that He is in control. We will begin the climb in Daniel. It is through His Spokesman, Daniel, that God lays down the FRAMEWORK for all His prophetic revelation of future things.

The scope of prophecy is all pre-written history; it is history written before it happens. It involves all the future of the human race, and what God has in store for it. In prophecy we see what man's final destiny will be, and we see the events that will close man's life upon this earth. The prophecies in Daniel set the stage. They give to us the "program" of history so that we can know when the "play" of "The Last Days" will start; its makeup, and its conclusion. Without a knowledge and an understanding of the prophecies in Daniel, all the rest of prophetic truth is a jumbled confusion with no form or direction.

THE KING'S DREAM
(Daniel Chapter 11)

This study in Daniel is not to be a study of the Book of Daniel, but a study of the *prophecies* of the Book of Daniel. The first prophecy to be examined is found in chapter two of Daniel and concerns the dream of the King.

King Nebuchadnezzar was the ruling monarch of the Babylonian Empire. He was the world power at that time in history. He captured Judah and Jerusalem and brought away many people from the Southern Kingdom of Israel as captives to serve him in his Empire. He subdued Israel according to the will of God, and for His purpose.

Among these captives was Daniel, a teenager at the time of his captivity. With the passing of time God had placed Daniel, His servant, in a position of great influence in the Babylonian Empire, and in the confidence of the King.

King Nebuchadnezzar was a heathen King. His religion was idolatrous, and he worshiped many gods. He himself was considered a "god" and was worshiped by the people. His word was law.

God, as was His custom in days of old, and for the purpose of His program for mankind, spoke to the King by means of a dream; a common means of Revelation in the dispensation of the Old Testament. Now the King knew that his dream was important. He did not hear the voice of God, nor did he understand any of the meaning of the dream. In fact, in God's sovereign workings the King could not even remember anything of substance from the dream. It was gone from him.

God's purpose in this was to cause the King to trust and to have confidence in God's own spokesman, Daniel. The other "gods" had their spokesmen; but Daniel was the spokesman of the one true God, and God was going to prove this to the King. This dream was going to serve as a "sign" to authenticate God's messenger, who was to bring God's message to the King.

We will not go into all the details of this amazing story. They are all extremely important and very inspirational; but that is not the purpose of this study. I would encourage you, however, to read over

Daniel, Chapter Two; and let the Lord bless you with the thrill of the story as it unfolds before you. There are so many wonderful lessons to learn from the Lord's workings in Daniel, and He would teach us through him. But let us now go on to the dream:

THE IMAGE

In Nebuchadnezzar's dream he saw the vision of a huge statue or image. The image he saw standing tall was a man of royal appearance. This great image was divided into four distinct parts, each part being made of a metal differing from the others.

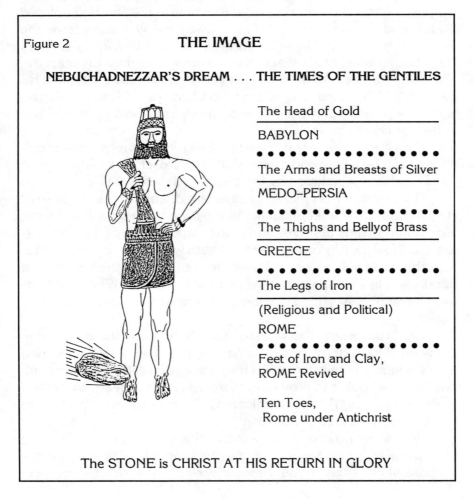

Figure 2   **THE IMAGE**

NEBUCHADNEZZAR'S DREAM . . . THE TIMES OF THE GENTILES

The Head of Gold
_____
BABYLON
• • • • • • • • • • • • • • •
The Arms and Breasts of Silver

MEDO–PERSIA
• • • • • • • • • • • • • • •
The Thighs and Bellyof Brass

GREECE
• • • • • • • • • • • • • • •
The Legs of Iron
_____
(Religious and Political)
ROME
• • • • • • • • • • • • • • •
Feet of Iron and Clay,
ROME Revived

Ten Toes,
 Rome under Antichrist

The STONE is CHRIST AT HIS RETURN IN GLORY

The kingly head was made of *gold*. The breast, or chest, and the two arms were made of *silver*. The belly, or abdomen, and the thighs or hips were made of *brass*. Last of all, the two legs of the image were of *iron*; and the two feet of the legs, included as part of the "legs," these were seen to degenerate to a mixture of *iron and clay*. This degeneration was extremely noticeable and is brought to our attention in the *ten toes*. Study figure 2.

As the King contemplated this magnificent, colossal image, there came a *stone*, not of man's making. This "stone" was something superhuman, or supernatural. This STONE fell upon, or struck, the feet and toes of the image, breaking them into pieces. With the breaking of the feet and toes of the image, the whole colossal structure came crashing down. It crumbled into powder and was blown away by the wind, never to be found again.

The dream was not yet over, for then the STONE became a great *mountain* and filled the whole earth. What a dream this was. This, in truth, was more than a dream; it was a REVELATION and the King seemed to understand that much. He had to know what it meant.

With the help of history and the understanding given to Daniel the Prophet, we now clearly know that the dream is divided into two major parts:

FIRST: The Image itself, representing four Gentile World Kingdoms, showed the continuous unity of Gentile rule of this period.

A. The HEAD of GOLD: Babylon, #1.

B. The Chest and Arms, SILVER: Media – Persian, #2.

C. Belly and Thighs of BRASS: Greece, #3.

D. The Legs of IRON: #4. Signified both strength and a divided rule-two legs. The feet and toes of iron mixed with clay represent the type of union that will bind the TEN nations together at the *final stage* of this last Empire.

SECOND: The STONE is CHRIST — the Son of God, who, at His coming, will put an end to Gentile political rule and will fill all the earth with His Glorious Kingdom.

(Keep in mind, always, these major parts of this important dream.)

Nebuchadnezzar was duly impressed, but completely baffled. He could not even remember the dream, yet he knew that it was of some great significance. He had no idea at all of its meaning for himself and for history.

Somehow, he was sure that the "gods" were communicating with him. He wanted to know what the message was. He called upon all of his heathen spiritual, scientific and political counselors, with all their wisdom and occult powers of the underworld. They, too, were found to be helpless in this situation. Somehow or other, Daniel had not been consulted. Then, perhaps as a last resort, the King called this one who was God's Spokesman.

Nebuchadnezzar was shrewd; he was not going to be fooled or deceived by any of these. He prudently demanded that before they tried to tell him the meaning of the dream, they should tell him the dream itself. No clues were given. This was a matter of life or death for all the "wise" men. Daniel, of course, went to God in prayer.

God, who had given the dream to the King, now gave to Daniel, His prophet, both the dream and its interpretation. Daniel at once proceeded to give it to the King, who instantly recalled and confirmed the dream. Henceforth, he recognized the TRUTH of the interpretation as given by Daniel. The King recognized that this dream was a message from God, DANIEL'S GOD.

DANIEL'S INTERPRETATION, GOD'S MESSAGE

Because this message came straight from God via His spokesman, Daniel, with enough PROOF (signs) to convince the King, you, too, can believe it. Accept its truth by faith. There is also the added witness of HISTORY, for much of the dream is now fulfilled. Since that which has been fulfilled was fulfilled LITERALLY, we can expect and be sure that the remainder also will be *literally* fulfilled. It will actually happen as given in this dream.

The four parts of the image, the gold, silver, brass and the iron, plus the iron mixed with clay, signify or represent the *four* Gentile World Powers that were to rule upon the earth. God would use these four Gentile Powers, or Kingdoms, or Empires, to subjugate the Nation of Israel and to chastise his chosen, but disobedient and rebellious, people. This time of Gentile Rule is that time our Lord called

THE TIMES OF THE GENTILES.

> *And they shall fall by the edge of the sword, and shall be*
> *led away captive into all nations: and Jerusalem shall be*
> *trodden down of the Gentiles,* **until the times of the**
> **Gentiles be fulfilled.** [emphasis added] (Luke 21:24.)

Jerusalem speaks of and for the Jewish people or the Nation of Israel, of which it is the Capital. Just as Washington speaks of and for the American people and the United States of America. Jesus is saying that the Jewish people would be subjugated by Gentile powers until this time of Gentile rule, according to God's plan and purpose, is brought to an end.

Look in the book of Nehemiah to prove this truth from Scripture and to identify the overriding moral principle by which the Lord is here working. In dealing with His people, Israel, God says:

> *Testifiedst against them, that thou mightest bring them*
> *again unto the law: yet they dealt PROUDLY, and*
> *harkened not unto thy commandments, but sinned*
> *against thy judgments . . . and withdrew the shoulder,*
> *and hardened their neck, and would not hear.*
>
> *Yet many years didst thou forbear them, and testifiedst*
> *against them by thy spirit in thy prophets: yet they would*
> *not give ear: THEREFORE GAVEST THOU THEM INTO THE*
> *HAND OF THE PEOPLE OF THE LANDS.*
> (Nehemiah 9:29-30.)

It is clear that this is God's chastisement. Its purpose (please remember this) is to break their rebellious pride and to "bring them again unto thy law." Nehemiah goes on to say that because of their prideful rebellion, they were even then "servants" in the very land promised to them by God:

> *And it yieldeth much increase unto the kings whom*
> *THOU HAST SET OVER US BECAUSE OF OUR SINS: also*
> *they have dominion over our bodies, and over our cattle;*
> *at their pleasure we are in great distress.*
> (Nehemiah 9:37.)

This divine principle of chastisement is still in effect today. It is being enforced by our sovereign Lord. We may not like the thought of it, and many refuse to recognize or admit it, but it is true. This also is the basic cause of the trouble in the Middle East, even in our day.

Israel may be a nation in the affairs of the political world. This is according to the prophetic plan. But she is still completely dependent upon the whim and support of Gentile nations for her insecure peace and safety, limited as she is.

Getting back to the dream of Nebuchadnezzar, we find that, beginning with Babylon and her King, there would be four world kingdoms, four and only four. They would follow in order one after the other.

Daniel said to the King of Babylon: "Thou art this head of gold." So the head of the image represents the Kingdom of Babylon, which is represented by its king.

Following Babylon came the Media–Persian Empire, which is here represented by the breast, speaking of unity; and the two arms that speak of the two principle powers of this empire. This empire is of silver and the differing metals serve to differentiate one kingdom from the other, a definite line of demarcation.

The Grecian Empire follows and is represented by the belly of brass together with the hips, all speaking of strength and speed.

The fourth empire to follow in order was to be the Roman Empire, and is represented by the two legs of iron. The iron speaks of strength and the cruel rule of this empire crushing all who oppose it. God has more to tell us of this fourth, or Roman Empire because it involves times and circumstances of great importance.

It is during this Empire that Christ the Messiah would come. It was to be during this Empire, controlling Israel with its rebellious pride, that the Messiah would be "cut off." It is to be this empire that continues to rule until the end of time, when Christ returns as the Divine Judge and the King of Glory.

A close look at this fourth empire reveals several important factors which HISTORY NOW CONFIRMS:

1. The two legs represent the two branches of the Roman Empire: Political and Religious.

2. There has been no Empire to follow Rome, which still "Rules" the world through the Vatican.

3. The last stage of this empire, represented by the two feet and the ten toes of an iron and clay mixture, is a time of instability and political division and

diversification.

4. The Roman Empire, the Western Confederation of Nations, North Atlantic Treaty Organization (NATO), and the European Common Market (EMC) must therefore be seen to be the empire of the Antichrist , who will be its final "king," "president" or political leader.

THE TWO LEGS

Let us consider the above four points. There are those who view the two legs as representative of the Eastern and the Western divisions of the Roman world. There is nothing significant in this implication, for it seems to lead nowhere. It is a dead end street with nothing at the end. It seems that the Lord is showing us something much more significant.

Consider this: The Roman Empire is very clearly and correctly represented by TWO VERY REAL AND POWERFUL BRANCHES TODAY. These "legs," of course, upon which the Roman world stands are its POLITICAL "leg" and its RELIGIOUS "leg." One is the political harmony and growing unity of Western nations bound by treaty. The other — without fear of contradiction — is the ROMAN CATHOLIC CHURCH with its SEAT at the VATICAN.

It has for many years been called the HOLY ROMAN EMPIRE. Even today world leaders from every part of the globe pay homage in recognition of the Papacy. Papal power "rules" over the lives of millions of the world's peoples scattered among many lands and nations. This is the only understanding acceptable because it is in complete harmony with the unity of the witness of Scripture.

For example, in the last stage of the Roman Empire we clearly are given, in Scripture, two leaders. The one is Political and is the Antichrist. The other is Religious and is called the "false prophet." It will be this second leader who will lead the whole world in the worship of the image of the Antichrist.

Like the emperors of old, this First one also will be recognized as, or acclaimed to be, Divine by the Second; and the Second will enforce the worship of the First. Thus we are given in the Scriptures a picture of this evil "trinity": Satan, Antichrist, and the False Prophet.

ROMAN RULE

Now consider the facts given in this revelation of the dream of Nebuchadnezzar. This Roman Empire will be the LAST world empire, or world power, before Christ returns to establish His Rule. THERE WILL BE NO OTHER.

What does this mean? Well, for one thing, we know that Rome was and is a WESTERN power. Today it is seen in that alliance of nations of the old Roman world. This means, among other things, that Russia will NEVER be victorious in her desire for world conquest. She will never conquer the West. IT IS NOT IN THE BOOK. It simply cannot happen.

The only one who will Conquer the West, and the rest of the world also, is CHRIST. His kingdom will be a righteous kingdom. It will be a glorious kingdom of world peace for one thousand years.

It will not be the "church" that conquers the world to bring in righteousness as is taught. The "church" in its corrupted and compromised form will become part of Antichrist's kingdom. It will become that world's religious system, catholic in nature, under the leadership of the False Prophet. This "church" is spoken of in condemning words by Christ when He says:

> . . . *I will spue thee out of my mouth.* (Revelation 3:16.)

Revelation 3:14-22 gives us the total picture of that apostate church. This same "church" and religious system is seen again in Revelation, Chapter 17, where she is depicted as an evil woman and is called "THE GREAT WHORE," because she has "committed fornication" with the kings and inhabitants of the earth. This is plain talk, but remember, IT IS SCRIPTURE.

THE FEET

The feet of the legs are seen to be a mixture of iron and clay. The feet, of course, end with the ten toes. This represents the final stage of the Roman Empire. This represents the final stage of the Roman Empire. It is speaking of a lack of cohesiveness; of peoples and political systems joined together without the stability of a united kingdom. Instead they are bound by accord or treaty.

The description as given in Daniel 2:41-43 is one of instability, and even division or contention. "Partly broken" is the term used to show the elements of the "kingdom" not existing as a unified whole, but that its union is by agreement. In other words, even as we have it today, there are the individual nations of peoples bound together for economic and security protection against common enemies. Note this phrase:

> . . . *they shall mingle themselves with the seed of men: but they shall not cleave one to another* . . .
> (Daniel 2:43.)

As you do a word study of these statements you come up with a picture of the final stage of the Roman World. You will find it to be the exact condition of our day and of our Western World. WE ARE LIVING IN THE LAST STAGE OF THE ROMAN EMPIRE.

It is described as a mixture of people, of governments, and of governmental systems that will be united by agreement or accord. This simply means that the Western World, and last stage of the Roman Empire, will not be held together by one central government, but by treaties or alliances. This is exactly what we have in our NATO Alliance, and even more clearly in the European Common Market.

We, in our day, are living in the time period represented by the ten toes of Nebuchadnezzar's dream so many years ago. THIS IS THE END TIMES.

Praise God, Christ is coming, but before He does, the Antichrist will. This is not reading into Scripture. It is reading current events by means of the Scriptures. It is "WATCHING."

The Western World, of which we are a part, is UNITED by alliances for ideological, economical, social, religious and security purposes. Yet the states remain independent and interdependent competitors of each other. There is disagreement, but there is unity.

After some two thousand years, no one would expect an empire to be confined to the same territorial boundaries that it had at first. In every empire, with the passing of time, there is a give and take of boundaries, but the empire retains, characteristically, its own identity. Even so with ROME.

Upon the basis of the above conclusions, therefore, (Are you ready for this?) we can regard our day and our time, in every possibility, probably, to be the TIME in the Roman Empire when the

Antichrist can be expected to appear. We can expect his APPEAR-ANCE at any time.

Notice how I have stressed the word *APPEARANCE*, lest you be confused. When the Antichrist *appears* on the scene of world history he will not be recognized, or *known* as to his identity. His true identity will come only at his REVELATION, a short time later.

He will arise out of one of NATO's allied nations. After some difficulties, he will gain the full support and backing of the European Common Market Community. And he will become THE leader of the Western World.

Keep these facts in mind. God gives to us some important clues in Chapter Seven of Daniel. Added to these, they make the picture ever more clear, and certain our understanding. But before going on to that very important and helpful chapter; return to the conclusion of Daniel's interpretation of the image of King Nebuchadnezzar's dream.

THE STONE

. . . in the days of these kings shall the God of heaven set up a kingdom, which shall NEVER be destroyed . . .
(Daniel 2:44.)

This is a simple statement of FACT, an objective truth of revelation which must be taken at face value BY FAITH. If there is a God in heaven, then it is true. If not, then we are all dead meat and it does not matter.

The FACT of this revelation is *proven* by the RESURRECTION of Jesus Christ. For the believer there is no problem. It is the godless and the unbeliever who has a problem. The above quoted Scripture gives us an overview of the eternal Kingdom of Heaven with Jesus Christ our Lord as its glorious King. Many more details dealing with this Kingdom are given throughout Scripture. Here it simply states that: It is at the time of the close of this period in the history of Gentile supremacy, THE TIMES OF THE GENTILES, that Christ will return.

He will put an end, forever, to the godless rule of heathen nations; because His purpose for Israel has been accomplished. Christ will rule. Jesus is coming again. COMING IN GLORY AND POWER.

We can be sure that He is coming SOON, imminently, for we are living now in the closing years of Gentile rule. The period of the solidarity in the Roman World is long gone. We are living in the time of the FEET, the iron and clay mixture. We can even now count the TOES of the image.

Some would say, "Don't panic, it could be a thousand years yet before Christ comes."

Not so, fellow believer. The picture simply does not lend itself to that kind of understanding. That is the voice of unbelief. Some say that we should not major on the minors. Since when is Christ's return a "minor" subject? Since when are the prophetic truths of Scripture to be understood as of MINOR IMPORTANCE?

It is this kind of thinking that blinded Israel to the prophet's message concerning the Messiah's FIRST coming. No, these truths are of major importance. Look at the amount of Scripture dealing with the subject. Our Lord Himself told us again and again to WATCH.

We remember with great joy that: BEFORE Christ comes back to establish His Kingdom, He must come for His Church and remove us, as He has promised. His Church will be taken from the scene of the outpouring of His wrath, in the Tribulation Period, just prior to His return. The hour is late; it is almost the midnight hour. Time is short.

NOW is the time to know WHO you are and WHERE you are spiritually. Now is the time to KNOW why you are where you are, no guessing, no playing games, no playing religion. Who are YOU? Are you a Christian in the know, or floundering and drifting with the tide of indifference, compromise and apostasy?

These are very significant days in which to be alive. You can be certain that the Lord does not want His children to be indifferent to the prophecies of the day in which we live. Don't be a sleeping Christian.

The end of life as we know it is upon us. The STONE is about to fall upon the feet of the image. The image is about to crumble. I hope that your faith is strong enough to stand the shock waves that are about to reverberate throughout the world. Their rumblings we can already hear and feel. Are you Ready?

The STONE represents CHRIST, the Son of God, heir to the THRONE. The FALLING of the stone represents His return, and He is seen to fall upon the feet and toes. You will notice that it is in the days of *these* kings, as represented by the toes, that He comes. The picture is just too clear to misunderstand. Now is the time. How many days we have left is no longer the question to ask. We should be asking how FEW do we have. CHRIST IS COMING.

DANIEL'S DREAM
Daniel, Chapter Seven

As we read the seventh chapter of Daniel, it becomes very obvious that Daniel's dream covers the same period of history, and the same truths, as given in the dream of Nebuchadnezzar in Chapter Two. Here we find much more detailed information and greater insight given into the workings and foreknowledge of our sovereign Lord.

The prophetic truths of Scripture, as revealed by God and given to us by His prophets, do not come to us in a chronological order of events, prophecy by prophecy. There is an overall progression, which may be seen in prophecy; but one is often built upon, or is an enlargement of one already given. A particular prophecy may deal with one small aspect of a previously given prophecy; and, thus, not follow the sequence of events. One prophecy may even precede another in the order of occurrence. These thoughts are important to prophetic understanding and correct interpretations of Bible prophecy.

Much of the confusion and misunderstanding concerning the book of Revelation is simply because many teachers and preachers FAIL to recognize and apply this principal of prophetic revelation. In their failure to recognize this principle they proceed to interpret the book of Revelation chronologically, causing them to misrepresent the Word of God. The book of Revelation simply cannot be rightly and correctly understood that way. Yes, there is progression in the book of Revelation, but it is NOT verse by verse, or chapter by chapter, or prophecy by prophecy.

In this dream of Daniel's, in Chapter Seven, we see this principle clearly applied. The four kingdoms of Chapter Two are again brought before us; but now great emphasis is put upon the FOURTH kingdom. Seven comes after two, but they are not chronological. They cover the same time period, the Times of the Gentiles.

In Chapter Seven the focus of attention is drawn to the Roman World kingdom; the legs and feet and toes of the image of Chapter Two. Notice here that *only one verse* in this chapter is given to the three kingdoms of Babylon, Media-Persian and Greece, while two long verses pertain to the one kingdom of Rome.

In the interpretation given to Daniel, again, only one verse is given as a general explanation of the four beasts. Then EIGHT WHOLE VERSES are focused upon the FOURTH beast exclusively!

So here is a subsequent prophecy, focusing in on a portion of a previous prophecy, but not representing subsequent events.

In this manner, we are given to understand that ROME is of extreme importance to us in our understanding of Bible prophecy concerning these last day events. ROME IS NOW.

THE FOUR BEASTS

In Chapter Two of Daniel, in the dream of Nebuchadnezzar, there were four kingdoms that would exist during the Times of the Gentiles. They were represented by the IMAGE made up of four different kinds of metals. In Daniel's dream, or vision, of Chapter Seven we have these same four kingdoms of the same time period represented by FOUR BEASTS.

Daniel saw these four creatures coming up out of the sea. The "sea" in Scripture is a symbol of the masses of the peoples of the earth. It also can be understood as nations, because nations in Scripture can be correctly translated as "peoples." In these terms the thought also includes the political systems that govern or control the inhabitants of the earth.

The first beast is a lion, king of the beasts, and corresponds to the head of gold in Chapter Two. The lion is Babylon. The second beast is like unto a bear. Its description corresponds to the two arms and the breast of the image. It is the Media-Persian empire that followed Babylon in history.

Then there arose a third beast, a leopard, fleet and swift in its conquest, depicting the Grecian empire; and the rapidity of the conquests of Alexander The Great. The four heads of this third beast symbolize the four generals of Alexander's army, who divided the empire upon the untimely death of its ruler.

Then there comes ROME, the fourth beast, dreadful and terrible, ruthless, cruel and strong. It is said that it had *ten horns*. And it is to be understood that these ten horns correspond to the ten toes of the image in Chapter Two.

It takes no great imagination to see the relation between these beasts and the image of Nebuchadnezzar. We do not need to rely upon our imagination, however, for the interpretation is made for us in the chapter. We can, however, understand certain implications. For example: we can understand without difficulty that, as with the toes, the ten horns represent the ten prominent nations of the Roman World at the time of the end. It is to be in their time that Antichrist comes first to *appear* upon the world scene as the "Little Horn."

So far, there is not too much that differs between the two dreams; except that Daniel's dream depicts the beastly character, the animal, cruel, carnal nature of the rule that these heathen kings wield over their subjects and among nations. Still, it is just at this point, with the description of the beast, that God focuses, very significantly, upon events relative to the ten horns. Details are given here that could not be seen in the illustration of the ten toes. Notice these important facts:

> *I considered the horns, and behold, there came up*
> *AMONG THEM ANOTHER LITTLE HORN, before whom*
> *there were three of the first horns PLUCKED UP by the*
> *roots: and, behold, in this horn were eyes like the eyes of*
> *man, and a mouth speaking great things. (Daniel 7:8.)*

This is important information added to the revelation of Chapter Two. In this verse we encounter Antichrist. Several clues are given about the events, the time, and the character of the APPEARANCE of the Antichrist, and to his person.

Daniel continues to relate his dream, in verse nine, to show that: While beholding the vision of the "Little Horn," the thrones, or seats, of governmental powers were "cast down," or destroyed, by "the Ancient of Days." This is Christ, in His return, as He sits upon His throne. Judgment is given unto Him as the books are opened.

Pause here for a moment and read Revelation Chapters One and Twenty. You will find that you are reading of the events which Daniel saw in his dream. Daniel describes in perfect detail the judgment of the Antichrist as given in Revelation 19:20. You would do well to compare the two verses:

> *I beheld then because of the voice of the great words*
> *which the horn spake: I beheld even till the beast was*
> *slain, and his body destroyed, and given to the burning*
> *flame. (Daniel 7:11.)*

> *. . . the beast was taken, and with him the false prophet*
> *that wrought miracles before him, with which he*
> *deceived them that had received the mark of the beast,*
> *and them that worshiped his image. THESE BOTH WERE*
> *CAST ALIVE INTO A LAKE OF FIRE BURNING WITH*

BRIMSTONE. (Revelation 19:20.)

These are two separate prophecies written centuries apart. The prophecies of Revelation contain many more details, given to help in understanding these great events of the end of time.

The rest of Daniel's dream is the reiteration of the coming Kingdom of Christ. Daniel calls the King of that final Empire the "Son of Man," which is a common title for our Lord in the New Testament. Daniel says that all people, nations and languages shall serve Him in His everlasting Kingdom. John, in Revelation, puts it this way:

> *After this I beheld, and, lo, a GREAT MULTITUDE, which no man could number. Of all nations, and kindreds, and people, and tongues, stood before the throne, and before the Lamb clothed with white robes, and palms in their hands;* (Revelation 7:9.)

It almost sounds as if we are reading out of the same book, doesn't it? Well, WE ARE. We are reading of the same events in the integrated Word of the Living, sovereign Lord. What Daniel saw is that which John saw, and what they saw we shall see.

If we truly know the Lord, we will be part of that great multitude that John and Daniel both saw. If you do not belong to the Lord Jesus, then you will be among those who are condemned with the Antichrist. Christ, the Son of Man, will sit upon His throne to judge this wicked world.

It is true that we live in a world divided, the "haves" and the "have nots." I trust that you are among those who HAVE a saving FAITH in JESUS CHRIST. Do you BELIEVE GOD?

INTERPRETATION OF DANIEL'S DREAM

At this point give your attention to something important. It is noted here because we can easily slip over it as we often do. Listen carefully to Daniel:

> *I came near unto one of them that stood by, and ASKED HIM THE TRUTH OF ALL THIS. So he told me, and MADE*

ME KNOW the interpretation of the things. (Daniel 7:16.)

The thing all should see is that, as Daniel did, WE MUST *SEEK* TRUTH and understanding from the Lord. Don't be the least bit interested in a man's opinion on these things. Although, if he has some insight given by God, after diligent search of the Word, listen to him. But, if we WANT TO KNOW THE TRUTH, we must ask and wait upon the Lord for understanding.

It is good to read the works of godly men on this subject; but, you may be amazed at how much of their "teaching" is nothing more than defending their opinion. Sometimes it simply does not matter what the Scriptures say ever so clearly; because men are going to believe what they want to believe. At times even godly men can get off on this self trip.

My, how we take pride in SCHOLARSHIP. If so-and-so says it, then that must be the way it is whether Scripture is in agreement or not. This is the way most people think when it comes to prophetic understanding. Usually, because they are too lazy or un-knowledgeable to study in their own in search of truth.

Daniel was GIVEN the interpretation of the four beasts:

These great beasts, which are four, ARE FOUR KINGS,
which shall arise out of the earth. (Daniel 7:17.)

This is a clear statement of FACT, interpreting the symbolism of the dream. "Earth" here is the symbolic way of saying that these four kings will rule over literal earthly kingdoms. We must not spiritualize this — that tends to destroy the truth being given — but accept it as a statement of actual future fact.

These four kings do not rule all at the same time. They follow one upon the other as is seen in verses four through seven.

One point of understanding needed here is the importance of remembering that, often, the term "king" is synonymous with the *kingdom* over which he rules. This term in prophecy may have in focus the individual ruler, or his kingdom or both; the context will determine. For example, a president may speak for himself, or he may speak representing the nation.

There is a cartoon taken from a news magazine some time ago. It shows the President of the USA standing upon the outline of that country, on a globe of the earth. The Prime Minister is standing upon England, the Chancellor upon Germany, the President of France upon that country, and the Pope standing upon the Vatican in Italy. Each figure is clearly identifiable. Everyone who saw this cartoon knew that it depicted England, Germany and France in a political exchange with the USA. The Pope was there in representation of the Vatican. The Vatican represented the Roman Catholic Church with its world wide influence in political affairs.

THERE WERE NO WORDS, but the message of the cartoon was loud and clear. Each man represented a country or kingdom or empire, and so it is with the term "king" in prophecy. This understanding of the relation of the king and his kingdom is important for you to keep in mind. As in the cartoon, there were three prominent "kings" or HORNS in Europe, so shall it be, according to Daniel's dream, at the end of time. Without this factual understanding, many things in prophecy will make little or no sense at all.

THE FOURTH BEAST

Daniel is heard to ask specifically about the FOURTH beast or kingdom. God is, again, directing thought to the great significance of the prophecy concerning this fourth kingdom and its leader in end time affairs.

Something special to consider is the fact that Antichrist will NOT suddenly arrive. He will not suddenly come upon the scene saying, "Here I am. I'm the Antichrist and filled with satanic powers." OF COURSE NOT. Who would trust him in that case?

He will come and he will DECEIVE the nations. He will arise within the political arena of ONE NATION and become the political leader of THAT NATION; elected by due process of law. It will be the will of the people because they will not know who he is; or what he will be a very short time from then. He will gain the respect and confidence of our Western World, BEFORE he becomes the ANTICHRIST. He will *appear* among men as a leader of men, and his *appearance* will be normal, unheralded and almost uneventful.

The interpretation given at first is simple and direct. It states that the Fourth Beast represents the Fourth World Empire to come in order in history. It suggests that it would be cruel, hard, demanding, and that it would be very strong. We know ROME to have been all these. The interpretation then skips over many years of time and history, and takes us to the end of that dreadful empire.

It is again the time of the ten toes and of the ten horns. But, here the principal thing revealed is the RISE of the "LITTLE HORN." Many clear statements are given concerning him; so that we will not be mistaken about the importance of this man soon to come upon the world scene.

THE LITTLE HORN

Consider this marvelously detailed revelation. And remember that God is here sharing many FACTS of prewritten history. History before its occurrence. God expects us to use our BRAINS. He has given them to us for this purpose. There are certain logical conclusions and deductions that can and must be made before these prophecies are applied to the time in which they belong.

If it is this point of time and history, our time, then we should begin to see many things shaping up to these events of recorded prophetic history, both generally and specifically. It is not wrong to make certain deductions, nor is it wrong to come to conclusions based upon a true Scriptural understanding of clear Scriptural statements.

In prophetic studies we must carefully and clearly know that DOCTRINE cannot be based upon deductions. Doctrine must be based solely upon the OBJECTIVE TRUTH OF GOD. Often, prophetic deductions are based upon understanding and not upon clear Scriptural statements, and this is very shaky ground. TIME will tell whether our deductions are correct, for *prophecy can be fully understood only in the LIGHT of its own FULFILLMENT.*

Yet, we should not be afraid to allow the prophetic Scriptures to lead us to a logical conclusion or understanding. If we are afraid to venture upon the prophetic seas we will make no progress at all. And we will never gain an understanding of God's wonderful program. This certainly would stunt our growth and weaken the message we preach.

PROPHECY IS A SCIENCE. If you put the right facts together in the right way, you will come up with the right answer. It is something like a chemistry equation; certain quantities added to other quantities produce a certain result. If you add two parts of hydrogen to one part of oxygen (H_2O), you will get water. As this principle is true of mathematics, it is also true of the prophetic Scriptures.

Relying upon the operation of this principle, let us look at some Scriptural FACTS concerning the "Little Horn" and see what deductions can be drawn from them.

FACT LIST:

1. He comes up "among" the other ten. Daniel 7:8

2. He comes up "after" them. Daniel 7:24

3. Before him three of the ten are "plucked up by the roots." Daniel 7:8

4. Before him three "fell." Daniel 7:20

5. He shall "subdue" three kings. Daniel 7:24

From these facts, we are given some very important information about this political leader, and of the end times, to consider. First is HIS RELATIONSHIP TO, AND WITH, THE TEN LEADING NATIONS AND THEIR LEADERS IN THAT FINAL HOUR.

As we look at the FACTS, let us keep our eyes upon today's world situation and the relationships between nations. As noted, there is already a loose confederacy of nations consisting of those powers that make up our Western World — the modern, twentieth century Roman World. Remember the cartoon.

Is it possible that these "Horns" of prophecy depict these "Horns" of today? "Horn" is symbolic of governmental authority. Today we have a group of "Horns" united as NATO. We also have some of these same united as THE EUROPEAN COMMON MARKET (ECM). There are *three prominent leading nations of the ECM*. Everyone knows that they are ENGLAND, GERMANY AND FRANCE. These are always the most vocal. They are the most powerful. They are the most influential powers of Europe. These same three powers, other than for the United States, are the three predominant powers of NATO. Could it be possible that Daniel's vision views these three nations of our day? We must admit that it is *possible*.

Let us go back to our FACT LIST, for there we saw that the "Little Horn" came up *AMONG THEM*, also *AFTER THEM*. These two FACTS then lead us to three deductions:

1. The TEN HORNS *existed before he did.*

2. The "Little Horn" must have some kind of *relationship* with the TEN, but is NOT one of them.

3. He was of the *SAME BEAST*. The word "among" has the basic significance of "in the company of" or "surrounded by, as among friends."

We can, therefore, conclude the following as a perfectly logical understanding in agreement with our Scriptural FACTS:

1. The nation in which the Antichrist will arise as a political leader will not be an older nation of Europe.

2. The nation in which the Antichrist arises as a political leader will be in a friendly relationship with the European Nations of the Old Roman World.

3. The nation in which the Antichrist arises will be newer, or younger, than the old nations of Europe and will spring forth from *the same beast*, its European background.

Upon these logical, Scripturally compatible deductions and conclusions, we are then led to ask: What nation might that be? What nation BEST fits the picture given? What would YOUR answer be? You MUST answer; you must come to some conclusive answer or remain in prophetic darkness. Don't be afraid to step out — let the Holy Spirit guide your thinking.

Most often, we are afraid to think because we are afraid of the implications. We are not really interested in TRUTH. Let's face it; God is telling us *something*. What could it be? Before coming to a premature answer, we must return to consider more of the facts given.

What about the three that *fell*? As we look at the text, we find that there are actually three terms for us to consider here. The first is *"plucked up."* This word or term is describing what Daniel saw in the vision of his dream. It is Daniel's word depicting what he saw, and is, therefore, symbolic and in need of interpretation. The next word is *"fell,"* and is the word used by Daniel as he relates his dream without knowing the interpretation yet, but remembers what he saw in his dream or vision. The third word is *"subdued."* It is this word that is used by the Holy Spirit in the Divinely inspired interpretation of the dream, with its symbolic meanings clearly explained.

This last word, then, is the word that carries the weight of the meaning of the teaching involved. We find in Wilson's *Old Testament Word Studies* that this word, "subdued," has only ONE meaning and that is to HUMBLE.

It does not mean to destroy, or to conquer. It simply could not mean such, because the Ten Horns continue to exist and be in power with the Little Horn. We properly can conclude that the Antichrist, and the nation he leads, will have some kind of POLITICAL struggle with these three principle nations of Europe. And, that somehow, while maintaining their national integrity, they will acknowledge his leadership. It will not, however, be a MILITARY STRUGGLE. We can further conclude:

1. The nation from which the Antichrist will arise as a political leader will have some major point of conflict in POLICY concerning world affairs.

2. This political leader, who will become the Antichrist, will seek to become the controlling figure in the Western Alliance of nations.

3. After some kind of POLITICAL and international pressure and intimidation, a compromise will be NEGOTIATED.

4. This leader will then be given recognized leadership over the Ten Nation Alliance. This may be to insure greater economic and military strength and unity in the Western World; seemingly to bring greater stability to the international world scene.

Remember, and keep in mind, that these deductions have their basis in the VERY WORDS OF SCRIPTURE. This understanding shared with you is, of course, influenced by my knowledge of the rest of the prophetic Scriptures dealing with the subject at hand. Again, the question, "What nation might this seem to suggest?"

A personal leader cannot be identified now. He has not yet reached that point in his career where the identifying clues that the Bible gives to us can be specifically applied. His time of *revelation* is not yet. Still, *his nation* is in operation, and we can even see a shadow of the political struggle that he will have with the three European nations. That is, IF WE ARE AWARE of world events. There is more to help our understanding.

"LITTLE HORN"

Now we come to the importance of the doctrinal STAND on the *VERBAL* INSPIRATION of God's Word. God CHOSE the word, translated for us as "*LITTLE*" Horn. Did he mean to do so? Did God choose THIS word because of the meaning of the word? If not, then words do not mean anything at all. Language loses its value for the communication of ideas, and the Bible becomes a worthless book of meaningless gibber. We must recognize that GOD CHOSE "LITTLE," the Hebrew word, BECAUSE IT CONVEYED THE IDEA HE WANTED US TO SEE.

It is one of God's important CLUES to our correct understanding of His message to us of the End Times.

This word that we are here concerned with is altogether different from the word translated "little" in Daniel, Chapter Eight. There it applies to a TYPE of Antichrist and has a different meaning completely. The word "LITTLE," now under the microscope of examination, found in Chapter Seven in Daniel's dream, is defined in our WORD STUDY book by Wilson as: "A FEW, A LITTLE; *EITHER OF* MEN, THINGS, OR TIME."

Look at that definition closer: The "EITHER OF" implies that it does not mean ALL THREE, but ONE of the three. "LITTLE" means *A FEW MEN*, or *A FEW THINGS*, or *A LITTLE TIME*. But it means only ONE of these. We must pick ONLY ONE to have the proper understanding of "LITTLE." Look through the microscope of logic:

1. "A FEW MEN," speaking of a nation under a political leader, would indicate this to be a nation having a *small population*. Such a nation would have a small standing army. It would not be in a position to have a mighty military capability that would give its leader the influence demanded in this prophecy. Such a nation would not have the ability needed to take control of the Western World. We, therefore, reject this as the meaning desired.

2. "A FEW THINGS." Speaking of a nation, would signify a nation with few or little resources or wealth. This would suggest a poor nation, a nation such as one of our Third World Countries. The influence of

this kind of nation is small, and our arrived at deduction is again negative.

3. This, then, brings us to the one remaining choice. See how it looks and how it fits into the prophetic puzzle. "A LITTLE TIME" — TIME, in the life of a nation, is measured by years and centuries. This is the measurement of the AGE of a nation. A nation having existed for A LITTLE TIME is a YOUNG NATION. There is *nothing* in this understanding that makes it unacceptable. Thus, this deduction is positive: *The political leader who will become the Antichrist will arise in a YOUNG NATION* of the Western Alliance of nations.

This is logical understanding of Biblical words and terms. It is completely within the proper manner of prophetic interpretation. If our deduction is correct, it will be confirmed by the rest of the prophetic picture.

There are many YOUNG nations in our world today. But there is only ONE nation that fits, entirely, the picture given to us in Daniel's dream and its interpretation. What nation could that possibly be? Is there another nation that could even remotely fill the requirements of this prophecy? Remember, the United States recently celebrated its SECOND BIRTHDAY as a nation. We threw ourselves a great big wonderful BIRTHDAY PARTY and rejoiced in the bicentennial of our honored and beloved Constitution. We are just two centuries old. That is YOUNG, but look at the great influence, in all the world, that the United States exerts today.

Yes, and we have had and do have differences with the nations of Europe and especially with ENGLAND, GERMANY AND FRANCE. They do not always agree with us and our thinking. They do not always cower to us. They still make up their own minds and go their own way while maintaining our alliance. Yet, we are clearly told that the Little Horn shall subdue or humble three of them. That is just what the Bible says.

No. I don't like it any more than you do, but I have to listen to what God is saying. Watch closely the developing relationship between our country and the big three of Europe. Keep your eyes open to our own political trends and elected officials. It is later than you think.

Could it really be possible that the good old USA might be the "seat" of the Antichrist? Well, let me ask you, why not? Well, you might say, because we are a Christian nation. Are we? Because America loves the Bible and honors God?

Yes, sure, we honor God and His Word so much that we have booted them both right out of our schools. We even forbid our children to pray to God in the public school buildings. We are, in actuality, an immoral, AIDS infested, blaspheming nation of people who have turned their backs upon God; running hell-bent for judgment.

We are a nation of baby killers, and even demand our RIGHT TO KILL our unborn babies. We are home wreckers and family destroyers. We promote the vilest kinds of lustful, violent, degrading dehumanizing behavior, and pump it right into our homes via television. We have dethroned God and enthroned SEX as the god that we worship. We excuse our animal behavior because we come "from apes." Thus, we declare war on decency.

We promote, accept, and even ordain to the Ministry, as spiritual leaders, the kind of person that the God of heaven judged and destroyed in Sodom and Gomorrah. Very recently, we have seen some two-hundred-thousand Americans march on Washington in defense of such depraved behavior. They demanded protection and equal rights under the law. I might ask, what law? Certainly not God's law.

If you will look closely, you, too, will come to the conclusion that America is not only the BEST candidate for the seat of the Antichrist, but it is, perhaps, the ONLY nation that can qualify. It has been justly said that if God does not judge America, then He should apologize to Sodom and Gomorrah. There are more clues given to us in Daniel, Chapter Nine that confirm this conclusion.

We cannot reject the above conclusion simply because we do not like it or because we do not want it to be so. Many writers say that America is not mentioned in Scripture, and this is true in as far as her name is concerned. Rome was not mentioned in these prophecies, either.

In spite of that, there is absolutely no doubt at all that Rome is referred to in the prophecy of the Fourth Beast. HISTORY PROVES THAT. God had ROME in mind when He revealed the truth in the legs and feet of the image in Chapter Two. He had ROME in mind when He gave to Daniel the vision of the Four Beasts. All agree with this.

Though we do not find the name AMERICA, or THE UNITED STATES OF AMERICA in the Bible, it does not mean that God did not have this country in mind when He revealed these prophetic truths. We can be sure that God, in revealing the future and end-time events, foresaw and foreknew the important and significant role this country would play in the world shaking events of these last days.

Many writers say that the Antichrist will be from one of the Ten Horn nations. That is clearly contrary to the prophetic picture. Also, because they recognize the unusually powerful place that she has today and because they cannot find her in Scripture, many are now saying that the USA must be destroyed before the time of the end. Such is a very illogical conclusion, and groundless. Still others say that she will be reduced to the status of a Third World power, and that all this is to make way for the rise of the Antichrist elsewhere.

Almost no one is looking at what God has said in His use of this word "LITTLE." This is God's adjective to describe the Antichrist and his country. When was the last time you heard someone preach on this?

One thing must be made clear. The Bible does not say that the United States will be the nation from which the Antichrist comes in his rise to political power. THE BIBLE DOES NOT SAY THAT. But, the USA does fit the description given to us as good as, perhaps better, than any other nation. Due to its YOUTH, its great INFLUENCE in world affairs, and due to its RELATIONSHIP with the nations of Europe, the United States appears to be the likely candidate. It seems a very good POSSIBILITY. Is there anything that would disqualify her?

It is true that even now the Western World does, indeed, look to the USA as its "Champion" against aggression. Each European country tries to secure itself; but, and at the same time, they all know that their real defense rests with WASHINGTON. In its dealings with Russia, who speaks for the Eastern Block, WASHINGTON generally speaks for the WHOLE of the West. THIS IS TRUE OF NO OTHER NATION. Here is a Scripture that clearly shows this relationship between the Ten Horns and the Antichrist:

And the Ten horns which thou sawest ARE TEN KINGS, which have received no kingdom as yet, but receive power as kings one hour with the beast.

These have one mind, and shall GIVE THEIR POWER AND STRENGTH UNTO THE BEAST. (Revelation 17:12-13)

Our great nation is going downhill spiritually so rapidly that it makes your head spin. We are being consumed with greed that is feeding the drug trade. It is causing the moral collapse within our political leadership, and in the economic center of our business basis, Wall Street. It has come to the point where you cannot trust anyone anymore, and that includes the man in the pulpit.

It is entirely conceivable that one of our political leaders of TODAY may turn out to be the MAN OF SIN who sells his soul to Satan. Daniel says:

> . . . *he shall be diverse from the first* . . . (Daniel 7:24)

There is going to be something different about this man and/or his country. In fact, there is something very different about the USA. Our Constitution is unique. Our system of government "for the people and by the people," with our guaranteed rights of "life, liberty and the pursuit of happiness," is something NO OTHER NATION ON EARTH has ever enjoyed. Not only is our government different, but our population is different. We are a mixture of ALL the peoples of the earth. No nation has EVER existed such as ours is. Also, concerning the Antichrist, Scripture says:

> *Even him, whose coming is after the working of SATAN*
> *with all power and signs and lying wonders.*
> (II Thessalonians 2:9)

This is clearly going to be Satan's man. He himself may not even fully realize it. But somewhere, sometime, and for some reason, he will have sold his soul to the Devil. Then, when the time is ripe, Satan will empower him with supernatural ability to accomplish his evil design.

> . . . *and the DRAGON gave him HIS POWER and HIS*
> *SEAT, and great authority.* (Revelation 13:2)

We should, therefore, watch the developments in the political arena of our nation. Keep one eye on Washington and the other on the Bible. Some might say that we do not need to worry about this because we won't be here then. It is true that we will be REMOVED by the RAPTURE before Antichrist is REVEALED and before he is empowered by satanic, supernatural powers. But we, THE CHURCH, will be here when he first comes upon the scene of world affairs. There is no indication in Scripture otherwise. Do not be spiritually naive and lulled to sleep by nice sounding words that have no foundation in the word of God. OUR LORD SAYS OVER AND OVER AGAIN, *"WATCH."*

ANTICHRIST'S TIME

The Lord gives to us many clues concerning the Little Horn, the Antichrist, so that we can both identify him, and for the church perhaps, even more important, identify the TIME OF HIS APPEARANCE. Daniel gives us to know that this Man of men will:

> . . . *speak great words against the most High* . . .
> (Daniel 7:25)

This man is going to be an outspoken ENEMY of Jehovah, God, and of our Lord, Jesus Christ. This, of course, will be as he has been revealed for whom he really is, the ANTICHRIST. We can assume that, even before that time, he will be no FRIEND of true Biblical faith. He may have a name as a Christian, but he will be an enemy of the Gospel deep in his heart.

Finally, he will declare HIMSELF to be GOD, or DIVINE, and demand the worship of all the world. He will be the ultimate HUMANIST and a promoter of the NEW AGE philosophy. He will be believed and accepted and followed by the multitudes of this world who have turned their backs upon the sovereign God and have rejected the Gospel of His love and grace as offered in Christ Jesus. Then Daniel informs us that he will:

> . . . *wear out the saints of the most High, and think to*
> *change times and laws: and they shall be given into his*
> *hand until a TIME AND TIMES AND THE DIVIDING OF*
> *TIME.* (Daniel 7:25)

The truth contained in this verse of Scripture (much of which we will look at later in our study) is clearly suggested here. It is so stated to give us the understanding that this MAN will have such a hatred for everything Christian or Jewish that it will express itself in his ceaseless persecution of the SAINTS OF GOD. This will by then be within that period known as THE GREAT TRIBULATION. Part of the reason that this time is so-called is due to the tremendous affliction brought upon this world by this man's endeavor to destroy faith in the Living God. He will then be the world leader, and a great deal must happen to bring that about. He will have a bitter hatred for those who profess faith and loyalty to Christ, the true Messiah. Antichrist will claim to be the Messiah of the world himself. He will seek to annihilate the Christian and the Jew from off the face of the earth; much as Hitler tried to do to the Jews in Europe during the Second World War. Many lives will be lost, and the blood of martyrs will flow freely. However there will be 144,000 of the Jewish peoples who will be SEALED with the SEAL of God. These will be protected according to God's purpose, and for His work of the preaching of the Gospel during this bitter time. *For three and one-half years* the Antichrist will roam and rule like a mad man; like a wild beast, hungry and rabid, seeking out the Saints of the Living God.

The time of his power, his rule, his reign of terror, is specifically stated to be, throughout the Scripture, three and one-half years. This is 42 months or 1260 days. THIS IS THE SPAN OF THE TRIBULA-TION PERIOD. The suffering will be such as the world has never seen from the time of creation until then; and so it is known as THE GREAT TRIBULATION. *Thank God we, THE CHURCH, will not be here!*

Many of our friends and loved ones will remain behind as we are called home: those who have not believed in Christ as Lord and Saviour. We must make every effort to bring them to Christ NOW. If they are left behind when we are "caught up," their fate will be far worse than that suffered by the Saints of God at the hands of the Antichrist. It is a horrible thing to fall into the hands of an angry God. Do what you can NOW to rescue the perishing. Daniel's dream ends with the coming of the Kingdom of God. Thank God that HE IS SOVEREIGN LORD.

In summary of these two chapters, Two and Seven, of Daniel, we understand:

1. The "Times of the Gentiles" will last from the time of the Kingdom of Babylon until Christ comes to establish His righteous Kingdom.

2. There will be four, and only four, World Empires and they are: BABYLON, MEDIA–PERSIA, GRECIAN AND ROMAN. These will be followed by the KINGDOM OF CHRIST.

3. The Roman Empire, consisting of a confederation of ten nations, will characterize the Western World at the end of this time.

4. An eleventh nation would arise as the seat of the Antichrist, from which he will spring forth in his political career of world rule.

5. The ten nations of Europe will give to him their power, or accept his leadership. After a brief time of political confrontation he will "humble" the three prominent ones among the ten.

6. The Antichrist will be anti-God, and he will pour out his hatred upon the saints of God. His reign will become a reign of terror and is identified in Scripture as "The Great Tribulation Period," and the "time of Jacob's trouble." More generally it is called, "THE TRIBULATION PERIOD."

7. Antichrist's designated time of rule and terror is given to be a "time, times and a dividing of time." This is understood throughout Scripture, being interpreted by Scripture as 42 months and 1260 days, or three and one-half years. (Revelations 11:2-3; 12:6, 14; 13:5)

8. When Christ returns in glory to establish His Righteous Kingdom, Antichrist will be judged and cast into burning fire.

These prophetic FACTS OF SCRIPTURE are generally accepted by faithful Bible teachers. They should be understood and be made to become very familiar in your thinking. Many more prophetic Scriptural truths will be added to these. Build your building of prophetic understanding with one brick of TRUTH at a time. After you have learned well these basic truths, you will be ready to continue to the very HEART of Bible prophecy as found in Daniel, Chapter Nine.

DANIEL'S SPECIAL DELIVERY MESSAGE
Daniel Chapter Nine

In coming to this most important chapter, Daniel Nine, we see something wonderful. It serves as a real example of the value of prophecy for each of us personally. Daniel had been studying prophecy. He had come to the conclusion that the time had arrived, according to God's predetermined schedule, for Israel to be delivered from their Babylonian captivity. God had revealed His plans to His spokesman, Jeremiah, the prophet, *and Daniel believed God.* He therefore says:

> . . . *I Daniel understood by the books the number of years . . . (*Daniel 9-2)

We find, then, that Daniel's understanding of PROPHECY drove him to his knees to seek God's favor in PRAYER. He prayed, confessing his sin and the sin of his people. It was not just the sin of disobedience and rebellion, but the sin of UNBELIEF. The two former are the fruit of the latter. Real understanding of prophecy, as is given in Scripture, WILL CAUSE US TO DRAW CLOSER TO THE LORD. It will drive us to prayer and confession. If it does not do this, it is because you simply DO NOT BELIEVE GOD.

Next, we find an example of one truth, previously shared with you, about "*friends.*" We find Daniel in sweet communion with God, as a true believer, and as a friend of God. Suddenly he has a glorious visitor. It is GABRIEL, God's SPECIAL DELIVERY ANGEL. He has come in his heavenly flight directly from the Throne of God; sent to Daniel with a very distinct and personal message for this very exceptional "friend" of God. Gabriel came and reached down and touched Daniel. What a touch that must have been. Then, in his heavenly voice, Gabriel said:

> . . . *O, Daniel, I am now come forth to give thee skill and understanding.*

> . . . *and I come to shew thee; for thou art GREATLY BELOVED: therefore understand the matter, and consider the vision.* (Daniel 9:22-23)

HOW GRACIOUS GOD IS. Because of His love for His faithful servant, His true friend, God would share with Daniel a wonderful ability. He gave Daniel the wisdom to understand the truth, God's truth. This act of the sovereign Lord is expressively sweet and kind. It gives to us a clear insight concerning John 15:14-15, where Jesus refers to us as FRIENDS. O, to be a friend of God!

Notice that there is a *condition* there in John expressed by the "if" of the verse. Do YOU qualify? It is simply a matter of loving obedience to the will and to the Word of our Lord. It is the difference between being *religious* and being *spiritual*. Gabriel's message to Daniel is for us, for you and me, IF WE ARE A FRIEND OF GOD. That unique wisdom to understand is given to us, also, by Christ through His Spirit as we abide in Christ, and His Word abides in us. It is NOT academic. It is spiritual.

GABRIEL'S MESSAGE

This divine message brought by Gabriel to Daniel is the basic KEY to all prophetic understanding. Without this KEY, and the ability to use it correctly, the DOOR of understanding will remain closed, as it is today for so many Christians. An improper use of this KEY will simply lead to wrong conclusions and a closed door.

There is a "right" way and a wrong way to "divide" Scripture, to arrive at Scriptural truth. We must always, and at all times, examine our understanding of Scripture. We must always be OPEN to new or fresh insight, for there is no one of us that can say we have all the truth. We do not have the last word. GOD DOES, and this is most certainly true concerning prophecy.

Someone has said: "It is not that we should have an open mind, for that can be filled with ANYTHING." We must, however, have a CLEAR mind to see clearly the Scriptural truth God would share with us.

One thing that usually clouds the mind, as it filters out truth, is OPINION. Opinion is a belief without foundation, being based upon no certain knowledge of truth. Instead, opinion is based upon that which seems true, valid or probable, according to one's own wisdom. Another thing that is equally effective in filtering out the pure light of truth is TRADITION or "custom." Do not believe something just because you have always believed that way, or because it IS believed, or because it is taught. Believe it only if God says it.

Men, often educated men, and sometimes "godly" men, are extremely good at spiritual gymnastics when it comes to the defense of what they believe. We should not get involved in defending our beliefs. Prefer to stand in defense of the Gospel, as Paul put it, and the Gospel is the Word of God. Stand in defense of Scripture and Scriptural truth always.

THE KEYS GIVEN BY GABRIEL

This KEY, as found in Daniel and given to him by the angel Gabriel, is specifically brief, just a few verses, but very detailed. It is a clear account of God's predetermined plan and purpose for humanity within a given time period. This period was to extend from the time of Daniel until the glorious Kingdom of Christ is established. This message, too, like Chapters Two and Seven, covers the "Times of the Gentiles."

There is a great difference, though, for the focus of Two and Seven is upon the Gentile nations and their leaders; while the focus of Chapter Nine is squarely upon ISRAEL. One thing becomes apparent. This message of Gabriel's has to do with events and times that specifically deal with and are concerned with Israel as a nation and God's dealing with her.

The Gentiles are not seen here at all except in so far as it affects Israel and the working out of God's purpose for Israel. THE CHURCH IS NOWHERE IN VIEW. Although we, the Church of Jesus Christ, can benefit from this prophecy, the message is not directed to us.

This is a specific message that God wants Israel to hear. Another thing that we should understand, that is immensely important to proper prophetic conclusions, is because God, in His dealing with Israel, is working on and within a *specified, predetermined time schedule.*

In that God's dealing with Israel is subject to a *given* time schedule; the history of the Gentile world is subject also to a designated time schedule. In other words, the "Times of the Gentiles" is not going to extend itself indefinitely, nor is it just going to peter out. It will come to a specified end, according to the predetermined, appointed time in the mind of, and under the control of our sovereign Lord.

We as Gentiles and as members of the Church of the Living God, the Body of Christ, can know with a good deal of accuracy OUR TIME. This, however, depends upon our ability to understand the TIME and schedule that God has determined for Israel.

NO, WE CANNOT KNOW THE DAY, NOR THE HOUR, of our Lord's return for His Church. Such knowledge the Father has reserved for Himself, meaning, simply, that He has not revealed that detail. We can, nevertheless, know much more than we are generally led to believe. The following verses show such knowledge:

> *But of the TIMES and SEASONS, brethren, ye have no need that I write unto you.*
>
> *. . . ye, brethren, are not in darkness that that day should overtake you as a thief.* (I Thessalonians 5:1 and 4.)

We may not know when the storm will hit, or when the first snow will fall, but we can tell the seasons. We know Fall is Fall. Everything in prophecy tells us that in our generation we are in the FALL of the prophetic year. The cold, cruel WINTER of God's judgment is about to be ushered in; bringing to a close the year of this dispensation of God's wonderful grace. Read the Book. The time is at hand. Be ready, for the Lord is coming, and we are going home. Rejoice, Christian brother, and praise His wonderful Name.

DANIEL'S TIME FRAME

I refer to this TIME FRAME as Daniel's when, in reality, it is GOD'S TIME FRAME that He revealed to Daniel, His prophet. It was Gabriel, God's special delivery messenger, who brought this most important bit of truth from heaven above. I call it a "TIME FRAME" because it encloses all prophecy until the Kingdom Age. Everything that is going to happen WILL HAPPEN *within the scope of this TIME FRAME.*

This time frame actually *frames* the time limits of the fulfillment of prophecy. It not only frames the outer limits, but it also "frames," if you will, some *inner limits* of prophetic events. Because this is so, everything that will happen in the prophetic picture will happen in its direct relation to this time frame. Underscore this truth in your mind. All that is to happen in the prophetic calendar will occur in its proper relation to this given, precise time frame.

It is most important that we know, inside and out, this time frame as it is REVEALED to Daniel. We *must not* change it by taking away from it or by adding to it, but learn to accept it as given.

It is not only the time involved, but also the events RECORDED in their proper relation to the times given that we must know and understand. It is a picture in a frame. Everything in the picture is within the frame.

It can be likened to a puzzle. Every piece of the puzzle has ONE SPECIAL PLACE where it fits; and they all fit within the frame of the straight edged pieces. When a child is learning to color in a coloring book, we often say to him, "Stay within the lines." Even so, it must be with prophecy. Stay within the lines, the FRAME.

Place every piece of the prophetic puzzle in its PROPER location, within that specified frame. To force a piece into an improper location is to violate the picture, giving a distorted view. You can tell by the shapes and by the color of each piece of prophecy where it belongs. As with a puzzle, some pieces LOOK ALIKE, but they are not. Some pieces will not fit, and so we know that the location is wrong.

Sometimes we simply have to wait until more of the puzzle is in place and the picture begins to take shape. The prophetic picture is now clear, and it is only when we try to force a prophecy, due to opinion or tradition, that we do violence to the whole.

SPECIFIED TIME FRAME OF *SEVENTY WEEKS*

Seventy weeks ARE DETERMINED upon thy people and upon thy holy city . . . (Daniel 9:24.)

Gabriel very precisely delivers this message stamped "UR-GENT." This is our sovereign God declaring His purpose. We cannot, in any way except through outright unbelief, deny the fact that God has designated here a specific TIME SCHEDULE. This simply cannot be spiritualized. God says that He has DETERMINED this TIME to be SEVENTY WEEKS, and it WILL be for seventy weeks. He is sovereign.

The word "WEEK," as used here, is, if you will, a "generic" word for *seven*. It is like our word "dozen," which means twelve, that is TWELVE OF ANYTHING. It could be twelve eggs or twelve cars. This word "week," therefore, we know to mean not seven days, but seven of anything, depending upon context. Thus we can understand Gabriel to have said that SEVENTY SEVENS are determined by God concerning Israel.

God's designated measurement of time we know to be the YEAR. For example, God promised Noah after the flood:

> While the earth remaineth, seed–time and harvest, and
> cold and heat, and summer and winter, day and night
> shall not cease. (Genesis 8:22.)

Here God is simply promising Noah and all humanity that the YEARLY CYCLE will continue as long as the earth remains. This, because the year is the basic measure of time. Without it man would have no way of calculating the space of time. The yearly cycle is a fundamentally important part of God's creation for man, animal and plant life. In the Scriptures, both Old and New Testaments, the word TIME is understood contextually to mean ONE YEAR. I might add here that the YEAR, in Scripture, is the SOLAR YEAR consisting of 360 days. This is always the length of the year as considered in the prophetic Word of God.

We find that Nebuchadnezzar, the infamous King of Babylon, was put out of office until "seven times" had passed over him. The Antichrist will rule for a "time, times and the dividing of time." This, then, is seen to be ONE YEAR plus TWO YEARS (plural) plus ONE–HALF YEAR, or three and one-half years (3 ½ years).

This truth is unquestionably proven in Scripture more than once. For example, we are informed that the "woman" fled and was cared for by God for three and one-half years:

> And the woman fled into the wilderness, where she hath

a place prepared of God, that they should feed her there a
thousand two hundred and threescore days.
Revelation 12:6.)

Then, referring to precisely the same event, the Word says:

And to the woman were given two wings of a great eagle,
that she might fly into the wilderness, into her place,
*where she is nourished for **a time and times, and half a***
***time**, from the face of the serpent.* (Revelation 12:14.)

One does not have to be a great mathematician to understand that 1260 days, in a 360 day year, is equal to three and one-half years. This time period is also confirmed in Scripture by the designated use of *forty-two months* as its length.

So, we understand that when God, in the message to Daniel, refers to the 70 weeks, using this generic term for time, He is referring to *70 weeks of years.* You perhaps might say, "Then why didn't God simply say YEARS?" In answer to such a question, I would simply refer you to Christ's answer, when asked by His disciples why He did not speak plainly instead of in parables. He said:

Because it is given unto you to know the mysteries of the
kingdom, but unto them IT IS NOT GIVEN.
(Matthew 13:11.)

There is just enough mystery to God's Word to prevent a person who will not believe from understanding those things in which he lacks interest. Faith is the key that unlocks the Word of God! It is not given.

It is not the will of God that the unbeliever should understand the things that belong to the believing heart. If we would KNOW, we must learn to believe God, and if we believe we will WANT to know. Jesus said:

Ask, and it shall be given you; seek, and ye shall find;
knock, and it shall be opened unto you.

For everyone that asketh receiveth; and he that seeketh
findeth; and to him that knocketh it shall be opened.
(Matthew 7:7-8.)

This might sound a little simplistic, but that is the way it is in the Kingdom of our Lord

So, getting back to the 70 weeks, we know that they are weeks of years. Therefore, we know that God has determined 70 weeks of years, or 70 x 7, or 490 years, as the time that He will be dealing with Daniel's people: the nation of Israel, AS A NATION, and His Holy City, Jerusalem, the capital of national Israel.

What is being said here is important for us to grasp. It is not a time when God is dealing with the Jew, or the individual as such, but with the Jewish Nation. This is one of the reasons that Israel had to become a NATION again, so that these end time prophecies could be fulfilled.

GOD'S PURPOSE

God now tells us just what he plans to accomplish during these four hundred and ninety years, regarding national Israel:

> . . . to finish the transgression,
>   and to make an end of sins,
>   and to make reconciliation for iniquity,
>   and to bring in everlasting righteousness,
>   and to seal up the vision and prophecy,
>   and to anoint the most Holy. (Daniel 9:24)

We have here six specific things that God will do regarding national Israel within the scope of these 490 years. Let us consider that: while these six things concern Israel and her covenant relation with the Lord God of Abraham, Isaac and Jacob, they also indirectly concern us. Because, by faith, we Gentiles are now, through Christ:

> . . . no more strangers and foreigners, but fellow-citizens
> with the saints, and of the household of God.
> (Ephesians 2:19)

It is not that we have become Israel. No, the Church is not Israel. But because of the covenant made in Christ, we who believe have also become partakers of His promises. We stand in relation with Israel, having been like them, circumcised of the heart.

Let us consider this six-fold purpose of God as given to us here.

1. "To finish the transgression"— This is God's primary purpose in His dealing with the nation of Israel during this time period of 490 years. His purpose is to bring to a complete end Israel's rebellious pride; and her stubborn straying from His way; as she seeks to establish her own self righteousness.

God will do this, through judgment and discipline until Israel finally repents and cries out to God for forgiveness; and opens her arms in faith to her heaven sent Messiah.

As it is with Israel, it is God's desire and purpose for each of us, individually, to come to Him in repentance and faith; accepting His gift of life in Christ Jesus, as the Scriptures declare:

> *The Lord . . . is long-suffering to us-ward, not willing that ANY should perish, but that ALL should come to repentance.* (II Peter 3:9)

2. "To make an end of sin" — This is another aspect of God's primary purpose. It is to deal with the sin question. The SIN question must be settled. It cannot be ignored, or swept under the proverbial rug. Sin must be removed from before God, and we cannot do it. God alone can do it. And He does, through the atonement of Christ on Calvary.

He COVERS our sin with the sinless blood of the Lamb of God applied to our hearts by faith; bringing forgiveness, cleansing and the imputed righteousness of Jesus Christ. What the Scriptures say concerning Abraham, they say concerning us as well:

> *. . . Abraham believed God, and it was counted unto him for righteousness.*
>
> *Now it was not written for his sake alone, that it was imputed to him; but for us also, to whom it shall be imputed, IF WE BELIEVE on him that raised up Jesus our Lord from the dead.* (Romans 4:3 and 23-24.)

3. "To make reconciliation for iniquity" — Through the atoning work of Christ on Calvary, the "seed" of the woman, the promised

Messiah; and upon repentance and faith in Christ, Israel will finally be brought back into sweet fellowship with God.

Scripture tells us that they will mourn because of their sin of unbelief and rebellious pride. It had caused them to reject the very One sent by the Father to bring them deliverance and peace. It is even so that we, as believers, are now reconciled through the blood of Christ.

> *Truly our fellowship is with the Father, and with His son Jesus Christ.*
>
> *. . . and the blood of Jesus Christ his Son cleanseth us from all sin.* (I John 1:3 and 7.)

4. "To bring in everlasting righteousness" — With the sin question out of the way, and with Israel again reconciled to God, the sinner to his Lord; Christ will come in Glory and destroy the godless, heathen world empire with its evil leaders.

The Antichrist and the False Prophet will be cast into the Lake of Fire, and Satan will be confined in the Bottomless Pit.

Christ will then establish His Kingdom and rule in righteousness, "a rod of iron."

It will be those who survive the haunting persecution and the horrible suffering of the Great Tribulation, having been sealed with the seal of God and protected in His grace, that enter the Kingdom and replenish the earth; much as Noah and his family did after the Flood. This truth is witnessed to in the Scripture:

> *Then cometh the end, when he shall have delivered up the Kingdom to God, even the Father; when he shall have put down all rule and all authority and power.*
>
> *For he must reign, till he hath put all enemies under his feet.* (I Corinthians 15:24-25.)

5. "To seal up the vision and prophecy" — This word "seal" is unique. It means to bring to a close, to complete, or the finish through fulfillment. So, God specifically says that He will perfect and achieve His stated purpose within the scope of this specified time period of 490 years. It will be done; you can count on it.

Yes, there are scoffers and those who say, "Where is the promise of His coming?" It is to these in their unbelief that He will come as a "thief in the night." When they least expect it, the end will come. It will be the day of the wrath of the Lamb of God, and they will be lost eternally. God has, in great mercy and love, taught the believer to live:

Looking for that blessed hope, and the glorious appearing of the great God and our Saviour, Jesus Christ.
(Titus 2:13.)

6. "To anoint the most Holy" — Jesus is the King of kings and the Lord of lords. Jesus, the Son of God, will be "anointed" of the father in His Kingdom. Anointing was the manner of appointing a king or priest to his official position, and prefigured the anointing of Christ as prophet, priest and King. The reality and glory of that day can be witnessed in the Scriptures:

. . . This is my beloved Son, in who I am well pleased; hear ye him. (Matthew 17:5.)

And I heard as it were the voice of a great multitude, and the voice of mighty thunderings, saying, ALLELUIA: FOR THE LORD GOD OMNIPOTENT REIGNETH
(Revelation 19:6.)

These six things God will do. He will do it all within the framework of the 70 weeks of years, the 490 years, as He has clearly proclaimed. All prophecy, therefore, is related to these 490 years.

It is important for us to understand the makeup of those years in just the way that God has revealed them for us. God's will and purpose for Israel will have been accomplished. He will have fulfilled His covenant made with Abraham and his seed and confirmed with David. It is well for us to remember that these prophecies have a special focus upon NATIONAL ISRAEL. Now that Israel is a nation again, it helps us to understand that the End Times are indeed upon us.

GOD'S DIVISION OF THE 70 WEEKS

As we read carefully this portion of Daniel, Chapter Nine, we become aware that meaning hangs upon every word. God has carefully said what He wanted to say to communicate to His children a precise understanding. The way God has related this prophecy is so very important. We must take great care not to do violence to it by hurried, sloppy, indifferent thinking.

Take notice, now, that the 70 weeks of years are divided into THREE parts. The FIRST TWO parts contain the major portion of the time involved. They are given in such a way as to expect their close relationship or proximity. They follow one upon the other, and together make up a given span of years.

The THIRD part, however, even in the text, is separated from the first two. Let us look, to begin with, at the FIRST TWO DIVISIONS.

> . . . *shall be seven weeks, and threescore and two weeks* . . .
> (Daniel 9:25.)

We have here, first, 7 weeks of seven years, or 7 x 7, or 49 years. This is the FIRST DIVISION. Secondly, there are threescore and two weeks or 62 weeks, or 62 x 7 = 434 years. This is the SECOND DIVISION.

We see, then, that these first two divisions span a time period of 49 + 434 years, or a total of 483 years.

We now can see clearly that the full 490 years of prophecy less these first 483 years leaves just SEVEN (7) years, or the one week that is the THIRD DIVISION. Thus we have:

Division #1 — 7 weeks =	7 x 7 =	49 years
Division #2 — 62 weeks =	62 x 7 =	434 years
	Subtotal	483 years
Division #3 — 1 week =	1 x 7 =	7 years
	Grand Total	490 years

It is this final week, or the third division, which we commonly know as the 70th week of Daniel. This is the week referred to in verse 27. It is the time span of the covenant or treaty to be confirmed by the Antichrist. This week is clearly, even in the text, separated from the first two divisions by the circumstances and events of verse 26.

It is a positive indication that there is a "break," in the time frame, between the first 69 weeks and the final week of the prophecy. This will become more evident as we examine verse 26 in a moment.

Before going on, I wish to point out the events that limit these first two divisions. You will notice immediately the STARTING POINT of these 70 weeks:

> . . . from *the going forth of the commandment to restore and build Jerusalem . . .* (Daniel 9:25.)

This is not the command to rebuild the TEMPLE, but the CITY. The temple had been rebuilt and worship begun some years before. The city was insecure, and the enemies around were not letting them alone; because the walls were broken down. This starting point was to be the command to restore the CITY. To make it a safe place for the Jewish people to live as they returned from captivity.

(I will not, in this present work, take the space to go into a detailed study to establish the time of the commandment. There are many who have done this already and they did it well. My focus is somewhat different. I would encourage you to research this on your own – I am sure that you will come to the same conclusions.)

This commandment went forth to rebuild Jerusalem in 445 B.C. by order of Artaxerxes I (465-424). An account of this event is recorded for us in Nehemiah 2:3-8. This date, then, *445 B.C.*, is the STARTING POINT of this prophecy of 490 years involving world history within this time frame. Next, notice the event that CLOSES the first two divisions of 69 weeks:

> . . . *unto the Messiah the Prince . . .* (Daniel 9:25.)

This is a prophetic statement of great importance. It does not have to do with the birth of the Messiah. But of His APPEARANCE and PRESENTATION to the nation of Israel, as He rode upon the back of a donkey into Jerusalem. This closing event is what we call the Triumphant Entry, and is remembered on Palm Sunday each year. On that day Messiah the Prince came, and it was the final day of the 483 years.

> *All this was done, that it might be fulfilled which was spoken by the prophet, saying,*
>
> *Tell ye the daughter of Zion, BEHOLD, THY KING COMETH UNTO THEE, meek, sitting upon an ass, and a colt the foal of an ass.*

And the multitude that went before, and that followed,
cried, saying, HOSANNA TO THE SON OF DAVID:
BLESSED IS HE THAT COMETH IN THE NAME OF THE
LORD: HOSANNA IN THE HIGHEST.
(Matthew 21:4-5 and 9.)

The starting and closing points of the first 69 years in the one verse shows their unity of succession. This unity is marked only by the stated divisions of the 7 weeks and the 62 weeks. Why this division? The walls were rebuilt in 52 days, and the city was restored before the 49 years were up, so it cannot be referring to these events. But, we do find an interesting event, or happening, at the very time. It is the time of the close of the Old Testament, and the beginning of what is generally known as the 400 silent years.

After Malachi, the prophet, there were no more revelations given from heaven until the time of Christ. This is why it is known as a "silent" time. God was not speaking.

Then, Christ came, according to the plan of God, right on schedule, as He presented Himself, The Prince, in Jerusalem that beautiful Sunday morning. Had the people of Israel not been blinded by their state of unbelief; had they been studying the Scriptures instead of fomenting rebellion in their hearts; they COULD HAVE KNOWN THE TIME OF THE COMING OF THEIR MESSIAH.

I cannot help but wonder just how many "Christians" are in the same condition today. How many will be caught unprepared when He comes again?

A BUILT-IN-HOLD

We are now going to see something extremely interesting, which current events help us to understand in a big way:

AFTER threescore and two weeks shall Messiah be cut off,
but not for himself: and the people of the prince that shall
come shall destroy the city and sanctuary . . .
(Daniel 9:26.)

Notice the stress that I have put on the word "after." It does not say that this is the close of the first two divisions, but it specifically says *after* the close of that period. That is *after* the 62 weeks, the second division of time, *after* that two major events were to take place:

1. Messiah, the Prince, would be "cut off." This is a direct prophecy of the crucifixion of Jesus Christ, and it refers to the substitutionary character of his death on Calvary. Calvary took place *after* the close of the 62 weeks.
2. The next major event that was to take place was to be the destruction of Jerusalem and the sanctuary or temple. This great event was predicted by our Lord as well, in His prophetic discourse in Matthew 24. It was fulfilled in 70 A.D. by the Roman Army under General Titus. It took place almost 40 years *after* the 62 weeks.

The thing to take note of here is the fact that these events happened in time and space history; and that when they took place the 70th week of Daniel had not yet commenced.

These two major events occurred *after* the first two divisions of Daniel's 70 weeks (69 weeks), and *before* the commencement of the last week. This clearly suggests to us that God *planned*, according to his purpose, a *break* in the prophetic time line. He included in the prophecy of the 70 weeks a *built-in-hold*. You can understand it like a "time out" period in a football game. Time, of course, goes on, but the time of the game has stopped. Even so, in this prophecy time has to continue, but the prophetic clock has stopped. God's time frame is a true "countdown," counting down to "0" hour when Christ returns in Glory. (Revelation 19.)

It can be understood if we consider our shuttle launches as an analogy. Every countdown has built-in-holds, as we have noticed often. We have heard this as we have watched it on our television sets at launch time. There is always a specified number of minutes just before launch, but within the specified schedule, a built-in-hold, in which certain things have to be done. We have heard, "T minus 10 and holding," or "T minus 9 and counting," many times. We can understand, therefore, that so it is with God's prophetic schedule.

When Christ rode into Jerusalem on the back of that donkey, GOD'S PROPHETIC CLOCK STOPPED. It has remained *stopped*. We are living in a built-in-hold. IT WILL START AGAIN. He controls the "clock." When the prophetic clock does begin to tick, there will be ONLY SEVEN YEARS LEFT!

If we are unaware of God's prophecies, we will be unaware of the significance of the events taking place. And we will be unaware that ticking of the clock draws to a close this dispensation. Our Lord says in warning of this very thing:

> . . . *take heed to yourselves, lest at any time your hearts be overcharged with surfeiting and drunkenness, and cares of this life, and so that DAY COME UPON YOU UNAWARES.* (Luke 21:34.)

In the mind of God, and because of His great love for all His creatures, it was His plan and purpose, from the beginning, to include the Gentiles in His provision of Grace and Salvation. Therefore, God, in His infinite love and wisdom, set Israel aside because of their sin, pride and rebellion. He sent them into captivity and scattered them upon the face of the whole world; ultimately using the Roman Empire to this end.

Israel as a nation was no more, and God ceased to deal with it as a nation. Her people were now scattered and shattered because they were under Divine judgment. God's clock for national Israel had STOPPED.

God then turned His attention to the Gentile world. Through the Gospel message and the call of Christ the Messiah to the individual, Jew and Gentile alike are now brought into a covenant relation with the Saviour. They are reconciled to God by the blood of the New Covenant shed on Calvary. God is thus calling out from the nations of the world a people for Himself, the Church. Israel is scattered in judgment and the gentiles are called in grace.

It is during this time of the built-in-hold that God is calling out of the world individuals, making up the "Body of Christ."

> *Who gave himself for us, that he might redeem us from all iniquity, and purify unto himself a PECULIAR PEOPLE, zealous of good works.* (Titus 2:14.)

In the book of Romans, Chapter Eleven, Paul teaches this truth. He likens Israel to the natural branches of a good olive tree. Paul likens us gentiles to branches of a wild olive tree. He says that we, the wild ones, have been grafted into the good olive tree. Then he says that the natural branches, ISRAEL, have been broken off.

It is here that Paul first introduces us to one of God's principle "secrets." When the Lord uses the word "mystery," He is referring to a truth that had not been revealed previously. The "mystery," or unrevealed truth that He was now sharing, was that He would in this age of the "hold" make both Jew and Gentile into ONE NEW BODY. This was not to be a NATION, but a SPIRITUAL body, and is called the BODY OF CHRIST, and THE CHURCH.

Now when the Lord has finished dealing with the Gentiles, including those who believe, when that time arrives, the age of GRACE will be closed. He will then graft the "natural branches" back into the good tree. The promise is that "all Israel shall be saved." That is, Israel as a nation will turn in repentance to Christ, in faith, and confess Him as their Messiah and King. This will happen even as shared by the Apostle:

> *Blindness in part is happened to Israel, UNTIL THE*
> *FULLNESS OF THE GENTILES BE COME IN.*
>
> *And so all Israel shall be saved.* (Romans 11:25-26.)

This was the "mystery," the thing not revealed in the Old Testament Scriptures. God was going to include the Gentiles in His grace, in His plan of redemption. During this time of Gentile rule, with Israel scattered among the nations of the world, God is doing principally three things:

1. He is chastising Israel because of their rebellious pride and unbelief.
2. He has sent forth His Son to be the sin-bearer and to die as a sacrifice for sin, thus providing atonement and making it possible for the sinner to be reconciled to God.
3. He is calling forth from among all the peoples of the world a "people" for Himself, in whom He puts His Holy Spirit, forming ONE BODY of believing Jews and Gentiles. This NEW entity is now identified as THE BODY OF CHRIST and the CHURCH.

This third work of God's grace is largely the focus of this parenthetical period — the built-in-hold. It is why this time in history is known as THE CHURCH AGE and THE AGE OF GRACE. It is only because of God's grace that He is including the Gentiles in His call to FAITH in Christ.

It is helpful, in our prophetic studies, to remember that THE

CHURCH, being made up of those that are "called" out of the world by the Gospel, is identified as the "Body of Christ." THE *CHURCH* IS THE *BODY OF CHRIST!* We are called TOGETHER, called out of the world. The word CHURCH carries with it the concept of our relation to each other, in grace, as a unified whole, because of union in and with Christ. The term BODY OF CHRIST speaks of our union with CHRIST who is the HEAD of the BODY. These are spiritual realities, and our understanding of them helps in our understanding of prophecies concerning the CHURCH.

Paul reveals the heart and purpose of God in this day of grace:

I have heard thee in a time accepted, and in the day of salvation have I succoured thee: Behold, NOW is THE DAY of salvation. (II Corinthians 6:2.)

He is telling us so tenderly that *NOW* is the time in which God is dealing with us. NOW is *HIS* acceptable time. One cannot say, "Oh, I'll get saved when I want to." We MUST be saved while the door of His grace is open to us, and that is NOW.

The day of salvation came to an abrupt end in the days of Noah when God closed the door to the ark. It came to a close suddenly and irrevocably for Sodom when Lot was taken out of that evil city. This day of grace also will come to an end. The door will be closed when Christ takes His Church home.

The unbelieving gentile world will then be judged in God's all consuming wrath just as assuredly as the flood waters covered the earth; and as Sodom was burned in God's righteous wrath. Paul speaks of the closing of this door of salvation for the unbelieving world:

. . . they received not the love of the truth, that they might be saved.

And for this cause GOD shall send them strong delusion, that they should believe a lie:

THAT THEY ALL MIGHT BE DAMNED who believed not the truth . . . (II Thessalonians 2:10-12.)

SLAM! And the door is shut, closed by God, and no man can open it, ever. This is an intensely clear statement.

When God closes the door of grace and salvation to the gentile world, He will then turn again toward Israel. Israel has ALREADY become a nation again in preparation for this occasion. The "natural branches" will again be grafted into the good olive tree. Israel became an independent FREE nation in 1948, after approximately two-thousand five-hundred and seventy (2,570) years of servitude, suffering and persecution.

Can we not realize that even now she is being prepared for her final hour? Her pride and rebellion will at last be broken; as her cry for mercy and forgiveness is heard in heaven because of the unbearable suffering so long endured.

Now, Messiah and Saviour comes in the fullness of His eternal glory, she is humbled in remorse looking upon HIM WHO SHE HAD PIERCED. *Our* time is running out! The prophetic clock is about to begin ticking again. JESUS IS COMING.

THE PRINCE THAT SHALL COME

The "prince" spoken of in Daniel 9:26-27, is a very important figure because he will play a major role in end time events. He is the man who will BECOME the ANTICHRIST. He is called, in Scripture, "the man of sin," and "the son of perdition." He is seen in Daniel, Chapter Seven as the "Little Horn," and in Chapter Eleven as the "Willful King." He will be the embodiment of evil and wickedness. He is identified in Revelation, Chapter Thirteen, as the "Beast" and is filled with satanic power.

It is he who will do that which Christ refers to as the abomination of desolation. This he does when he sets himself in the temple of Jehovah, God, in Jerusalem. He will declare himself to be God, and demand the worship of the whole world. So, it is of vital importance that we know and understand ALL that the Scriptures say concerning him.

We must not allow ourselves to fall into the deep sleep of indifference where many Christians are found today. They have taken the Devil's sleeping pill labeled "It doesn't matter; we won't be here." Lest you think I am unfounded on this exhortation, I have people actually say to me that they would not come to a prophetic meeting because, :"I am not into prophecy." I had one associate pastor (not of my church) say to me that: "It is not important that we know the details of prophecy." Can you possibly imagine that?

If it's not important, then why in the world did the Lord take up so much of the Bible with prophecy? I have had pastors tell me that to emphasize prophecy is "to major on the minors." Sounds clever and maybe even "spiritual" to some, but in reality it is just plain ignorance. It is an insult to the intelligence and wisdom of our Lord.

The truth of the matter is that this "prince" may already be among us. He may be one of our own politicians in Washington. God wants Christians to be aware of what is going on. The day of salvation is about to close, and there are souls yet to be saved. "Lot" has not left the city yet!

What does Daniel tell us about this "prince?" It will be helpful to review what he relates concerning the "Little Horn," where we see this figure in his political context. Note that he is seen as a "prince" or leader. This word does not speak of royalty, but it does signify a LEADER. He will not be a religious leader, but a political leader in the Western World.

He will rise to power and world wide influence in the political system of a YOUNG and mighty nation that is allied with the powers of Europe. Have you ever given thought to the fact that the UNITED STATES OF AMERICA is, primarily, ethnically "Roman." The vast majority of our peoples are English, German, French, Spanish or Latin, Italian and other ROMAN EMPIRE nationalities. Yes, we are basically "Roman." Even RELIGIOUSLY this is so. Because Christianity, with a good mixture of paganism, was the religion of Rome; and it is the predominate religious system in America.

IMPORTANT CLUES

A significant clue is given to us in Daniel 9:26. Who destroyed Jerusalem in 70 A.D.? It was not the "prince," but the "people of the prince that should come." The prince has not come even yet; he is still future. But, his people, or his ancestral people from which he would come, THEY would be the ones who were to destroy the temple and the city of Jerusalem.

It was, as all the world knows, the ROMAN EMPIRE with an army under the command of general Titus that, in that fateful year, not only destroyed the city and the temple, but the very NATION of Israel. It ceased to exist until its regathering in 1948. "Rome" is the people of the prince! Rome signifies the ROMAN EMPIRE. We can understand then, with assurance, that the Antichrist will be a leader in the "Roman" or Western World.

You will notice that in Daniel 9:25-26 there are TWO princes mentioned. These two are different persons. It is easy to distinguish between them for the Bible makes that clear distinction. One is "Messiah the Prince," with a capital "P"; the other is "the prince that shall come," with a small "p." The One is Messiah, Christ the Lord who shall be "cut off, but not for himself." The other is the "Little Horn" who will sign a covenant for seven years, starting the prophetic clock ticking again. The first is Christ and the second is Antichrist.

THE COVENANT

Another clear-cut statement informing us that the prince that shall come, who will be Antichrist, is going to do something that will enable the alert student of prophecy to identify him BEFORE he is REVEALED to the world.

> *He shall confirm the covenant with many for ONE WEEK:*
> *and in the midst of the week he shall cause the sacrifice*
> *and the oblation to cease, and for the overspreading of the*
> *ABOMINATIONS he shall make it DESOLATE; even until*
> *the consummation, and that determined shall be poured*
> *upon the desolate.* (Daniel 9:27.)

This is one of the most significant verses in Daniel, and it is indispensable to the understanding of prophecy. Here is the remaining, MISSING *week*, the 70th week of Daniel's prophecy; the LAST SEVEN YEARS before Christ comes in glory.

Sixty-nine weeks had passed long ago. Many years were to come and go in this parenthetical built-in-hold; while Christ called forth for Himself a "great multitude, which no man could number," from among the gentiles.

Now the time had come in God's prophetic plan. Through His providence the world scene would be ready, as in the days of Noah. The stage was set for the final act. Nations were in their proper alignment. Spiritual apostasy had set in upon the professing Christian

Church. Compromise had weakened the witness of the Gospel, and the love of many had grown cold. The "prince" was in his place. The world, having turned an unbelieving ear to the Gospel and rejecting the wonderful message of God's love in Christ Jesus, was ready, even anxious, to welcome and to follow this promising leader.

The peoples of the world do not want a spiritual deliverer. They want hope NOW. They want a solution to the political and economic turmoil of the world's nations. They want to be free from the threat of nuclear war and annihilation. The world is looking for a POLITICAL leader. One who will give them their pleasures in a new freedom from the moral restraints of Christianity. They are more than ready to follow, wholly, the sensual philosophies of the gods of the new age and worship the creature and not a Creator.

ENTER THE PRINCE: The Western World acclaims him, his wisdom and his leadership as he offers solutions to the global struggles. He then focuses his attention upon the overriding dilemma of the Middle East. Peace is wanted, and peace is acclaimed, as the Western World gives its new leader full support after a brief political challenge from three of the nations involved. There is now no disapproving voice.

Israel is finally recognized as having a right to exist, and is given secure boundaries after giving up some of her occupied land. Her safety becomes the responsibility of the prince, with the backing of the Western Powers now united in a new "Empire." Israel is given religious liberty and the use of her religious shrines. Jerusalem is established as the recognized Capital, and the Temple is authorized to be quickly rebuilt and its worship restored. Israel was now, after all her suffering years, to live in and enjoy real, lasting PEACE. It looked like God's Kingdom had come to Earth in truth.

The whole world watched via television, and the multitudes everywhere applauded in reverence as their leader came forward in the global assembly of the United Nations. With great pomp and pageantry the World Peace Covenant is presented. War is now forbidden, and there is world wide celebration as international hostilities are outlawed for this seven year treaty's duration. The whole world is to become ONE, living in peace and love. PEACE! PEACE! PEACE! The world shouts and dances and parties. All acclaim their new World Leader form his great wisdom and divine human spirit, and as a SUPER HUMAN. He is the MESSIAH OF THE WORLD.

Few know it, but this beautiful peace will be short-lived. No one, except those faithful Christians who diligently study the Word of God, will really know what is about to happen. Many Christian brethren are asleep and cannot understand the significance of what is taking place in the world today. They have been assured by sincere teachers of the Bible that they will never see these events. In their way of thinking, and in accord with what they have been taught, the events taking place before their eyes are not of importance.

You see, Christians have been told for some time, "Nothing more has to happen before we go home." Therefore, when the "prince that shall come" APPEARS on the scene, he will be UNKNOWN and not recognized by any, other than a faithful few who have been "watching." Only these will recognize him and realize that God has once again started the ticking of His prophetic clock. The countdown will then have resumed. At that moment the world will have just seven years before the Prince of Peace comes in all His glorious power. What a traumatic seven years those will be. They will conclude with that dreaded event called ARMAGEDDON.

Here we have a basic truth. The last seven years, the 70th week of Daniel, will BEGIN with the confirmation of a peace accord. Be extremely careful not to add anything to that truth. Many are saying that this week will begin with the Rapture of the Church, or just after the Rapture takes place. THE BIBLE DOES NOT SO SAY. Many say this last week is called "THE TRIBULATION PERIOD," but again, the BIBLE never refers to it as such. We should call it, or label it, what the Scriptures call it. It is the "End Time," the "Last Days," the last "Week," or the 70th week of Daniel.

It begins with the confirmation of a covenant, which is an accord, or treaty, among many nations. The principal figure in this event will be the "prince that shall come," the "Little Horn." He will be the leader of the Roman, or Western alliance of nations.

The big question is: Will the Church be here when that treaty is signed? We should have an answer to this question that is based upon the clear teaching of God's Word. Our answer should not be based upon opinion or upon traditional teaching. It should be a BIBLICAL answer.

There is nothing in Daniel that tells us anything at all about the Church. The concept of the Church was a "mystery," an unrevealed truth at that time. Therefore, we have to find the answer to our question elsewhere in Scripture. It will be a help, however, in finding the answer to this important question, to have a correct and full understanding of this last week as it is described in its context in Daniel

9:26-27.

First, it will be helpful for us to understand that we have in these verses the APPEARANCE of the "prince." It is at the signing of this treaty where he first APPEARS on the prophetic scene. At that time, it will not be generally known or internationally comprehended that he will BECOME the Antichrist. The facts about his true character and identity will not became known until the MIDDLE of the week, when he is REVEALED for what he really is. It is of major importance, for a correct understanding, to clearly distinguish between his APPEAR-ANCE and his REVELATION.

Just as it was with our Lord, His appearance was when He came into His own, and His own received Him not because they did not KNOW who He was. He rode into Jerusalem on the back of a donkey, and this great event was the APPEARANCE of their MESSIAH. He came into the city among cries of "Hosanna, blessed is He who cometh in the name of the Lord"; but then, that very week, they crucified Him. It was because they did not understand that He was the Lord of Glory; though He had appeared among them with heavenly power. This is so stated in the Word:

> We speak the wisdom of God in a mystery, even the
> HIDDEN wisdom: which NONE OF THE PRINCES OF THIS
> WORLD KNEW: for had they known it, they would not
> have crucified the LORD OF GLORY.
> (I Corinthians 2:7- 8.)

The son of the living God, the promised Messiah, Jesus Christ, came VEILED in human flesh. The people who saw Him did not KNOW Him at the time of His appearance among them. At the time of Christ's REVELATION it will be far different, for ALL SHALL KNOW WHO HE IS THEN:

> And then shall appear the sign of the Son of Man in
> heaven: and then shall all the tribes of the earth mourn,
> and they shall SEE THE SON OF MAN COMING in clouds
> of heaven WITH POWER AND GREAT GLORY.
> (Matthew 24:30.)

There will be no confusion about who Christ is at the time of His REVELATION:

The REVELATION of Jesus Christ . . .

*Behold, he cometh with clouds; and EVERY EYE SHALL
SEE HIM, and they also which pierced him: and all
kindreds of the earth shall wail him and all kindreds of
the earth shall wail because of him. Even so, Amen.*
(Revelation 1:7.)

That is REVELATION! No one, but no one, will be in doubt about
the identity of our Lord when He comes in glory.

So shall it be with the coming of the "prince." He will first APPEAR
as a wise, trusted, confident, political leader among men. He will bring
the divided, hostile world together in a peace accord. He will be hailed
by the world as a great leader. It is only after he seems to have
everything under his control that he will ultimately be REVEALED,
showing his true nature and purpose as he is filled with satanic power.

You may be asking, and you always should ask, "Do you have
scriptural proof for the above statement?" The answer is a resounding
YES! When the "prince" breaks the covenant in the middle of the final
week and causes the oblation to cease; he will be performing that
which is called by Christ, in Matthew 25:15: "THE ABOMINATION
OF DESOLATION, SPOKEN BY DANIEL THE PROPHET," here,
warning the Jewish people who will be living in that fateful hour to
understand the significance of this most important event. It is a "sign"
to them. When they see this take place, they are to flee to the
mountains to escape the destructive wrath and hatred of the now
revealed Antichrist.

*For then shall be a great tribulation, such as was not since
the beginning of the world to this time, no, nor ever shall
be.* (Matthew 24:21.)

This is the unique time of suffering and affliction known as THE
TRIBULATION PERIOD. Because the suffering of this time will be
such as the world has never known, it is called THE GREAT
TRIBULATION. These are not two different times, but the same time
period, and it begins in the middle of the week.

It will commence with the Abomination of Desolation, which is
the REVELATION of the Antichrist. We, therefore, know that it will last
just THREE AND A HALF YEARS. This time is so stipulated in the
Word of God as a period of "42 months," or "1260 days," according

to the prophetic year of 360 days. This is the time of the DURATION of the RULE of the Antichrist. We know from Scripture, for it is so stated THREE TIMES OVER, that it is at this time that the "prince" is REVEALED. This you will see in reading II Thessalonians 2:1-9. Notice these clear statements found in verses THREE, SIX and EIGHT:

> . . . *the man of sin be REVEALED* . . .
>
> . . . *that he might be REVEALED* . . .
>
> . . . *then shall that Wicked be REVEALED* . . .

These three statements are positively connected, in their context, with the abomination of desolation that occurs in the midst of the week. There simply can be no confusion or misunderstanding concerning this truth.

THEREFORE, we CANNOT put his REVELATION at this time of his signing of the covenant at the start of the week. To mix these two events, his APPEARANCE and his REVELATION, is to bring confusion and wrong conclusions into the entire understanding of the prophecies of the End Times. When it comes to prophetic truth, it is of utmost importance that we tell it like it is IN THE SCRIPTURE. We should never use wrong terminology. Correct terminology is SCRIPTURAL terminology, and it will always be Scripturally harmonious.

In accord with the Word of God, then we see the "prince" appearing on the scene of world history, and among men, as a leader of men. He will sign, or confirm, a covenant of seven years, bringing peace among the nations of the world. Then we find him three and one-half years later as he violates that covenant. His mask drops away and his true personage is revealed.

From this we also can learn that he will not be the persecuting, wicked, evil enemy of all good and godliness during the first half of that week, at least not openly. This, of course, means, and correctly so, that those first years WILL NOT BE and *cannot not scripturally* be classified as "TRIBULATION" years. It will be a time of relative peace.

It will be a broken peace as the prince vies for world power, but it will not be that which the Bible classifies as TRIBULATION. During this first half of the week the "prince" will be regrouping his power after the destruction of the NORTHERN INVADERS of Israel. He will consolidate his control and leadership over the surviving world; following the nuclear destruction in the North that will have destroyed one third of the world. But, then, this is a study reserved for a later chapter.

Let us try to sort some of this out in our minds so that we can grip the facts involved. Here are some "nails" to hang our thoughts upon:

1. The "Times of The Gentiles" is that time of Gentile rule, from the time of Daniel's captivity and extending until Christ comes in His glory to reign.

2. The "70 weeks" of Daniel's vision is the time schedule of God's prophetic "countdown" to the hour of Christ's coming in glory.

3. The "70 weeks" include 7 plus 62, or 69 weeks plus *one* final week. That 1 week is a period of 7 years. Thus, it gives us an extended period of 49 + 434 = 483 + 7 = <u>490 years</u>.

4. This 490 year period is broken by a "time out" or a built-in-hold of undetermined length coming between the 69th and the 70th weeks.

5. During the "Times of The Gentiles," Israel is under divine chastisement because of her rebellious pride and unbelief, and is subjugated to Gentile rule.

6. During this time of the "hold," God is calling out of the world a people for Himself, which is largely gentile.

7. This "calling out" began with Peter, who was given the "keys to the Kingdom," and continued through Paul and beyond him. It ends, finally, at the "Rapture," when Christ calls His Church home.

8. This "holding period" is therefore known as the Church Age and the Dispensation of Grace.

9. The "confirmation of the covenant" by the "prince that shall come" is the "sign," given to' us in Scripture, that the countdown has resumed and the Prophetic Clock has begun to tick again.

10. There is NO Scripture that specifically relates the timing of the Rapture with the signing of the covenant.

11. The "appearance" of the "prince" in the prophetic Scriptures is related to the signing of this covenant.

12. The "revelation" of the Antichrist in the prophetic Scriptures is clearly associated with the "abomination of desolation." It occurs three and one-half years AFTER the signing of the covenant, or at the middle of the 70th week.

THESE ARE INDISPUTABLE SCRIPTURAL FACTS. Perhaps it will help the reader to reexamine Figure 2 of Daniel's Time Frame. Study it carefully and seek to understand its various parts, its times and events and their interrelationship. In our study of the Time Frame, we are to understand that Daniel gives to us the bare facts. It is the "skeleton" of prophecy.

The substance, or the "meat," or "flesh," which are the details of events recorded in prophetic history, will be filled in as the study of the prophetic Scriptures continues. The "picture" takes on a clear reality as we proceed from prophecy to prophecy. It is therefore important that we have a clear mind and a real desire to understand God's "Time Frame." After all, it is HIS revelation that we are seeking to understand.

Let these scriptural truths be STAMPED and RECORDED indelibly and unmistakenly upon your mind. In so doing, these FACTS will be available for INSTANT RECALL and review at will in your study, which is most needful.

Up to this point in our study, we have seen the "prince" confirm the covenant. We RECALL that this act of his starts again the prophetic clock ticking; resuming the countdown of the last seven years. God is letting His people know that the "last days" of the "Times of The Gentiles" has come. There remains just seven years before Christ comes in all His glorious power to reign.

THE ABOMINATION OF DESOLATION

With your INSTANT RECALL now available to you, you remember that this traumatic event takes place in the middle of the

70th week. Daniel does not linger or give anything more specific in the first half of the week. He proceeds to the "midst" of the week where we are told of great occurrences taking place:

> *And in the midst of the week he shall cause the sacrifice and the oblation to cease, and for the overspreading of ABOMINATIONS he shall make it DESOLATE, even until the consummation, and that determined shall be poured upon the DESOLATE.* (Daniel 9:27.)

There are three very important truths to be noted here in this verse, which are clearly substantiated in the prophetic Scriptures.

1. The Antichrist will break his covenant with Israel in the middle of that seven year period.

2. The Antichrist will then turn upon Israel and persecute her, seeking to annihilate her from the earth. Israel is the one called the "desolate." It is this that Jeremiah refers to in Chapter 30, Verse Seven, as "the time of JACOB's trouble."

3. The overshadowing and sovereign WILL OF GOD will be accomplished concerning Israel. She will be brought to repentance. Her stubborn, rebellious pride broken; and thus be made ready to receive her Messiah upon His return in glory.

These three things give to us three of the four principle characteristics of that terrible time known to us as "The Tribulation Period," or "The Great Tribulation." These three have to do with Israel.

The FOURTH has to do with the WHOLE WORLD, and it is to this truth that Scripture refers in Revelation 3:10. We will see this very clearly as we come to those studies in the New Testament. This FOURTH, and unutterably horrible characteristic is that of the outpouring of the WRATH OF GOD. Poured upon the unbelieving, Christ-rejecting world that has believed the LIE, upon those who accepted and worshiped the Antichrist.

BREAKING THE COVENANT

The statement in Daniel 9:27 gives us some insight into the substance about the terms to be included in that "covenant." It also reveals Antichrist's evil purpose as inspired by Satan. The SACRIFICE and the OBLATION both speak of the form of Temple worship practiced in the Old Testament times; when the Temple was the center of all Jewish life.

When the Roman Army under Titus destroyed Jerusalem in 70 A.D., the Temple was also destroyed and Temple worship ceased. It has never been reinstated. The Jewish Nation of Israel was destroyed and its people slaughtered by the thousands. Those that escaped death were sold into slavery, and have thus been scattered over the face of the globe for the past 1900 years.

Since then, they have continued to celebrate PASSOVER wherever they were found, saying, "Next year in Jerusalem." They have never lost this hope of returning and rebuilding their Temple. With this would naturally come the reestablishment of the Temple worship. We can clearly see that this statement in Daniel, concerning the Antichrist causing the sacrifice and the oblation to cease, surely shows that such had been resumed. That the Temple will be rebuilt is, therefore, seen as essential. The Jewish people cannot have the sacrifice and the oblation without the Temple. There have been many recent rumors about the Temple being rebuilt — in these days, now.

I do not put much stock in what people say. There is a lot of sensational teaching going on, and we must be careful to stick to Scriptural facts. Thus, we will not be mislead into something that is just not true. Don't get excited about what people say; get excited about what God says.

It is the clear indication from God's Word that the Temple will be rebuilt and the sacrificial worship reestablished. There is much that would hinder this today. So it is logical that these hindrances to Temple worship may be removed because of the covenant that is to be confirmed. The Antichrist, even before his REVELATION, will have no love for God and no love for the State of Israel. Israel will be a constant "thorn in the flesh" for him. In the midst of the week he will call a halt to their obstinate ways.

Antichrist will go into their Temple and declare himself to be God and their Messiah, demanding to be worshiped by the whole world.

Israel, of course, will never accept this, and so he sets forth to bring about the final solution to the Jewish question: total annihilation. He will seek to finish what Hitler started. This is that which is referred to by our Lord in Matthew 24:15. He identifies it as THE ABOMINATION OF DESOLATION.

Let us go back for a moment. Upon signing the peace treaty among the nations, with the prospect of true peace guaranteed and backed by the powers of the Western World, there will be an immediate change in the direction of Israel's economy. Now, without the need to defend herself from her age old enemies such as Syria, Iran, Iraq and her other Arab neighbors, Israel will be more than ready to stop spending her very limited resources on the military. DISAR-MAMENT will be both required and desired. The "WALLS" of defense will "come down."

We see this already exemplified in that Israel has even now been pressured to stop their fighter aircraft program, after spending many millions of dollars to develop this industry. Why? Because they can get planes from Uncle Sam. "You can depend on us," we say. They HAD to or else we would have pulled the financial plug on their pro-gram, leaving them dry — without planes.

So, finally, Israel's army will be able to go home and occupy itself in peaceful pursuits. A standing army will be no longer needed, for we will say, "You can depend upon us." Peace keeping forces are a PRESENT reality. So peace will be affirmed as promised; it will be proclaimed by all and provided by the "prince." All the world will marvel.

That first year may begin with world wide celebration, with the cry of PEACE! PEACE! People the world over will rejoice as they see the military walls of defense dismantled, plane by plane, gun by gun, tank by tank, ship by ship, missile by missile and man by man. Peace has come! Still, it will be necessary to retain the "PEACE KEEPING FORCES" of the PRINCE intact, ready for swift use if needed.

Wait a minute. Don't forget the RED BEAR in the FAR NORTH. Even she may appear to have been mesmerized by the PRINCE, but she becomes restless. What will she do? Israel will be dwelling safely in "UNWALLED CITIES," according to the Scriptures, as her "walls" of defense have been removed. She will be rejoicing in her new found freedom and economic abundance. Little does she realize how hungry and angry that Red Russian Bear to the North has become. Paul the apostle tells us:

*For when they shall say Peace and safety; then SUDDEN
DESTRUCTION cometh upon them, as travail upon a
woman with child; and THEY SHALL NOT ESCAPE.*
(I Thessalonians 5:3.)

Chapter Nine of Daniel closes stating, "THAT DETERMINED
SHALL BE POURED UPON THE DESOLATE." God has determined
his sovereign will concerning Israel. His purpose will be accomplished
as he uses Antichrist to chastise her, the "desolate." He will bring her
to her knees begging forgiveness and mercy.

She will turn to her Christ as He comes in Glory, her true Messiah.
She will find Him to be JESUS, who she pierced on Calvary so long
ago. Christ, in all His heavenly glory and power, will come to her
defense. He will destroy her enemies as she herself is finally reconciled
to her God by the Blood of the Lamb.

SPIRITUAL REALITY
Daniel, Chapter Ten

Chapter 10 of Daniel is another example of God's wonderful
grace. it is here that He gives to us a view, no where else to be found,
into the "spirit world." There is an awful amount of falsehood going
about concerning this "under world" or "other world." It is actually a
FOURTH DIMENSION. It is a dimension into which we can only look,
in fact, with the assistance of the Holy Spirit. Satan would have us
confused concerning this dimension. He does not want us to
understand him and his workings, his purpose, or the scope of his
influence; God does.

Perhaps the major significance of this great chapter is to help us
SEE, with the eye of faith, what truly is reality in the realm of the spirits.
There is something special in view here. There was a revelation of
truth given to Daniel that was to be completed in the plan of God at
an APPOINTED TIME. It was yet a long way off, but God wanted His
children to have a knowledge of its occurrence. Daniel wanted to
understand, and so God sent His special messenger to give this

understanding to His "friend," Daniel.

Daniel had a vision of Christ in His glory, and this vision had left him in a trance, something like a "spiritual coma." The angel came and woke Daniel, and said:

> *Now I am come to make thee understand what shall befall thy people IN THE LATTER DAYS: for yet the vision is for many days.* (Daniel 10:14.)

What was told to Daniel is given to us in Chapters *Eleven* and *Twelve. Before* we go into that, let us look at what is reported in the rest of Chapter 10.

After Daniel had received this revelation, he prayed for understanding; he prayed for THREE WHOLE WEEKS. That is how much he wanted to know the truth. (Would to God that Christians today could have such a desire for the truth of God's Word.) After 21 days the answer came by angelic courier. Upon arriving, the angel told Daniel that he had been dispatched by God with the answer when Daniel *first started praying.* He had run into some trouble on the way "down," which had delayed him these three weeks. He had found trouble between Heaven and Earth. This was related by the angel:

> . . . *The prince of the kingdom of Persia withstood me one and twenty days . . .* (Daniel 10:13.)

Persia (modern Iran) was the ruling world empire at that time in history. Understand, now, that the "prince" here spoken of could not, under any circumstance, have been the human ruler of Persia. Why not? Simply because flesh and blood cannot withstand and fight against a spirit being. We may resist the working of a spiritual being in our minds and upon our wills, but we have no power against such a being, nor can we soar into the heavens to do battle. We have no direct impact into this FOURTH DIMENSION.

This was clearly a SPIRITUAL battle. It was so fierce that finally, after *three weeks of struggle*, the angel could not win or break free. So help was dispatched from Heaven. Michael, "one of the chief princes," was sent to help him. Now, MICHAEL is identified in Scripture as the ARCHANGEL, and he is here called "one of the chief princes."

There are many things that we can comprehend from this incident. One of them is that there was an EVIL, DEMONIC SPIRIT, a fallen angel of immense power who was in charge of the spiritual darkness ruling over the kingdom of Persia. That spirit was directing Persia in her downward path of sin and rebellion against the creator, and keeping her in ignorance and wickedness.

After delivering the message to Daniel, the angel told him:

> *. . . Now will I return to fight with the prince of Persia, and when I am gone forth, lo, the prince of Grecia shall come.* (Daniel 10:20.)

We know that Greece was the kingdom that followed Persia. She, too, is said to have her own evil, spiritual governor of her spiritual darkness. This gives to us real insight into the frightful truth of the spiritual forces controlling the world of humanity in its constant rebellion against the rule of righteousness and the Kingdom of Heaven. It helps us to understand why there is so much suffering and sin in the world. IT IS NOT GOD'S FAULT! So let's stop blaming God.

This chapter helps us to understand the real, satanic organization of the spiritual powers of wickedness to which Paul the Apostle, under the guidance of the Holy Spirit, refers:

> *For we wrestle not against flesh and blood, but against PRINCIPALITIES, against POWERS, against THE RULERS OF THE DARKNESS OF THIS WORLD, against SPIRITUAL WICKEDNESS in HIGH PLACES.* (Ephesians 6:12.)

These "high places" are those areas above and around the Earth, the heavens of our atmosphere and space. Paul tells us in Corinthians of his having been "caught up" to the "third heaven." This was understood to have been the "heaven" where God was; it was God's throne room, or Paradise.

Between the "third heaven" and the Earth are to be found the first and the second heavens, or the earth's atmosphere, and then space. Satan DOES have access to God's Heaven, but only in his function as the accuser (Revelation 12:10) of the brethren, as is pictured clearly in the story of Job. Satan now, also, has access to earth, but the earth is not his true sphere of operation. Satan is identified as:

> *The PRINCE of the POWER of the AIR, the SPIRIT that now worketh in the children of disobedience.* (Ephesians 2:2.)

In II Corinthians 4:4, he, Satan, is said to be the "god of this world." This title suggests that he has usurped control of God's creation and is seeking to destroy, by his evil methods, all God's wonderful work. Especially, he wants to destroy those created in the image of the Creator, the human race.

This is why redemption has been wrought. God in Christ has "brought" us back, so that those who turn, through Christ, to God are FREED from satanic powers of dominion.

Satan has blinded the minds of them that believe not. Satan is the ruling prince of this godless world system. Under him are his special princes assigned to govern and control the evil affairs of each nation upon the earth. Is it any wonder, then, that we see the downward direction in which our own great nation is heading just as fast as it can?

Pornography, adultery, fornication, murder, and every crime one can think of; every type of sexual perversion imaginable; plus the horror of drugs: these are the EVERY DAY EXPERIENCES of Americans today. Gays and "gay rights" are actually defended by the multitudes today, though it was God Himself who judged Sodom for this very SIN. He is judging our society, without a doubt, today, with this AIDS epidemic. Babies are killed by the thousands every day while animals are protected. Alcohol, drugs and tobacco are in common use, and people love to have it so.

Religion is popular, but righteousness and truth are forsaken. WHY? Because the "prince" of the United States of America is doing a masterful job in his direction of this nation on the road to Hell. What we need to understand is that he is preparing THIS NATION for the "prince that shall come." THIS WILL BE *HIS NATION*.

Why is evil having such great success? The primary reason is that the sleeping, indifferent Christians have lost their "saltiness." People just don't care anymore. They don't care about prophecy and the future as God sees it. People want the NOW to be everything they desire.

Soon the Antichrist will appear upon the world scene. He will be a human being, and possibly the leader of our nation. He will be indwelt and empowered by Satan, with spiritual and supernatural powers far beyond our understanding. His appearance will mean the imminent end and damnation of our "home of the brave and the land of the free."

We hypocritically sing, *God Bless America,* and in the next breath tell God to leave us alone; all of which is nothing more than clear evidence that the "prince" of America has done his job well.

MICHAEL, YOUR PRINCE

A most stunning thought is this! Look closely and notice, in the last verse of Chapter 10, that MICHAEL, the archangel, is identified as "YOUR PRINCE." We find him referred to again by name in the twelve chapter as:

> . . . the GREAT PRINCE that standeth for the children of thy people . . . (Daniel 12:1.)

I do not know about you, but that does my heart good. Without question, we can understand the phrase, "THE CHILDREN OF THY PEOPLE," in *two different ways*. First, we know Daniel was a JEW from the land of Judah, and of the people that we know today as the Nation of Israel. We, therefore, understand that Michael has a special duty of watching over the Jewish people and the Nation of Israel. That is why we see so many unbelievable things happening in the Mid-east. Michael is on the job. God's purpose is being carried out for Israel.

Beyond this, we also know that Daniel was *more* than just another Jew. HE WAS A *BELIEVING* JEW. Every true BELIEVER is a member of the family of God. And, as we read in the Scriptures, by faith we are the children of Abraham.

It is so easy for me to understand that Michael STANDS for ME. He is there for ME, to protect me, for I am part of the BODY OF CHRIST, His Church. This is why Romans 8:28 is true. Michael is going to be there when the Lord takes me home, and if we go simultaneously, in the RAPTURE, Michael will be there. He will be very active, having a prominent place in that great event. The BIBLE comforts us with a wonderful truth:

> The angel of the Lord encampeth about them that fear

him, and delivereth them. (Psalm 34:7.)

This promise is not given just to the Jewish people; indeed, it is not even given to the Jewish people as a Nation. Psalm 34:7 is a specific promise of God ONLY to the BELIEVER. Many believe that this is a reference to Christ Himself. It may be, but it could very well refer to one of Christ's special servants, sent, in Christ's name, to do His bidding, as we see in Daniel 6:22.

So we have, in complete contrast, the evil princes of the godless nations in constant conflict with the prince that standeth for the children of God. The point here is: we are shown a sphere where the satanic forces of demonic powers have their "headquarters." It is not here upon the Earth, nor is it in Heaven, the "home" of our heavenly Father. It is therefore seen to be the sphere around the Earth.

One day, as we know, Satan will be cast down to Earth. But for now, we can understand his sphere of operation to be the first and the second heavens. From these he exercises his control over human affairs through his evil princes.

Consider, seriously, the fact of Gabriel's conflict with the "prince of Persia." Think of the spiritual resistance he encountered, and the length of his delay due to it. Do so and it will give you some significant insight WHY there, of necessity, will be a RAPTURE.

On our way to Heaven we must pass right through Satan's sphere of operation. I don't believe that Satan is going to be sitting on his front porch in a rocking chair, waving to us as we pass by. NO! A thousand times NO!

As with the pioneers of the early West, as with Joshua and the Promised Land, we, too, will have to face hostile forces seeking to prevent our crossing into our "promised land." But, we will not have to face these evil forces by ourselves, for we will be RAPTURED, and taken under divine escort and heavy guard.

Satan will have all his evil army out, in full array, to try to prevent us from reaching Heaven's shores. Attempting to thwart the purpose of God in bringing His children home. Remember how Michael came to help Gabriel? Well, would he do less for the children of God, the body of Christ?

Keep in mind that this very battle in the heavens is described in detail in Scripture in the 12th chapter of Revelation. We will look at that more closely later in our study.

Recall that during this built-in-hold in which we now live, the purpose of God for national Israel is on hold. We can, therefore, expect that Michael will be given charge, with all his army of good angels, of the people of God of this age, the Church. Michael is the "Chief Angel," the FIVE STAR GENERAL under the direct command of the COMMANDER AND CHIEF, who is Christ Himself. It is thus seen that under Michael's responsibilities is the care of the departed souls on their journey into the hereafter:

> *And it came to pass, that the beggar died, and WAS*
> *CARRIED BY THE ANGELS into Abraham's bosom . . .*
> (Luke 16:22.)

This is not reading into Scripture, but it is simply believing all the FACTS of truth given to us in Scripture on the subject. These conclusions are not inconsistent or incompatible with the Word of God. They have their very basis upon the clear statements of the Word of God. They are in total accord with all the Scriptural testimony about the subject. For example:

> *Take heed that ye despise not one of these little ones; for I*
> *say unto you, that in heaven THEIR ANGELS do always*
> *behold the face of my Father which is in heaven.*
> (Matthew 18:10.)

And then again:

> *And of the angels he saith, WHO maketh his angels*
> *spirits, and his ministers a flame of fire . . .*
>
> *Are they not all MINISTERING SPIRITS, SENT FORTH TO*
> *MINISTER FOR THEM WHO SHALL BE HEIRS OF*
> *SALVATION?* (Hebrews 1:7 and 14.)

The heirs of salvation make up the CHURCH of Jesus Christ. Yes, the very angels of God are sent forth to minister for us, according to and performing the will of God. They operate under their "chief" who is Michael. It is not out of line, therefore, to picture Michael as OUR PRINCE, or to understand that he "stands" for us, and he has direct responsibility to the Lord on our behalf. The Angels are all Christ's servants, doing His bidding for His people, even as it is promised:

> *For he shall give his angels charge over thee, to keep in all thy ways.* (Psalm 91:11.)

So, if you know the Lord, REJOICE and praise the Lord for His wonderful grace. YOU ARE NOT ALONE! It has been said that if God were to remove this protective care, even for a moment, Satan would KILL us in an instant. I believe that. We are God's people and Satan is our adversary.

I remember some missionaries we worked with in South America telling us of an incident in their work. They were making contact with an unreached tribe of Indians. At one point, as the missionaries were gathered in a home for prayer, the Indians approached the house, planning to kill them all. One missionary looked through the window and saw the Indians. Then he saw them suddenly stop and turn and run back into the jungle.

A few years later some of these same missionaries were gathered around a campfire in the Indian village. Many Indians had now become Christians through faith in Jesus Christ. Their pagan lives had been changed — including the chief of the tribe. This chief asked the missionaries about that day when the Indians went to kill them. The chief wanted to know: "Who were all those people dressed in shining white that stood surrounding the house?"

It was then that the missionaries realized that God's protecting band of angels were permitted to be seen by these savage Indians. This caused them to flee in fright.

THEY ARE ALL HIS MINISTERING SPIRITS SENT FORTH TO DO HIS WILL. I believe the account just related can be found in the book, *The Bird God*, by William Pencille.

THE WILLFUL KING
Daniel, Chapter Eleven

The subject is unbroken. Chapter 11 of Daniel is the continuation of the preceding chapter. The angel has come to give under-standing to Daniel. Now he is going to tell him what would befall his people in the latter days.

We are going to pass over the first 35 verses of this chapter because it is all history now. Prophecy that was fulfilled between Daniel's time and the time of Christ. It tells of the breakup of the Grecian Empire. The rise of Roman influence in the region. It describes the conflicts, struggles and suffering of the people of Israel caught in the middle of it under the chastening hand of God. Israel's suffering is clearly referred to:

> . . . *Yet they shall fall by the sword, and by flame, by captivity, and by spoil, MANY DAYS . . .*
>
> *to try them, and to purge, and to make them white, even to the time of the end: because it is yet for a time appointed.* (Daniel 11:33 and 35.)

We can see that this verse goes far beyond the time of Christ, and in a very few words shows the suffering of the Jewish people throughout this time of the prophetic built-in-hold. They will continue to suffer right until the time of the end.

You should take special note that it is FOR AN *APPOINTED* TIME. God is clearly working on a TIME SCHEDULE. This is a specific reference to the revealed TIME FRAME given in Chapter Nine. It will not happen just any time — it is for an *appointed time* — a given point in history already marked in the mind of God. This fact is doctrinally important and refutes some shallow teaching of today.

Then in the 36th verse of Chapter 11, Daniel takes us to the end time and tells us of the KING. This is the prince of Chapter Nine and the Little Horn of Chapter Seven. The last part of Chapter Eleven can be understood more readily if we recognize that: the SUBJECT of the remaining verses, from 36 on, is *the king* who does "according to his own will." I have named him, "THE WILLFUL KING." He is the Antichrist.

Thus, the clue to understanding verses 36-45 of this chapter is to remember that the *subject* is the WILLFUL KING. And *every personal pronoun*, proper or possessive, refers back to, and only to, the WILLFUL KING first mentioned in Verse 36. Wherever the "King of the North" or the "King of the South" are meant, they are so called — not once by pronoun. Using this clue we can learn many things about the Antichrist:

> 1. He shall do according to his own will. He will be unrestrained, strong and unopposed. He will be in control.

> 2. He shall exalt himself and be the highest expression of humanism: proud, boastful.

> 3. He shall magnify himself above every god. He will proclaim himself to be God: divine and worthy of all worship.

> 4. He shall speak against the God of gods. He will be "anti-Christ," the true meaning of the word. He opposes the God of creation.

> 5. He shall prosper till the indignation be accomplished. That is, until God is through with him in the chastening of the Lord upon Israel, to bring her to repentance.

> 6. He will not regard the God of his fathers. He will be an apostate in its purest form.

> 7. He shall not regard the desire of women. He is anti-Christ, the "seed" of the woman as promised in Genesis 3:15.

> 8. He shall not regard any god. He is to be worshiped as GOD, he alone, under penalty of death.

> 9. He shall magnify HIMSELF above all, the abomination of desolation, in the very TEMPLE OF THE LIVING GOD.

> 10. He shall honor and pay tribute to the god of force. He himself worships POWER. He will be the ultimate DICTATOR.

> 11. He shall acknowledge a "strange god" and "increase with glory." He sells his soul to SATAN and is empowered by Satan. See Revelation 13:2 and II Thessalonians 2:9.

> 12. He shall cause "them": satanic, demonic forces, to rule over men. His world rule will be demonic control; he is the "son of perdition."

13. He shall divide "the land" for gain. He will partition the land of Israel for his own purposes in seeking to control her. Provisions for this might even be seen in the peace treaty that he will have confirmed.

14. He shall destroy the King of the North and subdue the King of the South, and he shall enter into the countries. He will take control of the entire world upon the destruction of the Northern Red Bear.

15. He shall enter the glorious land, Israel, and possess her as his own.

16. He will, with insane hatred and great wrath, destroy all who stand in his way. He will seek to annihilate the Jewish people.

17. He shall place his throne, his headquarters, in Jerusalem.

18. He will be destroyed at the coming of our Lord as seen in Revelation 19, and in the "stone" of Daniel, Chapter Two.

This is an abundantly glorious chapter with so many details given in these very few verses. Everything here given is positively substantiated in the prophecies of the New Testament. Given with such clarity that it is impossible not to see them unless one knows nothing of prophecy; or unless one is a total unbeliever.

The thing that so stirs my heart is that so many Christians are sound asleep. Often it is the PREACHERS who have put them to sleep, with teachings based upon custom, or traditional teachings, or even personal opinion. WAKE UP! Wake up Christian; the time is now!

MICHAEL STANDS UP
Daniel, Chapter Twelve

Daniel captures our attention, as we begin reading Chapter

Twelve, with the words, "And at that time . . ." Of course, we are then forced to ask ourselves, What time? It is not an hour, or a day on our calendar, but a specific time in relation to God's calendar. His Prophetic Time Frame and the events occurring in relation to that specific Time Frame of pre-declared history. These words take us right back to the closing verses of Chapter Eleven, Verses 36-45.

The "that time" is the time of the Antichrist. More specifically, it is the time of the REVELATION of the Antichrist.

Remember that this is to take place three and one-half years AFTER he has signed a covenant of peace. NOW we will see him as he really is. We see how he is going to act, and what he is going to do to. He is no longer just the "prince." He now performs the abomination of desolation, declares himself to be God, and demands to be worshiped by all the world's population. He BECOMES the Antichrist! He is the great opposer of Christ, the Son of the Living God.

Don't forget that the Church was a "mystery" in Daniel's time. It was a concept never revealed to the Old Testament prophets. So when we read Daniel 12:1, we know that it is not talking about the Church DIRECTLY. But, in the mind of God, the Body of Christ was always in His thoughts and in His plans. We can read this first verse now with a more complete understanding of all the events involved:

> And at that time shall Michael stand up, the great prince
> which standeth for the children of thy people: and there
> shall be a time of TROUBLE, such as never was since
> there was a nation even to that same time: and thy people
> shall be delivered, everyone that shall be found written in
> the book. (Daniel 12:1.)

This is a very comprehensive statement of prophecy. I always ask myself, "What is Michael involved in? What is he going to do? What made him get up? Remember that he is UNDER ORDERS and that as the Chief Angel he ISSUES ORDERS. We instantly recall that the Bible is God's INTEGRATED BOOK; it is all interrelated. To get the full understanding, we must learn to study the Bible in that light. In this verse then, we find Michael:

1. He STANDS: His PURPOSE is to take a STAND for
   the people of God in general and Israel in particular.

2. He is heard: as a military commander would give

direction or orders to his troops, his VOICE is a command tohis ARMY of ANGELS. This VOICE is heard at the TIME Christ returns for His Church. I Thessalonians 4:16 speaks of the "voice of the archangel."

He is seen to be leading this mighty angelic army into battle against Satan and his demonic fallen angels. Satan is defeated in this heavenly battle and is then cast down TO EARTH.

Satan comes down here, banished from the heavens, with GREAT WRATH because he knows that he has a SHORT TIME in which to do his evil work (Revelation 12:7-12). Then, we see the BEAST of Revelation 13 RISE and the GREAT TRIBULATION begins, even as it is here so stated in Daniel 12:1.

From this first verse in Daniel 12 we see that it is when Michael STANDS that this unique time of TRIBULATION comes upon the earth. It is so easy to see a clear, specific correlation between these three Biblical events concerning Michael, if we are not blinded by tradition.

First we see him STAND. His grand purpose is the defense of God's people. He then leads the charge to do battle with Satan and his army. His reason: Satan has mobilized his army to prevent the saints of God from reaching their heavenly home.

A trump is blown to begin these earth shaking events: Christ descends with a SHOUT, and the resurrection and transformation of believers takes place. Michael gives his command to his troops. The RAPTURE occurs with the Saints of the Most High being "caught up," under armed guard, as the heavenly battle rages in all its supernatural fury. The powers of the heavens are shaken. The Saints go marching in, and Satan is cast down to earth. NO WONDER HE'S MAD.

Satan has lost this long awaited event for which he has prepared over the years and centuries. The Saints got through, and now he himself has been confined to this planet. Well, Satan was really mad. He was going to take it out upon those down here who claim to be God's people. Especially those Jews, the nation of Israel which God had chosen for Himself.

This makes sense! It makes good *Scriptural* sense! If this is not the picture then, so Michael stands up, so what? So his voice is heard? Why is HIS VOICE HEARD AT THE RAPTURE? He is not just going to be shouting, "Praise the Lord." So why pick on Satan after all this time? Why be so unkind to mankind? Why, indeed? If we look closely, we can see this great drama of indescribable glory and horror taking place. The END TIME has come. These events are about to become HISTORY.

With the signing of the covenant the "countdown" will have resumed. The world accepts this magnificent leader. The world wants no more restraints, no more talk of a "holy," sovereign God. The world wants no more preaching of the Gospel, no more talk of sin, redemption and judgment. The world wants to be FREE from the bonds of Christianity and its conservative thought and moral implications.

The world wants to enjoy, to the fullest, the new liberties now afforded in this New Age of spiritual enlightenment. Each man is taught to recognize the DIVINE spark of absolute goodness within himself. No more of Jesus. No more of the Church, the Bible and God. Give us life in its fullness, liberty without limits, and the RIGHT to satisfy the desires of our own hearts. Sin, sex and sensuality with all the vices, give us pleasure. These are our "rights" as human beings who are accountable only to our inner selves. There is peace and there is pleasure; passion is good, and "evil" is nonexistent.

Utopia has come under the able leadership of this great world governor – Antichrist. All acclaim his wisdom and glory. He is the "messiah."

Suddenly, the sky lights up with the brilliance of a million suns. There is what sounds like a tremendous clap of thunder, strangely comparable to the blast of a thousand trumpets sounding as one, echoing and reechoing across the heavens. There is a sound similar to an earth shaking shout. It definitely has the quality of a voice, but unlike anything ever heard before. It is analogous to stereo sound that comes from every direction at once. The very atmosphere shakes with the sound. It may say: COME FORTH, or, perhaps, COME HITHER! What could it mean? What on earth was happening? Is everyone going crazy?

All life stands still, as if frozen in death in an instant of time. The scene is indescribable and incomprehensible, frightful and terrible, glorious and awesomely breath-taking.

In that eternal moment and that infinite instant, millions of people have suddenly disappeared. They are just — GONE!

The heavens rumble and the sky becomes dark after such glorious light, and the earth itself seems in the throes of some kind of celestial storm. The people on earth cry out in fear. But their fright turns to joy when it becomes apparent that it is only those hated "Christians" that seem to have been affected. None of them can be located. They are nowhere to be found!

These Christians were nothing but a "thorn in the flesh" anyway. They continually HINDERED the enjoyments and pleasures and sinful delights of the people. The masses embraced the leadership of the new highly praised leader. The presence of God's followers is not wanted, and now that they are gone, there is great rejoicing world wide.

The restraining moral force, which had held back the overriding tide of evil, had now been removed. The Holy Spirit of God, residing in the Body of Believers, was left without a BODY through which to work.

The Spirit of God turns then to the People, Abraham's people, David's people, Daniel's people, ISRAEL; and He seals 144,000 of these so that they will be protected from the Antichrist's attempts to kill them. He sends forth His Two Witnesses to lead them in their endeavors. They must reach every Jew upon the face of the earth with the Everlasting Gospel of Grace, confirmed in the New Covenant and sealed with the Blood of the Lamb of God. The rapture has taken place. The Saints are in Glory. The Great Tribulation has begun and time is running out.

While all this is going on down here upon the earth, a view into the heavens reveals Satan leading his wicked, fallen angels as one gigantic, mighty, evil army of demons. The "fly" to intercept the great cloud of believers which has just left the planet Earth on their way to heavenly glory. This cloud is accompanied by, LOOK! It is none other than Jesus Christ, the Lord of Glory.

As Satan closes in, we suddenly see MICHAEL and his band of holy angels charging in to confront the evil forces. We hear Michael SHOUT, "Attack, attack!" The forces of good and evil join battle, and the very heavens shake and the earth trembles as the heavenly struggle rages. The stars are seen to fall and the universe shakes. The earth reels and wobbles as a drunkard. Men's hearts fail them as unknown dread grips them in fear of an uncertain future. People begin to run about here and there, anywhere and everywhere, thinking that this is the end of the world. It is just MICHAEL sweeping the "trash" out of heaven. Satan and his demons are then defeated and cast down to earth, never to have access to the heavens again.

Satan has "come down," but not of his own will. What rage he has. What hatred for anything and everything and everyone remotely connected to Christ and the Creator. Satan now gives to the "prince" his supernatural powers and takes up, his abode in his body. This is an evil that goes beyond demonic possession. It is SATANIC POSSESSION!

Satan now, personified in the Antichrist, goes forth in terrible devastation to control absolutely the whole earth. This is the time of "Jacob's trouble," spoken of so long ago by the prophet. It is the trial that is to "come upon all the world, to try them that dwell upon the earth." This is the Tribulation Period of unique character. It is the Great Tribulation; the time of the Wrath of the Lamb.

While this terrible situation is found upon the earth, there is great rejoicing in heaven: the land of pure holiness. The saints go marching in following the KING. There is praise resounding from all sides and shouts of Hallelujah, Home at last!

Yes, we read Daniel 12:1 with a limited understanding, but God sees the whole picture. He gives to us the whole picture; but it is in "puzzle" form with pieces of the picture scattered throughout the prophetic scriptures. We have to "put it together" by study and diligent search; as we ask the Holy Spirit to give us the understanding and wisdom to "rightly divide the Word of truth."

I encourage you to try to get sight, even a glimpse, of the whole picture. Never be satisfied with a hodgepodge of disjointed thoughts. Know where you are going in your study.

As you read Daniel 12:2, you will notice that the resurrection is included in the events just described, and so it should because Paul tells us:

> *. . . The dead in Christ shall rise first:*
>
> *Then we which are alive and remain shall be caught up together WITH THEM in the clouds, to meet the Lord in the air . . .* (I Thessalonians 4:16-17.)

This is a resurrection of believers only at this time in prophecy. Daniel knew nothing of the Church. The verse that he gives us concerning the resurrection is a GENERAL statement; stating the FACT of the resurrection involving both saved and the unsaved.

It is in the New Testament that we find the resurrection of the saved in the rapture of the Church. Daniel tells that those written in the book would be "delivered." Those who are members of the Body of Christ will be delivered in the rapture. Those who are sealed by the seal of God will be delivered by the power of God from the Tribulation horrors and Satanic powers. Those who profess Christ during the

Tribulation will pay for it with their lives and be delivered by martyrdom:

> And they overcame him by the blood of the Lamb, and by the word of their testimony, and they loved not their lives unto the death. (Revelation 12:11.)

You do not overcome Satan by surrendering to him, but by resisting him in the Name of Jesus Christ. What a privilege to DIE for the Lamb of God who died for us.

Notice, the last thing that the angel told Daniel was that the prophecy he was writing was to be CLOSED and SEALED *until the time of the end.* He thus suggested, not only that those prophecies dealt with the time of the end; that AT THAT TIME they would be unsealed and opened, or that understanding would be given to God's people.

In recent years there has been a great increase in knowledge through scientific research and study. The computer age has hastened the increase of knowledge; but Scriptural, or spiritual, knowledge can only increase as we are taught by the Holy Spirit of God. It is notable that at the close of the book of Revelation these words are found:

> Behold I come quickly: blessed is he that keepeth the sayings of the prophecy of this book.
>
> And he saith unto me, SEAL NOT THE SAYINGS OF THE PROPHECY OF THIS BOOK: FOR THE TIME IS AT HAND. (Revelation 22:7 and 10.)

Indisputable is the fact that God is here saying that "the time of the end" has come, and the prophecies are to be *no longer sealed or closed* to our understanding. According to His divine will and sovereign purpose, understanding of the prophetic scriptures would now be given. This truth is emphasized because God promises a BLESSING to all who read and keep the prophetic scriptures (Revelation 1:3).

It is certain that the closer we get to the end, or to ZERO in the countdown, the more the prophecies become clear. We cannot understand by simply running "to and fro," or by human endeavor alone. We must study and look to the Lord for the truth of the matter. We must have a clear mind, a mind that is not cluttered with the trash of tradition. We must not have a mind that is closed to truth because it is clouded by custom or personal opinion. Let the Holy Spirit guide you into the TRUTH of God's secrets.

HOW LONG?

The Book of Daniel closes with this question. This question is urgent. It has to do not with the length of time from Daniel's day to the end; but the TIME involved in the prophecy under immediate consideration: THE LENGTH OF THE TIME OF THE RULE OF THE ANTICHRIST; the TIME of TROUBLE, such that the world has never seen.

Daniel is not just asking for himself. The question is prompted by the Holy Spirit speaking for the People of God; especially those living near or in the TIME OF THE END. This becomes evident when you notice that it was not Daniel that asked the question at all; but he overheard this conversation among the three celestial Beings in his vision, one of them being, perhaps, Christ Himself.

So many times we are like Daniel; we want to know the truth, but we do not even know what questions to ask to get at the truth. Did you ever consider that if we ask no questions, we get NO answers? So this angel asks the question on our behalf because it is so important for us to know and understand the answer. The whole question is:

How long shall it be TO THE END OF THESE WONDERS?
(Daniel 12:6.)

Surely he is asking concerning TIME, the time it would take to fulfill the prophecies just related in Chapter Eleven, and about the statement in 12:1, *"At that time..."* It is the TIME involved in the great END TIME events, the time of the GREAT TRIBULATION, or that time we call the TRIBULATION PERIOD. It is the time when God's purpose for Israel will have been concluded, as she returns to Him in faith and repentance. It is the TIME OF JACOB'S TROUBLE. It is the time of the Willful King, the "prince," the Little Horn, the Antichrist.

The answer to this most important question is given, and it is given very specifically with utmost clarity. Included in the answer is the statement of the accomplishment of the Divine purpose for Israel. The breaking down of her sinful and rebellious pride and bringing her to repentance. This Heaven-sent messenger lifts both of his hands toward heaven, the Throne of the Sovereign God, Creator of the universe, to show that this answer is from Heaven itself. He "swears," or declares, or proclaims with the divine authority of the Living Lord, Eternal God, the SPECIFIED TIME according to GOD'S TIME FRAME:

> . . . *It shall be for a TIME, TIMES, and an HALF; and*
> *when he shall have accomplished to scatter the **power** of*
> *the holy people, ALL THESE THINGS SHALL BE FINISHED.*
> (Daniel 12:7.)

It is true. That is the way it will be! Please notice carefully that it is NOT SEVEN YEARS as is generally taught. Tradition can be unscriptural. Tradition leads you to erroneous answers and conclusions and misleading understandings. It is clearly specified to be just THREE AND A HALF YEARS. This, then, is the final half of Daniel's 70th week of the given TIME FRAME of Chapter Nine. God's dealings with mankind, both Jew and Gentile, in this present dispensation will be concluded and this AGE closes. A NEW AGE, the KINGDOM AGE is then to begin.

Concerning the statement here given, "to scatter the power of the holy people"; research and word studies reveal that the word SCATTER carries the meaning of TO BREAK; TO DASH TO PIECES; TO DISPERSE. You will remember in the verse under consideration, it is not the *people* that are the focus of the scattering, but the *power* of the people. This word means their power or agency or dominion. The thing that God is dealing with is their independent, self reliant, self confident and self righteous attitude. It is this, their PRIDE, that causes them to think they can get along without God.

They had forsaken God long, long ago. God had chastised them. He sent His prophets to them and they killed them. He finally sent them off into captivity to remain under the dominion of the

Gentiles throughout the TIMES OF THE GENTILES.

Finally, it will be this awful time, with suffering such as the world has never known, that will break Israel's pride. It will cause her to turn to her Lord, her Messiah, who she nailed to the cross when He came to them as the Lamb of God.

This terrible, rebellious pride that has caused them to reject the Saviour, resist the message of God's grace, His will and His leading for centuries. This pride will at last be broken as Israel is humbled before her Lord. This is a truth that you can see clearly reflected in the following Scriptures:

> *When thou art in tribulation, and all these things are come upon thee, even in THE LATTER DAYS, if thou turn to the Lord thy God, and shalt be obedient unto his voice;*
>
> *. . . he will not forsake thee . . .* (Deuteronomy 4:30-31.)
>
> *Is not this laid up in store with me, and sealed up among my treasures?*
>
> *To me belongeth vengeance, and recompense; their foot shall slide in due time: for the day of their calamity is at hand, and the things that shall come upon them make haste.*
>
> *For the Lord shall judge his people, and repent himself for his servant, when he seeth THAT THEIR POWER IS GONE . . .* (Deuteronomy 32:34-36.)
>
> *. . . If ye will not yet for all this harken unto me, then I will punish you seven times more for your sins.*
>
> *And I will BREAK the PRIDE of your POWER . . .*
>
> *I will walk contrary unto you in fury; and I, even I, will chastise you seven times for your sins.* (Leviticus 26:18-19, 28.)
>
> *. . . My determination is to gather the nations, that I may assemble the kingdoms, to pour upon them mine indignation, even all my fierce anger; for all the earth shall be devoured with the fire of my jealousy.*

[This is the TIME of *great tribulation* involving the whole world and lasting three and one-half years.]

In that day shalt thou not be ashamed for all thy doings, wherein thou hast transgressed against me: for then I will take away out of the midst of thee them that rejoice in thy PRIDE, and thou shalt no more be HAUGHTY because of my holy mountain:

I will leave in the midst of thee an afflicted and poor people and they shall trust in the name of the Lord. (Zephaniah 3; 8 and 12.) [emphasis added]

These Scriptures of prophecy concerning God's dealing with Israel very clearly and unmistakably depict what is going to happen to Israel. After years of suffering under God's judgment, her pride in being God's chosen people and her self confidence is finally shattered, and scattered, and broken as she is humbled and brought low. As an "afflicted and poor" people, mourning in true repentance for her sin, she will at last turn to God and TRUST in the name of the Lord.

As of yet, today, Israel still trusts in her own name, her abilities, and her tradition and her religion. She glories in her land and in her people. SHE IS A VERY PROUD NATION. God is going to break that pride! God will break her down, bring her low, and humble her. Daniel tells us that this will be finished after the three and one-half years of the Great Tribulation; and it will bring to an end the fulfillment of these prophecies.

THE END

Daniel, of course, is astonished by all this. He does not understand. In his confusion he cries out in great concern for his people:

. . . O my Lord, What shall be the end of these things? (Daniel 12:8.)

Not just how long; that had been answered. He was expressing great concern for Israel and wanted to know what it all meant for her. What does it all mean for the people of God? The answer that comes to him is that it was not then the time to reveal more of these important matters. It was to be reserved until the time of the coming of the Messiah, who would teach concerning these things to His disciples. Then the Holy Spirit would open the understanding of the Children of God and "show them things to come."

The answers to Daniel's question are given to us in the New Testament. It is the entire subject of the Book of Revelation.

Still, God, through Daniel, does give to us some important and very interesting CLUES concerning these end time days. Prophecy is often given as CLUES. It has bits of factual information concerning future events. It informs us of what is going to happen in the predetermined plan of our sovereign Lord. It is most often given to us as a "problem" to solve through study. It always requires an in-depth study of the Word of God. A comparing of Scripture with Scripture, and rightly dividing the Word of Truth. It requires diligence in our walk with the Lord and faithful, confident trust in His Word. We must look to the Holy Spirit for enlightenment, insight and understanding of truth. Here are some of God's clues found in Daniel 12:10:

> 1. "Many shall be purified, and made white, and tried." This is a clue concerning the terrible persecution Israel will undergo under the rule of the Antichrist. Many will die for their faith in the Lord, the Messiah. This truth is seen in Revelation 13:7 and 15.

> 2. "But the wicked shall do wickedly: and none of the wicked shall understand." Those who follow the Antichrist, including the Gentiles who will have rejected the Gospel and Jesus Christ, will receive the mark of the Beast and be lost forever. This precludes the possibility of a "great multitude" being saved during that time. There will be no great revival occurring among the gentiles after the rapture has taken place. It is just not in the Book! See: Revelation 13:8, 16; and 14:9-11.

> 3. "The wise shall understand." Concerning this, look at Daniel 12:3; John 8:47; Ephesians 5:15; also II Timothy 2:15 and 3:15. The "wise" are the saved, the saints of God. They, through their study of the Scriptures, will have come to understand who the

Messiah is. These prophecies of the End Time events will have become meaningful to them in faith. These "wise" will include some from among the Jewish people as they turn to God and His Word during this terrible time of the Great Tribulation.

4. "From the time that the daily sacrifice shall be taken away, and the abomination that maketh desolate set up, THERE SHALL BE a thousand two hundred and ninety days." Here the heavenly messenger clearly states that the ABOMINATION OF DESOLATION is the *beginning* of this time; and it includes the disruption of TEMPLE WORSHIP. This takes place, according to Daniel 9:27, in the "midst of the week." We, then, have here given to us an additional clue or fact. We know that three and one-half years of the solar year equals 1260 days, and here we are told that there will be 1290 days, or an added 30 days beyond that 1260 day period. This tells us, for one thing, that Armageddon is NOT the end of the world; time goes on. We are not told what will take place during those added 30 days.

5. "Blessed is he that waiteth, and COMETH to the thousand three hundred and five and thirty days." WOW! Here is another clue. We are now informed that there will not only be the added 30 days; but there is an *additional 45 days* to consider in this time. Knowing prophecy, WE KNOW that the next Dispensation is the Kingdom Age of Christ. This is why there is a special "blessing" pronounced upon those who come to, or live to that time.

Thus, we can safely conclude that *at this time* of 1260 + 30 + 45 days, the one-thousand-year *reign of Christ will begin*. We, therefore, understand that the Millennial Reign of our Blessed Lord will begin 75 days AFTER Armageddon!

About the extra 30 and additional 45 days and their purpose, WE ARE NOT TOLD specifically. Possibly, the earth may have to be cleansed after the devastating years of the Great Tribulation. It closes with the great slaughter of the peoples of the world at Armageddon. It will take some time for the fowls of the air to consume the dead scattered upon the face of the earth, as is recorded in Revelation 19:17-18.

The Jewish remnant will have been gathered from the four corners of the earth and brought to Jerusalem. Judgments, rewards, thrones and the Kingdom will now be established. These will be real, living people and it will require some time.

It seems that these 75 days allotted for all this is a *short* time. But then, God is working. What we have to remember is that this is the way God says it will happen.

Daniel was now told to ask no more, for he would die long before these things were to take place:

> . . . *Thou shalt rest, and stand in thy lot at the end of the days.* (Daniel 12:13.)

He is assured by the Lord that his resurrection would come, and that he would occupy his place in the plan of God at that wonderful, glorious time. DANIEL BELIEVED GOD. He did not understand nearly as much as you and I might understand, but he believed God with an unwavering faith.

Do you? Can you TRUST what God has said? Are you standing firmly upon the Word of God? Do you really believe that it will be as God has said it would be? If you really do believe, it will be reflected in your daily living. It will be expressed in your undying loyalty to Christ — and your faithfulness in His church — with your personal involvement in Christ's program for His people: The reaching out to the world with the Gospel of His love, as he calls sinners to faith and repentance WHILE THERE IS YET TIME.

> . . . *For the same Lord over all is rich unto all that call upon him.*
>
> *For WHOSOEVER shall call upon the name of the Lord SHALL BE SAVED.* (Romans 10:12-13.)
>
> *We then, as workers together WITH HIM, beseech YOU also that ye receive not the grace of God in vain.*
>
> *For he saith, I have heard thee in a time accepted, and in the day of salvation have I succoured thee: behold NOW IS THE ACCEPTED TIME, NOW IS THE DAY OF SALVATION.* (II Corinthians 6:1-2.)

Jesus is coming. He is coming SOON! Are YOU ready for Him?

Is it possible that you have trusted in your religion and your church membership, and that you are not SAVED? Will you be left behind when the Saints go marching into their heavenly home? Will you be left to encounter the Antichrist and those horrible days of the Great Tribulation? Come to JESUS now. Call upon His name. He will save you now, before TIME runs out for you and the door of grace is forever closed.

Trust the Lord now to enlighten you, and increase your understanding, as we next look at the prophecies of Ezekiel.

THREE

Learning From Ezekiel

Turning now to the prophet Ezekiel, we begin to examine scriptures written by a special spokesman of God. He was given many important details that fill in the picture. Details that fit the TIME FRAME shown to us in Daniel. It is important for us to remember that every prophecy of the END TIMES *must* fit comfortably into, and harmonize with, this basic time frame. Everything is related to it and is given to us with that divine schedule in mind. We, in continuing our study, must have instant recall concerning the information available to us in Daniel 2, 7, and 9 through 12. If we are fuzzy on these basic prophetic foundational truths, *everything* else will be out of focus as well. It cannot be stressed enough: students of the scriptures of prophecy must climb their individual ladders of truth carefully and diligently.

Ezekiel was a Jew of priestly heritage. He grew up in Judea as a witness to the devastation and suffering of his people, in the loss of their independence, and their deportation into the Babylonian captivity. Ezekiel was a contemporary of both Jeremiah and Daniel. He was taken to Babylon in 597 B.C., about eight years after Daniel. Jeremiah remained in Jerusalem until he was taken to Egypt where he died. Ezekiel's entire prophetic ministry spanned twenty-two years. It took place in the land of his captivity, and he died in exile in that foreign land. He knew, however, that God would ultimately deliver his people.

In this portion of our study we are concerned with his prophecies of the LATTER DAYS, and will limit our consideration to Chapters 36 through 39 of his book.

THE LAND

As we read Chapter 36 we are immediately informed that the subject of this prophecy is the LAND, or the COUNTRY itself. It is the LAND promised to Abraham and his seed so long ago. In our day there is much controversy concerning the land of Israel or Palestine. To whom does it really belong? If people would just read this chapter in the Bible and BELIEVE GOD, it would settle many disputes. Upon reading this chapter one can say that it is very dangerous to claim that land unless you are an Israelite. A study of this chapter also would straighten out much theology currently being taught in Christian circles. There are those who actually teach that Israel lacks a place, now, in God's program. If only we would learn to listen to God! Hear HIM. BELIEVE HIM. Make no mistake:

> *He that sitteth in the heavens shall laugh: the Lord shall have them in derision.*
>
> *Yet I have set my king upon my holy hill of Zion.*
>
> *I will declare the decree: . . . Thou art my Son; this day have I begotten thee.* (Psalm 2:4, 6, and 7.)

There can be no mistake that the prophecy of Chapter 36 is directed at the very land of Israel, the territory of her possession. It is addressed to "Ye mountains of Israel," and this is specifically clarified as:

> *. . . Thus saith the Lord God to the mountains and to the hills, to the rivers, and to the valleys, to the desolate*

> *wastes, and to the cities that are forsaken, which become*
> *a prey and derision to the residue of the heathen that are*
> *round about.* (Ezekiel 36:4.)

God gives to us His purpose for addressing the land of Israel:

> *. . . Because they have made you desolate, and swallowed*
> *you up on every side, that YE MIGHT BE A POSSESSION*
> *unto the residue of the heathen . . .* (Ezekiel 36:3.)

> *. . . because ye have borne the shame of the heathen:*

> *Therefore thus saith the Lord God; I have lifted up mine*
> *hand, Surely the heathen that are about you, they shall*
> *bear their shame.* (Ezekiel 36:6 and 7.)

We can understand, therefore, that God, in His jealous wrath, will punish the "heathen" round about Israel, BECAUSE they have envied her and desired her land for themselves. As we look at history we find that, indeed — from the time God gave the land to Abraham and confirmed it so down to Moses, and then on to Joshua under whom it was claimed and conquered in the name of Jehovah, and on to this present hour — the land of Israel has been a battlefield for the armies of the world seeking to claim it for themselves. Egypt, Assyria, Babylon, Syria, Persia, Greece and Rome have all fought to possess her, to enslave her people, and to claim her riches.

Israel herself has been rebellious and disobedient to her Lord by forsaking His commandments and in following the idolatrous prac-tices of her heathen neighbors. We understand that it is because of this rebellion of unbelief and her unfaithfulness to the covenants that God has allowed these nations to punish her. They dragged her into captivity and left her cities and her beloved temple in ruins.

This was done at various times and in varying degrees. God gave Israel every opportunity to repent of her rebellious pride. The Babylonian captivity was just one of those chastening acts of a gracious God who loved His people. In His desire to bring her to repentance, God allowed nations to punish her.

Although she was restored to her land, she never fully learned her lesson. She had not learned to listen and to obey her Lord. He would have to chastise her more and to an ever greater degree until, finally, she turns to Him in true repentance and faith.

But, we must understand that God has never forsaken Israel. He has never cast her away. Nor has He abandoned His purpose and His promise to Abraham and David. God's promise and His Word are sure. There will be restoration ultimately, though now, for a time, Israel must continue to suffer:

> . . . *when the house of Israel dwelt in their own land, they defiled it by their own way and by their doings: their way was before me as the uncleanness of a removed woman.*
>
> *Wherefore I poured my fury upon them for the blood that they had shed upon the land, and for their idols where with they had polluted it:*
>
> *And I scattered them among the heathen . . .*
> (Ezekiel 36:17-19.)

Israel's history shows us that, after the return from Babylonian captivity, she suffered even harsher punishment under Roman conquerors. And about 400 years later, the Roman General, Titus, destroyed the city of Jerusalem and the temple for the final time. Then, again, many of her people were carried into captivity. Others were scattered over the face of the earth and did not, for the next 1900 years, possess their land. Yet, God's word is true and His promise has not been forgotten. He has not, even now, forsaken His people:

> *Yea, I will cause men to walk upon you, even MY PEOPLE ISRAEL; and THEY SHALL POSSESS THEE, and thou shalt be THEIR inheritance, and thou shalt no more henceforth bereave them of men.* (Ezekiel 36:12.)
>
> *For I will take you from among the heathen, and gather you out of all the countries and will bring you into your own land.* (Ezekiel 36:24.)

There can be no question at all about God's purpose for Israel and the land of Palestine. Please recall our studies in the Book of Daniel and the TIME FRAME. You will remember the "built-in-hold," and the "Times of the Gentiles." You should now be able to relate these to this prophecy in Ezekiel about God's purpose for Israel. Throughout this hold, Israel has been scattered and under discipline.

Remember that before the last week was to begin, Israel would have to be back in her land. The "prince" would make a covenant with her, and he could not do that if she did not exist as a nation. We, thus, can understand that Israel's return and her reestablishment as the NATION OF ISRAEL in 1948 was all part of God's plan.

It is in *preparation* for the fulfillment of the prophecies of the LAST DAYS. We can, consequently, be assured that we live in the TIME OF THE END!

The pursuit of peace in the Middle East between Israel and her neighbors is leading up to the signing of the covenant. When signed, it will begin the last seven years of the countdown. Watch it happen!

I want you to see something else that God has promised concerning Israel. It has not yet happened:

> *Then will I sprinkle clean water upon you, and ye shall be clean: from all your filthiness, and from all your idols, will I cleanse you.*
>
> *A new heart also will I give you, and a new spirit will I put within you . . .*
>
> *And I will put my Spirit within you, and cause you to walk in my statutes . . .*
>
> *And ye shall dwell in the land . . . and ye shall be my people, and I will be your God.* (Ezekiel 36:25-28.)

Here God is telling us in very plain words that Israel WILL be restored to His fellowship. Israel will be reconciled to God; and we know that this can only be through faith in the Redeemer and His redeeming work on Calvary. So Israel will come to faith in Jesus Christ. She will believe and recognize her Messiah. This can only take place in connection with true repentance. Thus we read:

> *Then shall ye remember your own evil ways, and your doings that were not good, and shall loath yourselves in your own sight for your iniquities and for your abominations.* (Ezekiel 36:31.)

Israel will be brought, as we have seen in Daniel, to this low estate of self esteem, when God has "scattered" her "power." This will happen in the time of the Great Tribulation under the cruel persecution of Antichrist. Following the destruction wrecked throughout the world during this period, Christ will abundantly bless her as His 1000 year Kingdom begins. It is then that she finally will possess her land and live without fear. God will bless the earth, and the land of Israel in particular. We know from Revelation that it is at this time the Antichrist is cast into Hell, and Satan is banished to the bottomless pit.

> . . . *In the day that I shall have cleansed you from all your iniquities I will also cause you to dwell in the cities, and the wastes shall be builded.*
>
> *And they shall say; This land that was desolate is BECOME LIKE THE GARDEN OF EDEN* . . . (Ezekiel 36:33 and 35.)

God tells us that His purpose in doing all this for Israel is not for her sake, but for His name among the heathen. God will be glorified in Israel and, "They shall know that I am the Lord." These are the last words of this chapter that so clearly declares God's purpose concerning Israel and her land.

Chapter 37 is directed specifically to *the people* of the land, the Jewish people as a Nation.

THE VALLEY OF DRY BONES
Ezekiel, Chapter 37

This portion of Scripture is well known due to the old spiritual, "Dem Bones, Dem Bones, Dem Dry Bones." Few people actually understand, today, what is meant by "Dem Bones"; and what it is all about. As you read this chapter in the Word of God and grasp the context of "Dem Bones," it will become clear. You will find it of great interest. Bear in mind that the Lord is sharing with us a basic TRUTH. We are to understand the figures of speech used, and take at face value the clearly stated factual truth. Don't attempt to spiritualize it.

Read this chapter in the knowledge that you now have of the preceding chapter. There you saw God's purpose in judging Israel. Learned that He scattered her because of her sin and rebellion. And, also read His promise to regather her INTO HER OWN LAND.

Remember, too, that God promised Israel that she would be, one day, reconciled to her Lord.

Now, in Chapter 37 we find Ezekiel sitting in the "midst of the valley which was filled with dry bones." God was going to give to him, through this unique object lesson, some important truths. We read about these bones:

> *There were very many in the open valley, and, lo, they were very dry.* (Ezekiel 37:2.)

Again, keep in mind: these are not idle words, for God does not use such. These bones are all there in the open valley so that Ezekiel could clearly see them. Two specific things are said of these bones:

1. There are very many, and
2. They are very dry.

Picture, in your mind's eye, this whole valley filled with bleached white, dry bones. The picture, of course, is of deadness. The dryness of the bones speaks of time. For it is time spent out in the sun and weather that dries the bones of dead bodies. We also know that these bones represent National Israel because we read:

> *These bones are the whole house of Israel.* (Ezekiel 37:11.)

Thus, we can understand that this vision or experience that Ezekiel had was: to represent the truth of the deadness of national Israel as her people were dispersed for a long, long time over the face of the earth. National Israel would be "buried" and disappear from the scene of history for many years. Israel as a nation would become non-existent. History, of course, bears out the truthfulness of this understanding that is so clearly brought out in this chapter.

Because Israel was a very small nation it would take many, many years to accumulate so many bones to fill the whole valley. The passing of time is surely suggested with this picture in that these bones are *very dry*. They have been lying in the hot sun of God's judgment for an extremely long time.

As Ezekiel sits contemplating this mysterious scene, he is asked:

. . . *Son of man, can these bones live?* . . . (Ezekiel 37:3.)

The demise of Israel as a nation is pictured by the deadness and dryness of these bones. They have been dead for a long time. This question now about their living has to do with their return to NATIONHOOD. This would, of course, require their return and re-gathering as a people in the land of Palestine, which is the land of Israel. Then, as we continue to read, we find God declaring His purpose by saying:

. . . *Behold, I will cause breath to enter into you, and ye shall live:*

And I will lay sinews upon you, and will bring up flesh upon you, and cover you with skin, and put breath in you, and ye shall live; and ye shall know that I am the Lord. (Ezekiel 37:5-6.)

His purpose is clear. God is telling the believer that He would bring NATIONAL ISRAEL back from the "dead." This is not the resurrection of the individual, but the resurrection of the nation. Mar-velous as it is, our generation is living witness to the fulfillment of this prophecy. We have seen the bones come together as the Jewish people returned to reclaim their land. They began to regather after World War I. In His sovereign way, God worked in the nations of the world, and Jews were given a place again in their own land — bone came to bone.

World War II forced many more to return. This war also set the stage for the rebirth of the nation of Israel. The "Star of David" is its symbol, and their blue and white flag flies, in liberty, over the Land. Israel is again a nation after being "dead" for 1900 years.

Never before in history had such a thing happened. But, in 1948 we saw it happen as the entire world watched. We witnessed the struggle that nothing seemed able to stop. The nation took shape with the "flesh" and "skin" of a new government. Israel is alive, indeed, but her life remains only physical. She has yet to receive the "breath" of God. Breath and spirit are the same word in Scripture, and one day Israel will live SPIRITUALLY.

Please notice the stress put upon their "living." There are two things that we should keep in mind: There is *physical* life, and there is *spiritual* life. Some do not accept the fact that Israel *is* again ALIVE as a nation in fulfillment of this prophecy; because they are still spiritually dead. They have not yet been reconciled to God through faith. People fail to understand that, before she can live spiritually, she must live physically as a nation. It is NATIONAL Israel that will be renewed in spirit. Today Israel is physically very much alive, but she will remain spiritually dead until the final hours of the Great Tribulation. At last, then, through persecution and judgment, she will finally repent and turn to her Lord, in faith, when he returns to Earth to reign.

Another important teaching in this chapter is that Israel, in her resurrection as a nation, would be a UNITED people. She would no longer be a divided kingdom. When placed under divine judgment she was ISRAEL and JUDEA.

> . . . *Behold, I will take the children of Israel from among the heathen, whither they be gone, and will gather them on every side, and bring them into their own land:*
>
> *And I will make them ONE NATION ion the land upon the mountains of Israel . . . They shall be no more two nations, neither shall they be divided into two kingdoms any more at all.* (Ezekiel 37:21-22.)

This we have seen fulfilled in our day. This is the condition of the Nation of Israel under the "Star of David." It is one united nation as predicted so long ago by the prophet.

Then, concerning their SPIRITUAL rebirth, God says,

> . . . *I will save them out of all their dwelling places, wherein they have sinned, and will CLEANSE them: so shall they be my people, and I will be their God.*
>
> . . . *and they shall all have one shepherd: they shall also walk in my judgments, and observe my statutes, and do them.* (Ezekiel 37:23-24.)

This is clearly not just their being a physical nation, but goes far beyond that to their SPIRITUAL rebirth. We must remember to relate this to the TIME FRAME; and understand that this will take place at the conclusion of the terrible time of suffering. It will happen at the return of Christ, when they see their King, the son of David, descend in full glory. Then they will bow before Him who they "pierced" in repentance and faith:

> *Behold, he cometh with clouds; and every eye shall see*
> *him, and THEY ALSO WHICH PIERCED HIM: and all*
> *kindreds of the earth shall wail because of him.*
> (Revelation 1:7.)

Jesus, the "son of David," will sit upon the throne of David, and will rule for ONE THOUSAND YEARS in righteousness and then on into eternity:

> *. . . I will make a covenant of peace with them; it shall be*
> *an everlasting covenant with them . . . and will set my*
> *sanctuary in the midst of them for evermore.*
> (Ezekiel 37:26.)

No, God is not finished with Israel. Not if His Word is true. Not if He is holy. Not if He is trustworthy. No, and He will never be finished with them.

These are great days in which to be alive. Israel is a nation, and her nationhood speaks loud and clear to all who will hear. God is at work. He is bringing His program for the peoples of Earth to a close. Israel has been restored as a nation, resurrected from the "dead." The seven year peace accord, or covenant, is being sought NOW. The countdown is about to resume. When that covenant is confirmed and the prophetic clock begins to tick again there will be just SEVEN YEARS remaining until Armageddon.

But, almost immediately upon the signing of that accord, something almost indescribable is going to happen which will leave the world, as we know it, forever changed. This is the subject of the next two chapters of Ezekiel.

GOG, AND THE LAND OF MAGOG
Ezekiel, Chapters 38 – 39

As we begin to look at these chapters and the major events

contained therein, we are struck at once with a clear picture of God's overriding sovereign will and power. Truly He does in the nations of men according to His own will and purpose. This is why the Psalmist says:

Why do the heathen rage, and the people imagine a vain thing?

He that sitteth in the heavens shall laugh: the Lord shall have them in derision. (Psalm 2:1 and 4.)

As the heathen take counsel together against the Lord and His Anointed, their evil actions will be under the superimposed control of our all powerful Lord. He will hold them in derision. This is why we absolutely know that God's prophetic TIME FRAME will be concluded exactly as he has declared.

Many people today feel a sense of hopelessness, as though everything is out of control. Some believe it is almost as though God has forsaken His creation. That He has abandoned us to be consumed by the unseen forces of evil; and the corrupting passions of our own sinful nature. God does, to a large degree, allow sin to run its course. He gives deliverance only when the cry of faith is heard from a repentant heart. But we should never lose sight of the fact that the total course of history is under His sovereign control and power.

Although God tells us of evil that will come, He Himself does not plan and purpose that evil. He will use even the evil designs of the heathen to accomplish His purpose.

Lest you become confused by the word "heathen," remember that this word in Scripture refers to: ALL THOSE WITHOUT THE SAVING GRACE OF GOD OPERATIVE IN THEIR HEARTS, THROUGH FAITH IN THE REDEEMING WORK OF JESUS CHRIST. It may refer to you even though you are educated and "civilized." Without God, man is a heathen!

Although this prophecy concerns Israel, it is directed at Gog, and the land of Magog. Gog is the chief "prince" or leader of Meshech and Tubal. Moscow is a derivative of Muscovy, which is itself a derivative of Meshech. It was the first name of Russia. Tobolsky, another city in Russia to the far North, is a derivative of Tubal. Unquestionably, the prophet, under the direct control of the Holy Spirit, was directing this prophecy, so long ago, to present day RUSSIA and her leader.

As we seek to understand all that happens in these chapters, we must remember that these events are all related to the TIME FRAME now familiar to us. They are specifically associated with the last seven years of that FRAME of time. The prophecy of these two chapters covers a specific period. It begins with the event that will interrupt the peace established by the seven year covenant; and it continues to the final restoration of Israel in her covenant relation with her Lord.

An important PRINCIPLE in Revelation to understand is that *prophecy is never given in absolute chronological order*. There is always a natural chronological *development* throughout, but time and events are frequently mixed with varying visions, and often within the scope of a single vision. God is most interested in our understanding of the FACTS about what will happen; thus, the timing of events is occasionally more hidden. It is understood only through careful, diligent study and comparison of those Scriptures that deal with God's revealed time schedule.

Consider carefully the FACTS that God gives to us here, and then, with specific clues given, seek to understand the TIMING of these events.

THE NORTHERN BEAR

I use this title because Russia is often symbolized as a giant, angry and ferocious bear. She is known today as the RED BEAR. This is not necessarily a Scriptural symbol, but it is the symbol used for Russia today, and the Scriptural mention of hooks in her jaw is fitting because of her militant, aggressive character. Today she has many "cubs" under her control or influence. There is little question about the composition of the great and powerful confederation of peoples that made up the mighty Soviet Union.

It is universally recognized, in Christian circles, that Gog and Magog represent this Russian Bear and her leader. The first seven verses of Chapter 38 give to us the coalition of powers bound together under the leadership of Russia. This coalition will become a threat to the world in general, and to Israel in particular. It, and its friendly neighbors to the south, have Israel surrounded.

It is not my purpose here to go into a lengthy and detailed

explanation of proof of the statements just made, because this has been ably done by several authors. I would encourage you to do some research on your own. You will soon see that what is here written will be confirmed in your daily newspaper.

In the light of these facts concerning this united military might, I would refer you to the clear yet elusive truth given in this verse:

> Be thou prepared, and prepare for thyself, **thou, and all thy company** that are assembled unto thee, and be thou a guard unto them. [emphasis added.] (Ezekiel 38:7.)

This leader of the land of Magog, Russia, is thus told to stand up, get ready, and establish himself, together with the company of nations "assembled unto thee." Russia is to be a "guard" unto them. This word means exactly what Russia has been, with the KGB and her military forces keeping close watch over all her "company." These verses call it a "great company," and this expresses great might or military force and power. A significant statement is made next:

> . . . I will turn thee back, and put HOOKS INTO YOUR JAWS, and I WILL BRING YOU FORTH, and all thine army . . . (Ezekiel 38:4.)

God's purpose and supernatural control, even over the movements of so godless a group of nations, is evidenced here. The "hooks" in the "jaws" speak of the irresistible force of the sovereign will of the Almighty, shaping the events and motivations of history. There will be some type of subconscious, spiritual influence (not religious) brought to bear upon the mind and determination of the leaders of the Russian Coalition by the Spirit of the Lord God. He will cause them to come forth. Their objective is clearly stated, for they will INVADE the Land of Israel.

ISRAEL INVADED

The timing of this action by God, that brings about this invasion by the mighty Northern Forces, is stated to be:

> *After MANY days . . . in the LATTER DAYS . . .*
> (Ezekiel 38:8.)

This corresponds to the passing of many years during the built-in-hold of the Time Frame, and brings us to the time of the 70th Week of Daniel. That week is known to be "the latter days" in prophecy. You will notice that we are not left to guess what Russia will do, nor are we left in the dark about the timing of her action. Although it requires a bit more diligent search and consideration.

> *. . . thou shalt come into the land that is brought back*
> *from the sword, and is gathered out of many people,*
> *against the mountains of Israel, which have been always*
> *waste: but is brought forth out of the nations, and they*
> *shall dwell safely all of them.* (Ezekiel 38:8.)

Plainly, there are stated here at least five important facts for us to consider:

1. This northern confederation will invade Israel.

2. They will come "against" her, speaking of hostile action.

3. They will come in great military might; this is the context of verses 4 and 5.

4. Israel will have been regathered and restored as a nation.

5. This invasion will occur AFTER Israel has been given assurance of protection from her enemies. This is known because it is specifically stated that Israel will be living in safety, "all of them." This will be the result of the Peace Treaty confirmed by the "prince" of Daniel's prophecy, the signing of the last seven years of the TIME FRAME.

The fact that this is indeed a military invasion is again brought out in this statement:

> *Thou shalt ascend and come **like a storm**, thou shalt be
> like a cloud to **cover the land**, thou, and all thy bands,
> and many people with thee. [emphasis added] (Ezekiel
> 38:9.)*

This is not only going to be an invasion, but it is going to be a
massive invasion. It will be so great, quick and strong that it will make
the blitz of the German army, in its invasion of Poland at the start of
the Second World War, look like child's play. It will be unexpected,
rapid and will catch Israel and the world off guard because of the
recently signed Peace Treaty. It will be gigantic in scope and over-
whelming in sheer magnitude, unequaled in all history.

We can understand that Israel will be totally unprepared for this
because, due to the treaty, she will have sent her army home and
disbanded her military defenses, for we read:

> *. . . thou shalt say, I will go up to the land of UNWALLED
> VILLAGES; I will got to them that ARE AT REST, that
> DWELL SAFELY, all of them, DWELLING WITHOUT
> WALLS, and having neither BARS NOR GATES.*
> (Ezekiel 38:11.)

All the expressions and terms used here speak of a total lack of
defenses. When this was written, WALLS were the major means of
defense for every city. Every city had its gates that were shut at night
or in time of attack. From its walls the army defended the city and its
people. No city could "rest" and be safe without these walls of protection. To dwell without walls was to dwell without any defense at all.

In our day the walls of defense are standing armies and military
might. Today, the specific application of this prophecy can only
mean to be without guns and tanks, planes and missiles, ships and
men, all prepared to fight off the enemy.

The "rest," here referred to, is the rest of relaxation, free from
worry, that would come from a reliance, not upon self protection, but
upon the safety of a truce among nations. Also, the absolute promise
of safety given by another who has one's full confidence. Such will
be the effect of the Peace Covenant among the nations that will be
confirmed by the "prince that shall come."

The Western Nations, under the leadership of the "prince," will have absolutely guaranteed Israel's full and total protection against all those who have for so long troubled her. The threat from the Communist Block will seem to have disappeared completely; because Russia also will have signed the Covenant.

Russia's own world is changing even as I write this today. We are NOW talking about disarmament because the Communist threat seems less dangerous. All the world is relieved.

The Red armies are being withdrawn from their European Theater of Operation; and it appears that the Red Bear is going to sleep. Some even think that she is dying!

It is easy to see why Israel will be at rest. She can then, energetically, give the focus of her energies to the development of her ailing economy. It will not be necessary to spend huge sums for defense.

This will be the condition of the world as people follow their new leader to develop this NEW AGE of peace for the benefit of mankind.

Deep in the heart of the hibernating Red Bear, its hatred for the Jewish people will again smolder into flickering images of reality. Jealousy, hatred, envy and lust will silently grow. Israel will become a tempting morsel which Russia simply will be unable to resist. All this, of course, is according to the plan of God, for God will judge and destroy this evil system of godless atheism. Her cup of iniquity will at last be full, and so God will bring her forth that He might slay her. The evil purpose of her mind and the aim of her invasion is revealed to us:

To take a spoil, and to take a prey . . . (Ezekiel 38:12.)

The riches and the wealth to be had in the Mid-East, such as oil, gas and minerals of many kinds, are the things that she needs. Russia will feel the need to keep these things out of the hands of the "prince," who has become so popular; whose influence is now enveloping the whole world. She must act while she can, and she must act decisively.

The real and overriding purpose and impulse of the Red Bear will be to "take a prey." She will come against a PEOPLE, the Jew. The anti-Semitic hatred consuming her will drive her insane. She will come to devour little Israel. These truths are given and reiterated throughout Chapters 38 and 39 of Ezekiel. We are really not left to guess about these facts.

Simply believe what God has shared with us, while our eyes are focused upon current events, enabling us to recognize events as they occur. We need not question it; it is not "if" but "when?" We should expect these things to happen, and not be surprised when they do. We should be ready for the news when it breaks.

Remember, there must *first* be the confirmation of the seven year treaty. God speaks to us of this event, of Israel's invasion, with all straightforwardness:

> . . . *it shall be in the **latter days**, and I will bring thee against **my land** . . .* (Ezekiel 38:16.)

The prophet continues with this fascinating news of worldwide importance. After we are told that this something that God Himself will do — cause this invasion; we are told that God also will see to the outcome of it all. God is going to judge the evil system of communism and the people who have embraced and promoted it. Communism is evil. It is godless, immoral and atheistic. It is wicked in practice and enslaving by nature. It is humanistic and selfish, robbing and brainwashing the people it controls. It violates every human decency. It destroys the human character and the human spirit. Russia is ripe for judgment.

The world is presently divided into two major factions:

- The Western, Democratic, Judeo-Christian Nations that make up the core of the revived Roman Empire. This empire will bring to the foreground the "prince" of Daniel's prophecy.

- The Eastern, Communist community of nations with their alliances among the non-Christian countries.

These two world factions stand opposing each other in principle and in purpose.

God will remove the eastern group, with Russia at its "heart," from its place of world influence through the events recorded for us in these two chapters of Ezekiel's prophecy. This will permit the rise of ROME to be at the head of a ONE WORLD GOVERNMENT under the Antichrist.

Into this great vacuum left by the destruction of Russia and her allies, the "prince" will come giving aid to the troubled world: help for the suffering; food for the hungry; medical assistance for the sick, the wounded and the dying. In this fashion he will gain complete control of the entire world, and their loyalty will be unquestioned. There will now be none to oppose him and Satan's evil plans for him. The fact that Russia's destruction will be by divine judgment is spoken with great clarity:

> *And it shall come to pass at the same time when Gog*
> *Shall come against the land of Israel . . . that my fury*
> *shall come up in my face.*
>
> *For in my jealousy and in the fire of my wrath have I*
> *spoken, Surely in that day there shall be a great shaking*
> *in the land of Israel.* (Ezekiel 38:18-19.)

God continues to speak through His prophet. He tells us that it will be because of "MY PRESENCE" that there will be a great earthquake in the land of Israel, and:

> *. . . the mountains shall be thrown down, and the steep*
> *places shall fall, and every wall shall fall to the ground.*
> (Ezekiel 38:20.)

This, of course, will bring great havoc to the invading army. Into this disorder, caused by the terrible shaking, the people will arise to defend themselves with help from the "prince" and his peace keeping forces. They will be present in Israel, to protect her, according to the treaty recently confirmed. Still, we must remember that God will be in control. God will call for a "sword" against them. God has always used people to punish people, and nations to punish nations while He ensures the outcome. They will seek out and kill every remaining communist invader:

> *. . . I will call for a sword against him throughout all my*
> *mountains, saith the Lord God: every man's sword shall*
> *be against his brother.* (Ezekiel 38:21.)

God Himself will then finish the work, as the great invading forces seek to escape. They are doomed. They are condemned to divine judgment which now falls swiftly with devastation from above:

> . . . I will plead against him with pestilence and with
> blood; and I will rain upon him and upon his bands, and
> upon the many people that are with him, an overflowing
> rain, and great hailstones, fire and brimstone.
> (Ezekiel 38:22.)

Like God destroying Sodom for its godlessness, so will He destroy the millions that swarm in upon defenseless Israel and the land God calls "MY land." As one reads these Scriptures he is struck with the absolute clarity in which they are written. You need no interpreter. They speak for themselves, eloquently. It is important to note the repetition of the fact: these armies come upon Israel from the NORTH. This again identifies Russia:

> . . . of the north quarters . . . (Ezekiel 38:6.)

> . . . from thy place out of the north parts . . .
> (Ezekiel 38:15.)

> . . . to come up from the north parts . . . (Ezekiel 39:2.)

THE TIME OF THE INVASION

We already understand that this invasion into the land of Israel must take place "in the latter days." We also know that it must harmonize with the TIME FRAME with which we are now familiar. We see the clear indication that it will occur sometime AFTER the signing of the Peace Treaty that will secure Israel's safety.

Sometimes, in the minds of a few, this invasion is confused with the Battle of Armageddon. It is not possible that this invasion of Israel, from the North, and Armageddon encompass the same event. The reason is because Armageddon, that final battle, will include the armies of the whole world, under Antichrist, in an attack against Christ. This will take place at Christ's return, at the conclusion of the Tribulation Period.

There are those who place this invasion of Israel at the middle of the 70th Week of Daniel. At the time of the revelation of the Antichrist, when he performs the abomination of desolation. It appears, though that this invasion will confirm and solidify, for Antichrist, his position as World Leader. It will give him undisputed control, when he performs that dreadful, blasphemous act, as he declares himself to be god; and demands the worship of all the world.

Notice that God tells us that even the countries from which this invading army comes will not escape His judgment:

> *And I will send FIRE on MAGOG, and among them that dwell carelessly in the isles . . .* (Ezekiel 39:6.)

There is an important clue, in Chapter 39 of Ezekiel, that will help us place the timing of this invasion with great certainty.

An astonishing thing is told to us in Ezekiel 39:2: Of the people invading Israel at this time, God will, " . . . leave but the sixth part of thee . . ." after it is all over; because the destruction caused by God's judgment will be so great. The destruction of these events will include the fire of God's judgment upon Magog, Russia and her cities, her allies, and her surrounding "islands" of people. God's judgment will be swift and it will be sure.

God will have marvelously preserved His people, just as we have seen Him do so often in the Old Testament history. The land of Israel will, you can be sure, be greatly affected by such tremendous destruction. Life will be different.

There is no question about what happened in Sodom, and there will be no question concerning the destruction of Communism. It's as though God's finger has again put "the handwriting on the wall."

Yes, the Western World will come to Israel's relief with food and supplies, as they have done in every modern day catastrophe. They may even be involved in the act of the judgment of God upon the enemies of Israel. God can use them, and He may. We cannot be sure.

Personally, I believe that God will use the Western nations and their defense systems to bring destruction upon the cities of Magog. It appears, from the Scriptures, that when Russia makes up her mind to invade Israel she will try to neutralize any attempt by other nations to come to Israel's aid. One of her first acts may be a preemptive nuclear attack upon the West, with the USA as her primary target. I will share with you the whys and wherefores of this conclusion when we get into the book of Revelation.

After the elimination of her enemies, Israel will have the difficult chore of day to day living amongst the ruins and chaos of the world shaking events she has survived. A great need of her people will be fuel. The need for fuel for machines, cars and trucks will not be as great as the demand for fuel for daily living — to heat with and to cook food. Her return to normalcy from such chaos will take time.

Remember the disruptions caused by recent natural disasters — the length of time required for the reconstruction and recovery of Europe, Japan and Russia after WW II. Can anyone not a survivor really comprehend what suffering those people went through after such great destruction? Try to imagine the condition of the peoples of Israel after this invasion: the fear, desperate needs, attempts to conserve everything that is usable. They must provide for themselves as best they can.

Here is the clue, mentioned earlier, that will help us to understand the timing of this invasion from the North. It also sheds some clear light upon this dark situation:

> . . . *they that dwell in the cities of ISRAEL shall go forth, and set on fire and BURN the weapons . . . and they shall BURN them with fire SEVEN YEARS.*
>
> *So they shall take NO WOOD out of the field, neither cut down ANY out of the FORESTS: for they shall BURN THE WEAPONS WITH FIRE . . .* (Ezekiel 39:9-10.)

The words used in this Scripture are words of God's choice. They tell us that this burning of weapons is not only for their destruction; but, also, their use as FUEL for heating and cooking. Israelites that survive this holocaust will not have a normal supply of fuels. Life will be reduced to an almost primitive state; wood will be scarce and expensive. Trees may be guarded heavily. But there is always much wood and other materials, on military equipment, that will burn.

Development may be underway on a process to develop a new type of wood that will be stronger than steel and that will burn slow and hot. I have been unable to verify such. Regardless, I know that the people of the Land of Israel will burn those leftover weapons as fuel, and that they will burn them for SEVEN YEARS. Think! Why *seven* years? Why does the Bible tell us this? Why not three, five, or ten years?

Seven years! The TIME FRAME includes the last WEEK of the

vision of Daniel, which was just SEVEN YEARS. We know that, at the conclusion of that time, Christ will come and He will establish His Righteous Kingdom. It will last for 1000 years. Christ is the Lord of Glory, the God of Creation, and it is impossible to think that he will rule from rubble; not the King of Kings. He will clean up the Earth, and the land of Israel in particular, after the battle of Armageddon, as indicated in Revelation 19.

The Earth, and Israel in particular, will again be like the "Garden of Eden." It is, therefore, impossible even to think of Israel scrounging around for fuel for their fires for years into the Kingdom age. No! It just could not be.

There is every logical reason to correlate these seven years of the burning (of the weapons of war left from their defeated foe) with the seven years of the last week of Daniel's prophecy. This is especially true when you remember that for three and one-half years of that time, Israel will be fleeing and hiding from her new persecutor, Antichrist. With this understanding as a real possibility, and much of Scripture to conflict with any other deduction, we arrive at the conclusion that the invasion of Israel from the North will take place *within the first year* after the signing of the Peace Treaty of seven years duration.

Watch and pray! Peace is in negotiation right now. Keep an eye upon the news. Do not be disarmed by what Russia is doing. Remember that God is in control, and that it will happen just as He has said. Don't let the sweet, soft words of reassurance from preachers put you to sleep. The time is at hand. Jesus is coming!

We know that Israel will survive all of this and that she will be restored to fellowship with her Lord. This we have seen to be the grand purpose of God, even in this horrible time of suffering. Yes, without question, many Jews will die, but it is of National Israel that God here speaks:

> *Then shall they know that I am the Lord their God, which caused them to be led into captivity among the heathen: but I have gathered them unto their own land, and have left none of them any more there.*
>
> *Neither will I hide my face any more from them: for I have poured out my spirit upon the house of Israel, saith the Lord God.* (Ezekiel 39:28-29.)

This account of these Earth changing events ends with these beautiful words of HOPE for Israel. God keeps His word. Those who love Him are thankful that he is in control. They can absolutely count on His promise to us through the covenant sealed in the Blood of the Lamb of God, Jesus Christ our Lord and Saviour.

We now have a fuller picture of the LATTER DAYS. We see the "prince" rising up through the political system of the leading democratic Nation of the Western Alliance. He will gain the confidence of these allies of the Roman World. We see him negotiating a seven-year peace treaty with those nations concerned over the Middle East situation. This will cause an apparent peaceful solution to the hostilities between Israel and her neighbors — the hostilities that have for so long kept the world in a state of constant turmoil.

This treaty will give to Israel not only access to the Temple site, but it will allow her to rebuild the temple and reinstitute her Temple worship. As this covenant is confirmed, the world will rejoice and proclaim the "prince" to be the "prince of peace." They will give to him world wide acclaim and total confidence.

Upon this action Russia will look with reserve, and as the weeks of that first year creep by, she will be moved by God to direct her great jealousy and growing hatred toward Israel. Russia will covet the riches of the Middle East. She will move to secure this great wealth and power, for herself and her allies, with a massive invasion into Israel before the need of that first year.

Russia will encounter in Israel DIVINE JUDGMENT. The massive army of millions of men and women of the Communist Nations will be annihilated in the land of Israel. Russia's cities will be destroyed by fire. Probably, this invasion will cause an immediate nuclear response from the West upon Russia and her Allies. And the peace keeping forces of the "prince" in the Middle East will move to mop up any remaining Communist military troops.

The peoples of Israel, under God's guidance and care, will have largely escaped; and they will acclaim victory in the Name of Jehovah. This may be the beginning of Israel's turning back to her Lord.

Israel will receive aid from the West, helping her to recover from the devastation in her land. But even with all the help received, the people will find it necessary to use the spoils of war for their daily needs for fuel. The almost limitless quantities of military equipment left by their enemy will be gathered and stored or stockpiled. It will be used as fuel for heating and cooking. It will be used for seven years until Messiah comes. Probably, secret stockpiles of this fuel may be hidden in the caves and rocky crevices for peoples' use in the troubled times just ahead.

Although, in general, they are unaware of what is about to happen, some, through reading the Scriptures, will begin to understand. As they study Scripture, they will be forewarned by the Holy Spirit and the Word of God.

The "prince" will move into the political vacuum created by the destruction of Russia and the Communist forces. He will seek to bring order out of the chaos. He will become the undisputed leader of the entire world. None will oppose him. He will do what he wants. He will promote himself as the World Governor as he becomes the "Willful King."

Perhaps it will be the credit Israel gives to God for deliverance, instead of to the "prince," that causes him to begin his inner hatred of the Jewish people. Whatever the cause, time runs out for the Jew as the "prince's" anti-Semitic feelings grow. For three and one-half years he will have been leading the World. Now he wants to be recognized as the greatest human being who has ever lived, as divine. He will go to the Temple in Jerusalem to be proclaimed god!

We will next pick up his story in the New Testament. Are you ready? JESUS IS COMING VERY SOON!

FOUR

Matthew, Chapter 24

As we begin to look at the prophecies contained in the New Testament, it is especially appropriate that we begin with some of those major statements given by our Lord Jesus Christ. He reaffirms the message of the prophets of old. Realize that our Lord is strongly commending them and their message as worthy of our full trust.

In His Olivet Discourse Christ enlarged upon and adds some important details to what we learned from Daniel and Ezekiel. Remember, Christ is not just another prophet. He was and is GOD Himself. Walking among men in the likeness of man himself. The Lord gave us the message of Matthew 24, which is reiterated with more or less detail in Luke 17 and 21, and again in Mark 13. By reading these accounts, one can get an even clearer view of the prophecies and certain details that are important to proper understanding.

First, open your heart and mind to all that Christ is saying in these prophetic utterances. Some have mistakenly suggested that the message of our Lord, given here, was not directed to the Church, but to Israel only. To believe that is to close the mind to His Words of warning. It also means that you would miss important prophetic clues that Christ gives to us. These clues assist one in a correct understanding of prophetic events and times.

The Christian era does not begin at Pentecost, but with Christ Himself. Yes, the Church, as such, did begin at Pentecost. But the origin of the Church resides in Christ, and with those whom He chose and taught about the "Kingdom of Heaven." Christ taught those who were to be the Church. And, through them, is teaching all of us who are His Church.

Christ also spoke to Israel as a nation. In His prophecies, He definitely had in mind national Israel; and the Jews who would be the object of God's grace, *after* the taking out of the Church at the Rapture.

Yet, His main message is directed to the Believer and His believing Church. This discourse of our Lord's covers the period of prophetic history from His time on earth until the time of His glorious return in power and glory to reign in righteousness.

As we study this discourse of our Lord, we must always keep in mind the TIME FRAME that we have now learned. Picture it in your mind; draw it on paper and be able to fill in the details as given in Scripture. Remember that Christ, when He gave this prophetic Discourse, had in mind this very same TIME FRAME. It is of His origin and is as He gave it to Daniel so many years before. Christ sees things happening in conjunction with this predetermined FRAME of time and events, of prophetic history, and declares the prophetic future. We must understand His word in that context, and be careful not to create our own "context" of time and events.

In this prophetic Discourse, Jesus is answering some very direct questions put to Him by His beloved disciples. Their questions were the result of His statement concerning the "buildings of the temple." The Jews took great pride in their temple, and of it Jesus said:

> . . . *There shall not be left here one stone upon another,*
> *that shall not be thrown down.* (Matthew 24:2.)

This statement of our Lord's clearly predicted the destruction of Jerusalem and the Temple. It occurred in 70 A.D., and was accomplished by the Roman army under General Titus almost 40 years after Christ had spoken these fateful words.

This statement by Christ caused the disciples to want to know more, in detail, about these events and the future of Israel. These men were familiar with the Old Testament prophets. They knew of the Judgment Day, The Day of the Lord, and they knew about the end of the world. Now their specific questions had to do with two things:

1. The TIMING of these events, and
2. The SIGNS that would show the TIME was at hand.

The disciples wanted to know the TIMING of the destruction of the Temple. And, the TIMING of the glorious coming of the Messiah to reign, which they knew would be at the end of the world.

The word for "world" here is "AION," not "Kosmos," and had to do with *time*. They were asking when the present AGE would end and the KINGDOM AGE would come.

The answers to these questions properly involve the Church and the dispensation the Church is in now. This period is largely within the scope of the BUILT-IN-HOLD. Remember this important fact, for the Scripture NOWHERE equates the two.

It is a wrong to assume that the age of the Church will end with the signing of the peace covenant. THE BIBLE DOES NOT SO SAY! The signing of that seven year covenant tells us one thing only. It is that the prophetic clock will have begun ticking again — the countdown to Armageddon will be resumed then.

We must look to other Scriptures, beyond Daniel 9:27, to find the clues to help us understand the timing of the end of the Church age. The disciples, as yet, had little or no understanding about the "Church age." This was something new to them. Their knowledge consisted of the age of Israel's judgment under Gentile rule. The age Christ called the "Times of the Gentiles:"

> . . . and Jerusalem shall be trodden down of the Gentiles,
> until the TIMES OF THE GENTILES be fulfilled.
> (Luke 21:24.)

Jesus commences His instruction with a word of warning against being deceived. He warns about listening to the teachings of men claiming to be messengers of Christ. They could even be ministers of the Gospel, and those who would claim to be the Messiah Himself. Jesus is telling us that FALSE teaching would abound, and that MANY would be deceived into believing untrue doctrines as they follow false teachers.

We can easily identify this fact through the rise of so many false cults with their false Messiahs; and in all the splinter groups of true Christianity. We can today identify many erroneous doctrines within the Christian community, or those who would identify themselves with Christianity. This should be no surprise to us, for this was to be one major characteristic of this, OUR age.

It will progress, often, in the direction of corruption and not purity of doctrine, with error ever on the increase until the end of our age.

From this statement of our Lord, we can see the fallacy of believing that the Church will convert the world and bring it into the kingdom. The testimony of Scripture is that it will be just the opposite. It posits: that the world and evil will have such a deadening effect upon the Church that it will cause a general apostasy within the ranks of so-called Christianity.

Conditions within Christianity, and the final state of the "Christian" Church, will be that of apostate religion where men profess godliness but deny the POWER of it. This truth is clearly stated by our Lord in His address to the Leodician Church. It is supported throughout the New Testament:

> *So then because thou art lukewarm, and neither cold nor hot, I will spue thee out of my mouth.* (Revelation 3:16.)

> *Knowing this first, that there shall come IN THE LAST DAYS scoffers, walking after their own lust . . .*

> *And saying, Where is the promise of His coming? . . .* (II Peter 3:3-4.)

> *But there were false prophets also among the people, even as there shall be false teachers among you . . .*

> *And many shall follow their pernicious ways . . .* (II Peter 2:1-2.)

> *For the time will come when they will not endure sound doctrine . . .*

> *And they shall turn away their ears from the truth, and be turned unto fables.* (II Timothy 4:3-4.)

> *This know also, that in THE LAST DAYS perilous times shall come.*

> *For men shall be lovers of their own selves . . .*

> *Having a form of godliness, but DENYING the power there of.* (II Timothy 3:1-2 and 5.)
>
> *Now the Spirit speaketh expressly, that in THE LATTER TIMES some shall depart from the faith, giving heed to seducing spirits and doctrines of devils;*
>
> *Speaking LIES in hypocrisy . . .* (I Timothy 4:1-2.)
>
> *. . . this is that spirit of antichrist, whereof ye have heard that it should come; and EVEN NOW ALREADY IT IS IN THE WORLD.* (I John 4:3.)

Let me add to these clear statements of evil and abundance of FALSE religious teaching, in these latter days, a statement that confirms what our Lord and his spokesmen have said. The following quotation is taken from the local newspaper here in New London, Connecticut where I am a pastor: *THE DAY*, dated January 14, 1990. This happened to be a Sunday paper. The following statement was made by a "Reverend" and "Pastor" of one of our local "Christian" Churches. This Pastor is presently working on her doctorate of divinity at Hartford Seminary. In the article she says that she believes that God is a FORCE in the universe and not a PERSON She is quoted as saying:

> "I do think that there is a divine something out there, but it doesn't intervene in history . . . The question is 'Who Needs God?'"

This statement clearly reflects the apostasy of TODAY *within* the Christian Church. It is widespread to a greater or lesser degree. Many churches and church leaders today might not go as far as the above "Pastor" in their denial of the faith once delivered to the Saints; yet they openly deny the AUTHORITY of the Scripture.

Scripture is the only foundation of true Christian doctrine. Any teaching not founded upon clear statements of Scripture, and in accord with the whole witness of the Word of God, is a false teaching. Its origin is in Satan the Father of lies. It is the spirit of Antichrist and the expression of apostasy.

History, to this present day, bears out the truthfulness of Christ's warning concerning false religious teaching. As the age draws to a close it will increase until the very person of the Antichrist appears. Then, with his false prophet, the two of them will lead the World to Armageddon.

The second great characteristic of the age in which we now live, as given by Christ, was that of constant unrest among the nations of the world.

> *And ye shall hear of wars and rumors of wars: see that ye be not troubled: for all these things must come to pass, but the end IS NOT YET.* (Matthew 24:6.)

Without fear of contradiction, this was to be and has been the experience of World History since the time of Christ. Peace was not to come! The Church was not to bring in "peace on earth, good will toward men." The Christian age would not convert the world and establish the Kingdom of Heaven. We are told specifically by our Lord that we are not to be troubled and filled with doubt, as though forsaken by God. These things were to be part of the prophetic picture for this age. THEY MUST COME TO PASS! We can see the unrest of our day and understand the news, available from all media, as we hear our Lord say:

> *For nation shall rise against nation, and kingdom against kingdom: and there SHALL BE famines, and pestilences, and earthquakes, in divers places.* (Matthew 24:7.)

In considering this verse, note that, according to Word Studies, the word given here as "nation" is the word for "people" and not "government." This is the prediction of racial upheavals, guerrilla warfare, civil war, ethnic and religious conflicts, revolutions, riots, and the general political and social unrest and violence that is our everyday experience.

The conflicts between "kingdoms" would be that of nations or governments going to war against each other. We have seen this in WWI and WWII, and in almost every part of the world since. These conditions of extreme unrest in our world would be accompanied by "famines." Who among us has not been witness to, or moved by, television reports of widespread famines in the world today.

Recently I read that the expected loss of life among children alone, over the next few years, may be as high as 100,000,000. We are constantly bombarded with appeals for help to feed and care for the needy around the world and in the streets of our own cities.

"Pestilences" or sickness and disease would follow, and it is an ever present reality. No one can deny the fact of AIDS. It has the whole world scared and even threatens the destruction of our economy. Think of the other types of venereal diseases that science is trying to conquer.

Earthquakes and volcanoes have become so common that they are hardly news anymore. Great loss of life and property have been experienced in many parts of the world.

HOW CAN WE DENY THESE FACTS? Or, if we do not deny them outright, why do we overlook them? Their increase is one thing that Christ told us would forewarn us of the END OF THE AGE.

These truly have been and are the characteristics of this age with ever increasing intensity. They make up the news covered by our newspapers and television networks every day. We see them clearly in Europe, in Russia, in the Middle East, in the Far East, in Colombia, Peru, Bolivia, Argentina, Chile, El Salvador, Panama, Nicaragua, Grenada, Mexico, and in the United States of America. Such characteristics are WORLD WIDE!

Who can deny that "wars and rumors of wars" are NOW? But, listen, hear the words of our Saviour saying that the end is not yet. There is more to come. The end is not far off, but it is not yet. There is MORE TO COME. It will get worse and worse, for Christ says:

These are the BEGINNING OF SORROWS. (Matthew 24:8.)

This is an especially significant clue. The actual word interpreted as "sorrows" has the meaning of "birth pangs." It is the expression of those pains or cramps and contractions that a woman experiences as the birth of her child draws closer and closer until the moment of birth. These contractions in the birth of a baby begin to increase in both rapidity and severity as the day and hour approaches. When the contractions are very close and very severe, THEN the woman KNOWS that the moment has arrived, and she should get to the hospital FAST. *The child is about to be born.* This is a CLUE given by our Lord Himself. It is of special significance. Keep it in mind.

These conditions of *this age* are the "contractions" leading up to a "birth." Mark this truth in your mind for instant recall. It will help you to understand an important prophecy a little later in our study. These "contractions" of society will increase and intensify over the years until suffering humanity cries out for deliverance. The contractions are almost constant and deliverance is very near; the time is now.

Immorality, homosexuality, crack, ice, drink, violence, hatred and murder are an everyday part of life. Divorce, broken homes and lives, the killing of the innocent, and the rejection of Biblical standards are clear witness to a world gone mad. Wife beating and child abuse, abortion and kidnapping, prostitution and every form of godlessness is the fruit of a society, not only without Christ, but it is ANTICHRIST. This IS THE TIME OF THE END. We are today, like Jesus said we would be, even as the days of Noah were:

> *The earth was also corrupt before God, and the earth was filled with violence.*
>
> *And God looked upon the earth, and behold, it was corrupt; for ALL FLESH had corrupted his way upon the earth.* (Genesis 6:11-12.)

Notice, please, that all flesh had corrupted "HIS" way, that is GOD'S WAY, upon the earth. What a picture of our day:

> *But as the days of Nōe were, so shall also the coming of the Son of man be.*
>
> *For as in the days that were BEFORE THE FLOOD they were eating and drinking, marrying and giving in marriage, until the day that Nōe entered into the ark,*
>
> *And KNEW NOT until the flood came, and took them all away, SO SHALL ALSO THE COMING OF THE SON OF MAN BE.* (Matthew 24:37-39.)

What we need to see first, here, is that the social conditions then existing were in exact parallel with those of our time. Notice, too, that the Lord emphasizes the total indifference of the people of Noah's day to the message of coming judgment. They paid no heed to the warning, and that was because they did not believe the Word of God and His messenger.

There was total apostasy. Noah's generation lacked care. There was one exception, their own lustful pleasure. Passion had replaced compassion. Sin had replaced sanity, and violence had replaced love. Such is the condition of our generation as well in its social pursuits of fun, pleasure and happiness.

People do not care anymore about right and wrong, about goodness and godliness. Instead of holy days we now have holidays. People love to "party," and they "worship" in the sports arena. Our generation also "worships" at the altar of the goddess of SEX, and they will not listen to the warnings of JUDGMENT.

The Churches are mostly empty, or they are going through a dead ritual. God has written the name "Ichabod" over the door because "glory of the Lord has departed." The name ICHABOD, a boy's name, literally means that the "glory of God has departed." Therefore, in a spiritual sense, one can say, of a Church that has left God's Word to follow its own teaching and its own tradition, that God has left it. His blessing is no longer with them, and "Ichabod" can be written across the doors of that church. See I Samuel 4:21-22.

There are many churches that are full. The people seem "happy" in the Lord. But there is no spiritual depth in their knowledge of the Lord and His Word. Yet, we would be wrong not to recognize that the Lord does still have His "7000 who have not bowed the knee to Baal." There are those who are true to the Word of God, but their number is few. The great masses of the people follow leisure, pleasure, sin, lust and evil; coupled with some form of vain worship foreign to the Word of the Living God.

All this tells us that we are living in the last days. Think of it: Runaway teenagers, teenage prostitutes, child pornography, adult bookstores, bars and dance halls, nudity on demand, this garbage is the appetite of the day. "Burgers, babes and Booze" is the way one sign put it.

Homeless people are in the streets. Children are being molested at the preschools and day care centers. Others are kidnapped, raped and beaten to death. Serial killers and mass murderers abound; these are everyday news items.

There are preachers who prostitute and steal from their people while living luxuriously. There is lying and cheating on every level, in many organizations, and corruption in police forces.

Who hasn't become sick of this daily diet? Recently, the MAYOR of Washington, D.C. was tried on drug charges. Is there no escape? Evil, sin and every form of corruption abound everywhere.

Our only hope is in the Lord! Not government. Not education. Not science. And not RELIGION! As David said:

In the Lord I put my trust . . . (Psalm 11:1.)

For the oppression of the poor, for the sighing of the needy, NOW I WILL ARISE, saith the Lord. (Psalm 12:5.)

The wicked walk on every side, when the vilest men are exalted. (Psalm 12:8.)

These, too, are the beginning of sorrows, and the signs by which the Believer can know that our redemption draweth nigh. These birth pangs are continuing, with greater frequency and intensity. The world is in a state of preparation.

Soon, it will witness the greatest event since the incarnation, crucifixion and resurrection of the Son of God, our blessed Saviour. Still, the Lord warns us of the hatred that will be focused upon His people:

Then shall they deliver you up to be afflicted, and shall kill you: and ye shall be hated of all nations for my name's sake. (Matthew 24:9.)

This word of prophetic warning is two-fold.
Within its scope:

• We see first the hatred and persecution of the Jewish
people down through the centuries. This because of
what they did in the rejection and crucifixion of their
promised Messiah, "for my name's sake."

Also, we have here a view of the hatred that will be poured out upon the Jewish people by the Antichrist and his followers. It will go even beyond those limits of Hitler's evil passion for their extermination.

• The second part of the warning is for the Christians.
They also will suffer "for Christ's sake," as they have
since the time Christ Himself suffered for us.

Read Fox's *Book of Martyrs* if you have never done so. True believers suffered horrible deaths at the stake and on the racks at the hands of the Roman Church. Millions have given their lives for Jesus' sake.

As this apostasy continues and the midnight hour approaches, many more will die for Christ as the Book of Revelation bears witness. This is no surprise to the Believer. Our Saviour has told us to watch for it, to find our peace in the Grace of God, and not in the world.

> *If the world hate you, ye know that it hated me before it hated you.*
>
> *If ye were of the world, the world would love his own: but because ye are not of the world, but I have chosen you out of the world, THEREFORE THE WORLD HATETH YOU.*
>
> *. . . If they have persecuted me, they will also persecute you . . .*
>
> *But all these things will they do unto you FOR MY NAME'S SAKE, because they know not him that sent me.* (John 15:18-21.)

We, therefore, must not be surprised when, in "Christian" America, our children are not allowed to pray in school any longer. Don't be surprised because groups of our children can meet after school, in the school building, for any kind of club except one that has to do with the Bible.

We should anticipate objections to the display of the manger scene and the Christmas story. People want the "joy" of Christmas without the HEART of Christmas.

When you take Christ out of Christmas, you just have a "mas," or better said, a MESS. You must have noticed that the "carols" sung today are not the real Christmas Carols, but secular songs of love, joy and peace. They are nothing more than emotionalism — Oh, a true carol is thrown in from time to time to ease the conscience.

The source of love, joy and peace is denied His place in the celebration that is supposed to be a celebration of HIS birth. He came into our sin-sick world so that we sinners might have love, joy and peace. That is the correct message of Christmas.

All the while we go about this "celebration" of love, joy and peace, we continue the killing of our babies. Of course, we have seen the necessity of killing these unwanted babies. It enables us to enjoy the freedom of our unnatural, unhealthy sexual immorality without the responsibility for our reckless, selfish lifestyles. It has nothing to do with freedom of choice, except that it is our freedom and choice to live without God and divine restraint.

We should not be surprised that our drinking and drunken law makers, those who practice every kind of immorality behind their closed doors, make laws to defend and uphold their evil ways. Justice is gone. It is crying in the streets of the USA. The innocent become the victims of the very system sworn to defend them; while the criminals walk free and are pampered by the law.

How can we expect such law makers, who are often themselves law breakers, to support Christian and Biblical values?

The drug infested, AIDS infected minds of the Sodomites of our day do not love the God fearing. They and the laws made in this country will frequently be directed against the true Believer, Biblical lifestyles, the Bible believing and Bible teaching Church.

Persecution may take the form of litigation and laws that attempt to stem the flow and influence of the Gospel, before it takes the form of clubs, stones and guns. Make no mistake about it, it will come. THE WORLD HATES THE BIBLE AND THE BIBLE BELIEVER! It always has and it always will. Satan has always, one way or another, sought to destroy the children of God.

The false teaching and teachers of the united ecumenical church, directed by its false prophets, will lead the way in these attacks upon Christianity. Many will flee to the "security" of this false church; because of the open persecution of those who dare to believe the Word of God. Many will be deceived by high sounding words and speeches of self appointed, sophisticated, Christ rejecting scholars. Those who openly scoff at and condemn others that believe the Bible.

We will be seen as nonconformists, as misfits in society, as "fundamentalists" whom are fomenting right-wing social and religious reform and censorship of freedom. We will be blamed for the ills of society. Hatred will grow and blossom in the garbage fertilized in the impure minds of the unbelievers as Satan has his way. Life will become hard for the Believer:

> And because iniquity shall ABOUND, the love of many shall wax cold. (Matthew 24:12.)

Distressful times are coming for you and for me; all those who love the Lord Jesus Christ. That is why Paul warns us of this, and tells us that the one thing to do is to:

> . . . *take unto you the whole armour of God, that ye may*
> *be able to withstand in the evil day, and having done all,*
> *TO STAND.* (Ephesians 6:13.)

Many have died for the Lord, and as that day approaches ever closer, we may be sure that many more will die for Him. It is because of this suffering for His sake that Christians will endure.

Though many are going to find their "love" for Christ growing cold. Many will turn away and be captured by the evil One.

In spite of this, those that truly do belong to Jesus Christ will endure unto the end. True, even if the "end" be death itself.

Throughout these troubled and terrible times there will be found those who remain faithful to the Lord. They will bear the Good News to all wherever they go.

A great clue of Scripture is: the Gospel Message, the Good News of Jesus Christ, will spread until it encompasses the entire world. Every nation, all peoples, everywhere, will have had the opportunity to hear the Gospel of God's grace and love in Jesus Christ. They will have had the opportunity to believe, and repent, and turn to Christ as Saviour and Lord.

> *This gospel of the kingdom shall be preached in all the*
> *world for a witness unto all nations; and THEN shall the*
> *end come.* (Matthew 24:14.)

There are two things to make note of here:

FIRST. We must understand that it does not say that the whole world will be won for Christ. It does not say that every tribal language will have the Bible in its tongue. It simply says that the Gospel will be preached, or proclaimed, in all the world — "for a witness unto all nations." There will be the ability, wherever man is found, to HEAR the Gospel, if men WILL HEAR.

This condition has been met in our day. Missionaries have encircled the globe with the Gospel. They penetrated into the far off reaches of the jungles and desert, the East and the West, the North and the South. They did it by airplane, canoe, motor launch, on the backs of horses and mules, on foot, by tape recorders, cassettes, transistor radios and even television. The Gospel has reached even where the missionary has not gone. The Gospel is preached every-where!

SECOND. We should understand from this verse of Scripture that the word "end" is a direct reference to THE LAST DAYS. It is referring to the 70th week of Daniel, that will begin with the signing of the Peace Treaty. It is time NOW for this to take place. That is why the uppermost objective on our political agenda is: PEACE IN THE MIDDLE EAST.

It is of great importance that we notice, see, and comprehend how our Lord relates this prophecy. He brings us right up to the TIME of the END in Verse 14. He does so without a single word about the BEGINNING of this seven year period.

Instead, we find Christ skipping over the first three and a half years completely. He takes us directly to the MIDDLE of the 70th week. He then gives us a *major clue.* Better yet, He gives us a *clear statement of fact* of how the TRIBULATION PERIOD will begin.

Until that time is reached, there will have been a general persecution, growing in severity, that God's people have endured for Christ's name sake. NOW comes that special time of unique persecution such as the world has never known. So, this Tribulation Period is called "THE GREAT TRIBULATION."

It is clearly set apart and distinguished from all other persecution. Uppermost in our understanding is the knowledge (Scripturally correct) that there are just two classes of "tribulation." These are the "general" and the "great."

General tribulation of the Saints of the Living God is to last until the Great Tribulation begins. Scripturally speaking (That, by the way, is the only way we should speak.) There is a "general' time of persecution, but no "seven year" period of tribulation distinct from the "great tribulation." To believe such Scripturally foundationless tradi-tion will always lead to contradictions, confusion, and wrong conclu-sions in prophetic understanding. Christ says clearly:

> When ye therefore shall see the ABOMINATION OF
> DESOLATION, spoke of by Daniel the prophet, stand in
> the holy place . . .
>
> . . . flee into the mountains . . .
>
> For THEN SHALL BE THE GREAT TRIBULATION . . .
> (MATTHEW 24:15, 16 and 21.)

This is the same message as that given to us in Daniel 9:27 and again in Daniel 12:7. Daniel was told that the length of the duration of end time events would be just three and a half years. These verses in Matthew 24:15-21 are the basis, in Scripture, from which theologians get the term "The Great Tribulation."

Specifically, Christ says that this time of tribulation will *begin* with the abomination of desolation. We know that this will occur in the MIDDLE of the last week, that is Daniel's 70th week.

These are important prophetic FACTS that we must keep straight in our minds. Prophetic teachers are extremely careless concerning these *facts*. They often confuse them in their writings with clever mixes of misunderstanding.

Notice that not one word has been said by our Lord about the RAPTURE of His Church in these verses. For a clear understanding of that great event, we must look at other Scriptures that relate to these verses now under consideration. If we do not have the FACTS given to us, here, firmly and correctly stamped upon our minds, we cannot properly relate the other Scriptures that deal with this most important event.

From Verse 21 through Verse 28, Christ gives us a glimpse of those horrible days of terrible persecution and judgment to come. He warns the "elect" of God, Jews who will be saved during that difficult time, not to follow the lies of the Antichrist and his false prophets. We are told that the time of Great Tribulation will end with a great judgment at the coming of the Lord in His glory.

He will gather together the believing Jews from wherever they have hidden in their flight from the pursuing Antichrist and his evil band of persecutors. It is important that you take note here of the blowing of the TRUMPET at this time:

> *And he shall send his angels with a great sound of a*
> *trumpet, and they shall gather together his elect from the*
> *four winds, from one end of heaven to the other.*
> (Matthew 24:31.)

THIS IS NOT THE RAPTURE! This is the picture of Christ gathering the believing Jewish people, His Elect of the Tribulation Period. Gathered from their hiding places to which they had scattered in fleeing the persecution ordered by the Antichrist. They will have been preserved by divine grace (See Revelation 12:13-17) and now they are gathered in divine love. THE TRUMPET IS BLOWN!

This is the LAST trumpet to be blown in prophetic OCCUR-RENCE. There is NO OTHER trumpet to be blown in prophecy as far as TIME is concerned in the sequence of events. Still, this is not the LAST TRUMP of I Corinthians 15:52 as we shall see.

Because this IS the last trump TIME WISE, many are led to believe in a post-tribulation rapture by confusing these two trumpets. Such a conclusion is wrong. It is based upon a false conception. It simply does not and cannot fit into God's clearly revealed TIME FRAME.

The day or the hour knows no man. This frequently quoted Scriptural truth is often misquoted and misrepresented regarding its context. The context is clearly that of the coming of the Lord in His glory as is seen in Verses 29-35 of Matthew 24. There follows, in the next verse:

> **But of that day** and hour knoweth no man, no not the
> angels of heaven, but my Father only.
> (Matthew 24:36.) [Emphasis added]

The "but" at the beginning of this verse takes us back to the preceding statement concerning the coming of Christ, and as that event is summed up in Verse 30. It is NOT His coming for His Church!

Once that peace treaty is signed, believers, familiar with the prophetic Scriptures, will then KNOW that there are only seven years remaining until Christ returns in glory. When the Abomination of Desolation occurs, believers will KNOW THAT THERE ARE BUT THREE AND ONE HALF YEARS LEFT for them to endure the hatred of the Antichrist.

What Christ is saying, then, is that the DAY and the HOUR of His coming in glory was not a REVEALED secret. It was to remain hidden due to the unspecified time length of the built-in-hold within the prophetic Time Frame.

Still, the Father knows, and all things run according to His schedule. Because of the unrevealed duration of this HOLD, it is impossible for man to calculate the time of His coming. We know that will be at the end of the 70th week of Daniel.

We do not know the time, year, or date that week will begin. Therefore, we cannot set dates about the rapture of the Church or of His coming in glory. Although we do not know when that last week will begin, we do know the EVENT that will signal the beginning of those last seven years. Thus, the thinking believer can recognize its commencement, and the significance of the resumption of the COUNTDOWN.

Next, we are, in our text, introduced to another "but." The significance of this second "but" in Verse 37 is to relate our thinking with the preceding statement given there, IN CONTRAST to what is to follow in Verses 38-41.

Verse 37 is the foundation for the admonition to "WATCH," in Verse 42. This second "but" of Verse 37 also gives us a clear contrast of the events of Noah's day and the events when Christ returns:

> *BUT as the days of Noe were, so shall also the COMING OF THE SON OF MAN BE.* (Matthew 24:37.)

It becomes obvious to us, as we read here, that our Lord is focusing in on the idea of JUDGMENT, and DELIVERANCE from that judgment.

Clearly the expressions used by Christ cannot be in reference to the deliverance of the Jewish remnant of the Tribulation Period. The idea of judgment is the core and the heart of this Scripture. It is emphatically stated:

> *And knew not until the flood came, and took them all away; so shall also the coming of the Son of man be.* (Matthew 24:39.)

The indifference of the generation of Noah's day to the message of grace and judgment that he preached for the 120 years of the building of the ark is unmistakably seen in Verse 38. They rejected Noah's message and their only opportunity of salvation.

They did not believe that God was going to judge the world, especially with rain and a flood. They probably thought that Noah and his sons were religious, fundamentalist fanatics. When the rains did come and the flood waters rose, after God had shut the door, they then realized their mistake. It was too late. THEY WERE TAKEN AWAY IN THE FLOOD WATERS OF JUDGMENT!

Jesus tells us that it will be the same at the time of His coming.

To understand this, we must recognize the fact of Christ's TWO COMINGS. One will be *FOR* His Church, and the other will be when

He comes *WITH* His Church at the close of the Tribulation Period.

Like Noah's generation, this generation will not believe that God will send His judgment upon the world either. Most of them, like the "Reverend" quoted before, do not believe that there is a God that intervenes in history and human affairs. They do not believe that a God of love could ever do such a terrible thing. They accuse us of being right-wing religious fanatics.

The objective, and purpose, of the Tribulation Period that will begin with the abomination of desolation at the middle of the 70th week of Daniel, is JUDGMENT. It is the Day of Wrath of the Lamb. Notice this fact so clearly stated in the following verses:

> *And said to the mountains and the rocks, FALL on us, and hide us from the face of him that sitteth on the throne, and from the WRATH OF THE LAMB:*
>
> *For the great DAY of his WRATH is come . . .* (Revelation 6:16-17.)
>
> *. . . If any man worship the beast and his image, and receive his mark . . .*
>
> *The same shall drink of the wine of the WRATH OF GOD.* (Revelation 14:9-10.)
>
> *. . . the great winepress of the WRATH OF GOD . . .* (Revelation 14:19.)
>
> *. . . seven angels having the seven last plagues; for in them is filled up the WRATH OF GOD.* (Revelation 15:1.)
>
> *. . . gave unto the seven angels seven golden vials full of the WRATH OF GOD . . .* (Revelation 15:7.)
>
> *And I heard a great voice out of the temple saying to the seven angels, Go your ways, and pour out the vials of the WRATH OF GOD UPON THE EARTH.* (Revelation 16:1.)
>
> *And out of his mouth goeth a sharp sword, that with it he should smite the nations: and he shall rule them with a rod of iron: and he treadeth the winepress of the fierceness and WRATH OF ALMIGHTY GOD.* (Revelation 19:15.)
>
> *And he was clothed with a vesture dipped in BLOOD: his name is called the Word of God.* (Revelation 19:13.)

This last verse is a picture of JESUS with His blood-soaked garments, stained with the BLOOD of the multitudes of this Christ rejecting world, as they were cast into the winepress of the WRATH of God.

The picture given is that of CHRIST HIMSELF trampling under-foot the "grapes" that are ripe unto judgment. His pure, white garments are stained with their "blood," as the wrath of Almighty God is poured forth upon the unbelievers.

This does not sound like a God that is indifferent or powerless to intervene. It is, in truth, the opposite.

It is a very strong warning to all unbelievers of the very real judgment that is soon to come. This is the reason that this period is characterized by the Biblical name, "THE GREAT TRIBULATION."

Those suffering then will be the godless, faithless unbelievers who have rejected the Love of God in Christ Jesus, and have followed the Antichrist. Yes, the Antichrist will pursue and persecute Israel and the Jewish people. Many of them will die for their new found faith in the Messiah. But, never forget that the Tribulation Period is so named, not primarily because of the suffering of believers; but because of the suffering endured by the ungodly, as the Wrath of God Almighty is poured out upon this Christ rejecting world and the kingdom of the Antichrist.

With this understanding, let us return to Matthew 24 and view the contrast of the Last Days with the days of Noah. There is a beautiful teaching given to us in Matthew 24:37-41. It is sad to realize that its beauty and truth are being obscured by many Bible teachers today.

I want you to have before you two important verses that Christ gives here in the CONTEXT of the wrath and the judgment of God, at the time of the Tribulation Period. That time more correctly and Scripturally known as THE GREAT TRIBULATION. Note the wording:

> *Then shall two be in the field; the one shall be **taken**, and the other **left**.*
>
> *Two women shall be grinding at the mill; the one shall be **taken**, and the other **left**.* (Matthew 24:40-41.) *[Emphasis added]*

Note Verse 39, where it says that the unbelieving of Noah's day were *taken away* by the flood of judgment. There are some who teach that individuals "taken," in Verses 40 and 41, are also taken in *judgment.*

These teachers would have us believe that those that are "left" are left and secured from the judgement. Left to go into the Kingdom of Christ that is to follow.

A simple, honest study of the words that are used by our Lord in these verses will reveal that this is a mistaken idea. It is a drastic misrepresentation of the Word of God.

First, you will find that the word "taken" of Verse 39 is a completely different word from the "taken" of Verses 40 and 41. It has a different meaning altogether. Please take note of the following FACTS from Word Studies:

1. *TAKEN*, as used in Verse 39, means (Greek word "Airoo") to take away, to take up, to carry away. (This from Bullinger's Word Studies.) In Verse 39 it simply means that the flood waters carried them up and away, away from all hope of being saved.

2. *TAKEN*, as used in Verses 40 and 41, means (Greek word "Paralambanoo") to take near, with or to one's self; to take from beside another. (Also from Bullinger's Word Studies.) Vine's Word Studies says of this word: ". . . besides its meaning to receive, denotes to take to (or with) oneself, to take a wife, of taking a person or persons with one."

These two words clearly are not saying the same thing. This second word is the *same word that is used by our Lord in His great promise to the believing Christian:*

. . . *I will come again, and* **RECEIVE** *you unto myself . . .* (John 14:3.)

We should all know that means: Christ will take us to be WITH HIMSELF in love, not in judgment. He will take us from beside the unbelievers, with whom we live now. He will receive us unto Himself; that where He is, THERE we may be also.

Now, if indeed this is what is being said in verses 40 and 41 of

Matthew 24, there should be further confirmation of this truth in our look at the word "left" as used in these same verses. Remember that there are some who teach that these individuals will be "left" to go through the Tribulation and into the Kingdom. Look at the word "Left."

LEFT, or TO LEAVE, (Greek word — "Aphiemi") means: "to send forth or away, to let go from one's self; then, to let go from one's further notice and care, to leave or to let alone." (From Bullinger's Word Studies.) Vine's Word Studies adds to this meaning, "to forsake."

At this point, with the help of our Word Studies, it should be CLEAR to all that the use of these words in Matthew 24: 40-41, in the context of the Judgment and the Wrath of God, can only be referring to one thing.

It is unquestionably stating, in accord with all other Scripture, that those who belong to Christ *will be taken unto Him*. We will be TAKEN from beside the unbeliever, TAKEN AWAY *before* the awful Wrath of God is poured out. We will be TAKEN BY CHRIST as a man takes a wife to himself. It will happen suddenly and unannounced: "two shall be in the field," "two shall be grinding at the mill"; probably working and talking together when, SUDDENLY, "one shall be taken and the other left."

This taking away will happen with the same certainty that the flood came in the days of Noah.

The one that is LEFT is ABANDONED, forsaken, and left to endure all the horrors of the Wrath of God Almighty as it is poured out upon the earth. This punishment will continue throughout the three and one-half years of the TRIBULATION PERIOD.

Remember these words of our Lord. Understand how clearly they speak in light of what we have just seen:

> *Because thou hast kept the word of my patience, I also will **keep thee from THE HOUR** of temptation, which shall come upon all the world, to try them that dwell upon the earth.* (Revelation 3:10.)

This is Christ's personal promise to the Overcomer, to His faithful servants, and the way in which He will keep us from that HOUR is to TAKE US TO HIMSELF even as He has promised:

> *And if I go and prepare a place for you, I WILL COME*
> *AGAIN, AND RECEIVE YOU UNTO MYSELF: that where I*
> *am, there ye may be also.* (John 14:3.)

According to the Word Studies, this word "RECEIVE," in John 14:3, is the same word used by our Lord in the verses of Matthew 24:40-41. There it is translated as "taken."

We will be TAKEN by Christ to Himself FROM the HOUR of His Wrath to which the others are "left." This is commonly known as the RAPTURE OF THE CHURCH. We are told to:

> *Watch therefore; for ye know not what hour your Lord*
> *doeth come.* (Matthew 24:42.)

There will be no last minute preparation. We are either OVER-COMERS looking for:

> *. . . that blessed hope, and the glorious appearing of the*
> *great God and our Saviour Jesus Christ.* (Titus 2:13.)

This, or else we will be, though religious but unbelieving in heart, LEFT to go into the TRIBULATION PERIOD with all its suffering — to experience, personally , the WRATH OF GOD.

There is no middle ground. We belong, right now, to either one or the other of these two groups.

Have you heard His call and heeded that call? Or, will you turn away in unbelief as so many have done already.

The rest of Chapter 24 of Matthew is a warning to be prepared. It is a warning to the unbelieving heart. Though professing Christianity, perhaps a member of some Christian Church, even baptized, if, after all, individuals are found to be unbelievers, they will be "left" behind by Christ when He takes His Church to Himself at the sound of the "last trump":

> *For the Lord himself shall descend from heaven with a*
> *shout, with the voice of the archangel, and with the*
> *TRUMP OF GOD: and the dead in Christ will rise first:*
>
> *Then we which are alive and remain shall be CAUGHT*
> *UP together with them in the clouds, to meet the Lord in*

the air: and so shall we ever be with the Lord.
(I Thessalonians 4:16-17.)

Now, in retrospect, let us recap what our Lord has taught us in Matthew 24, Mark 13, and Luke 21. Let us record these Scriptural FACTS in our memory bank. Available for instant recall as we relate them to the facts of the TIME FRAME now familiar to us. We will see the picture of Prophetic Truth becoming ever more clear and its image sharp in our minds.

FACT LIST FROM MATTHEW, CHAPTER 24

1. The characteristics of THIS AGE:
   A. False prophets, teachers and false Messiahs
   B. Wars and rumors of wars
   C. International and social unrest
   D. Racial conflicts, terrorism, nationalism
   E. Diseases of many kinds, uncontrolled
   G. Earthquakes and other disturbances in nature
   H. Hatred growing for Jews and Christians
   I. A growing apostasy within the Christian Church
   J. World wide missionary outreach
2. The above conditions characterize this age, but the end is not yet. This means that these characteristics are present before the Last Days, or before the 70th week of Daniel begins.
3. These characteristics are the "beginning of sorrows." That is: they will increase and intensify, with the passing of the years of this age, in frequency and degree.
4. After the 70th week has begun, having commenced with the signing of a Peace Treaty for "one week," in the middle of that week, the Antichrist will perform the Abomination of Desolation.
5. The Jewish people living at that time are warned to flee and hide when they see the Abomination of Desolation.
6. The GREAT TRIBULATION will begin, in the middle of the 70th week, with the ABOMINATION OF DESOLATION the starting point.
7. The Great Tribulation will last for three and a half years and is the time of the outpouring of the Wrath of God and of the Lamb.

8. The CHURCH will be RAPTURED, "caught up" and taken by Christ BEFORE that TRIBULATION PERIOD BEGINS. The unbelieving peoples of the world will be "left" to endure the Wrath of God.

9. The Tribulation Period and the Great Tribulation are seen to be the same *in Scripture*. It will last for three and a half years. It will be the time of the reign of the Antichrist and of the Wrath of God.

10. After the suffering of those days Christ will come *with* His Church in power and great glory. He will gather His elect, scattered under the persecution of the Antichrist, and establish His Millennial Reign. He will rule the world with a rod of iron.

I trust these FACTS are clear in your mind. Study them. Reread this chapter.

Know of a certainty that, as we continue in our search for prophetic Truth, each FACT will be verified. They will be strongly supported by many Scripture verses.

Refresh your knowledge until, you know the order, Scripturally, of prophetic events. Draw the TIME FRAME and fill in the details. Then, above all, REJOICE: JESUS IS COMING! WATCH AND PRAY! BE READY! Listen for the sound of the trumpet and the calling of *your name!*

Spread the Word, and comfort one another. Pray with me:

> *Lord Jesus, may we in all truth examine our hearts and know that we are Thine. May we not be deceived by false teaching, or even by the cunning deception of our own hearts. Here is my heart, Lord Jesus; I give it all to Thee. Here is my life, dear Lord, help me to live for Thee. Fill me with thy Holy Spirit, and let my life reflect thy glory. Fill my heart with thy love that I may reach out to others as they grope in the darkness of the world. I love Thee, and I long to see Thy lovely face. EVEN SO COME, LORD JESUS! Amen.*

We will now turn to I Thessalonians, I Corinthians, and then to II Thessalonians as we attempt to further comprehend what God is telling us.

FIVE

Caught Up
In the Clouds

The primary Scriptures that will demand our attention in this chapter of our research into prophetic truth are those of I Thessalonians 4:13-18, I Thessalonians 5:1-11, I Corinthians 15:50-52, and II Thessalonians 2:1-12. There is much more that could be studied in areas of prophetic truth. But, this study is limited to understanding the TIME FRAME of prophecy.

My purpose is not to answer all the questions one may have about our future as children of the Living God. It is to show His purpose and program as related to this TIME FRAME of prophecy. And, I do not want this work to become so cumbersome that it would discourage the reader. Thus, I find it necessary to help the reader develop his own study and understanding of the total PROPHETIC PICTURE.

We now have, fresh in our minds, the study of Matthew 24 and the many prophetic FACTS from that chapter. We can now focus on the event referred to in Matthew by the words of our Lord, "one shall be taken and the other left."

Paul is writing to the Church at Thessalonica concerning those who had died and gone to be with the Lord: "them that sleep in Jesus."

The subject of life and death had taken on a different perspective since the death and resurrection of our Lord. Many Christians were confused about what to believe about death and the future. New revelation was needed to clear up the confusion and misunderstanding. The Lord is now going to provide NEW FACTS of the FUTURE.

Paul encourages the Christian believer to understand that prophetic truth gives HOPE and COMFORT to the one who will believe. This is true even in times of bereavement. Those that had died in Jesus, that is, true believers only, God would "bring with him." This is a direct reference to the great coming event we are told to watch for:

> . . . *that blessed hope, and the glorious appearing of the*
> *GREAT GOD AND OUR SAVIOUR JESUS CHRIST.*
> (Titus 2:13.)

Christ was to bring the believing dead (John 11:25-26) with Him when He comes again. Then, Paul, under the direct inspiration of the Holy Spirit, tells us that the living saints, "we which are alive and remain" until the coming of our Lord, shall not "prevent" them — the believing dead in Christ.

This word *prevent* is the word, "to go before." The dead and we will be together and alike, neither having an advantage over the other. We will be together and we will go together in the day of the resurrection.

The reason given for this is that the dead will return with Christ when He comes for us. They will be resurrected and given a new body that is spiritual in nature. AT THE SAME TIME we will be changed or transformed from a physical to a spiritual being.

The together we will all be "CAUGHT UP" to meet the Lord in the air. This will happen when the Lord comes for His Church, His Body. That Body will be made up of the saints who have died, and those living at the time of the event. The Lord, thus, comes to take us, His Body, to be with Himself, where He is, forever. It is noteworthy to know that then:

1. The Lord Himself shall descend from Heaven.

2. Jesus will descend with a SHOUT!

Perhaps Christ will call each of us by NAME, and say "COME

FORTH," as He did with Lazarus in John 11:43. He has to shout something. When Christ called forth Lazarus the Scripture says, in the context of resurrection:

> . . . *he cried with a LOUD VOICE; Lazarus, COME FORTH.* (John 11:43.)

That was a SHOUT, and even so it will be. We know this because the very purpose of Christ's coming and bringing with Him "those who sleep in Jesus" is that of the RESURRECTION of the dead; and the TRANSFORMATION of the living members of His Body, the CHURCH. He will then "catch" us away to be with Himself. We know that the "dead" will hear His voice:

> *Marvel not at this, for the hour is coming in which all that are in the graves SHALL HEAR HIS VOICE,*
>
> *And shall COME FORTH . . .* (John 5:28-29.)

"The dead in Christ shall rise first," the Scripture says, that is, before the living and transformed saints leave in the RAPTURE.

When Christ raised Lazarus, it has been said, he specifically called him by name. Because, had He just cried, "Come forth," all the dead would have come forth! So, also, in the resurrection of the saints, Christ must limit His command to come forth. Because it is only for the "dead in Christ," at this time.

Thus, we might understand that those who sleep in Jesus will hear their names called, and the command to come forth. They will obey in their resurrection to LIFE.

Next in the sequence of events at that time, we see Michael, the Archangel, as he gets involved in the action. Remember him? We came across Michael back in Daniel 12:1. There he is called the "great prince," and we are told that he "stands" for the people of God. He is on our side!

He, the Archangel, under Christ, of course, is in charge of the angels. He commands the troops. We see this in Daniel 10:13 and then again in Revelation 12:7-9. We are assured of our conviction as we are told that Michael "and his angels" go to WAR against Satan and his angels.

Back in Thessalonians we are told that the coming of our Lord will be accompanied by:

> . . . *the voice of the archangel . . .* (I Thessalonians 4:16.)

You have just got to ask yourself, Why? What is he going to say?

We know that Christ is going to "shout" as the divine plan of action goes into effect for the resurrection, transformation and rapture of the saints. Christ's attention will be directed toward those "who sleep in Jesus" and those that are "alive and remain." Christ's attention will be given to His Body, the Church.

> *Verily, verily, I say unto you, the hour is coming, and now is, when the DEAD SHALL HEAR THE VOICE OF THE SON OF GOD: and they that hear shall LIVE.* (John 5:25.)

This, then, leads us to understand that Michael's voice will be directed toward a *different* purpose. Under Christ, Michael is the Five Star General of the heavenly army. His "voice" will be a voice of command to his angelic soldiers who have come because of the Lord's purpose in the RAPTURE.

You see, when we go home we must go THROUGH Satan's front yard, his territory. Satan is the "prince of the power of the air." You can bet your life that Satan is not going to be waving to us as we go by. NO!

Satan and all his demonic force, his fallen angels, are going to be out in strength to prevent our passage. They will try to STOP the parade "when the saints go marching in." Satan will seek, in this last-ditch effort, to destroy the Church of Christ on its way to glory.

Picture, if you can, the earth shaking, universe splitting battle that rages as Satan is finally defeated and is cast to earth. Here he will direct all his attention, finally, through the kingdom of the Antichrist, to his effort to destroy the Jewish people after his defeat in the heavens.

It is Michael who will command the heavenly troops in that battle, and the defeat of Satan in the heavens. When we get to Revelation, Chapter 12, I am sure that you will be spellbound by the events seen to unfold there.

The next event given to us in I Thessalonians 4 is the sounding of the "TRUMP OF GOD." It takes place at the moment of the Rapture.

This is the sounding of a very special trumpet. It does not specify that God blows the trumpet, but that it is blown at His command. This trumpet is to be blown ONLY at a specific time. That specified time dictated by the divine schedule given to us in His TIME FRAME.

This is a unique trumpet, and it plays a SOLO SONG OF THE BLESSED. We see something special involving this trumpet in the book of I Corinthians:

> *Behold I shew a mystery; we shall not all sleep, but we shall all be changed,*
>
> *In a moment, in the twinkling of an eye, AT THE LAST TRUMP: for the trumpet shall sound, and the dead shall be raised incorruptible, and we shall be changed.*
> (I Corinthians 15:51-52.)

This, it is clear, is the same event as that of I Thessalonians 4:16. There we saw the dead coming with Christ, and they are raised in the resurrection while the living believers are "changed" or transformed.

In I Corinthians we are told, straightforwardly, that "we," that is, those living, "shall be changed." We are CHANGED from this earthly, mortal body and transformed with a spiritual body BECAUSE:

> *. . . flesh and blood cannot inherit the kingdom of God . . .*
> (I Corinthians 15:50.)

The point of the thought now, however, is WHEN this great and wondrous event is going to take place. We know that it will be at the sound of the trumpet, but more specifically, the Bible clearly tells us that it is to be at the "LAST TRUMP."

We must know this: *God does not ever use words that are without meaning!* EVERY word is inspired by God. Every word of God is pure. God does not use empty, vain, meaningless words, *ever*. Know this for a fact.

I am absolutely amazed at how many prophetic writers discredit and discount this statement of Scripture. It is treated as though God did not really mean what He was saying. It seems that the reason for this "white wash" is that they cannot comfortably squeeze this statement into their *traditional* view of understanding. And so they force themselves to discredit the Word of God here.

But, we must understand that this statement DOES fit perfectly into God's view of the prophetic future. The LAST TRUMP is, and has to be, just that, the *last* trump. If we cannot understand this, then let us be honest enough to examine our understanding.

Through the process of instant recall, you will remember that a trumpet is blown, in Matthew 24:31, when Christ comes AFTER the tribulation. It is for this reason, and without further Scriptural proof, that many come up with an impossible idea.

They say that the Rapture will take place at the end of the Tribulation Period. If true, it would mean that the Church will go through that awful time, enduring the wrath of God for those three and a half years of immense suffering and hardship.

Such belief is in direct contradiction with Revelation 3:10, I Thessalonians 1:10, and I Thessalonians 5:9. Some, in an effort to smooth over their guilt of tampering with the Word of God, seek to deny the truth of a "secret rapture" at all. What is the answer to this problem?

It is really simple. We know that the trumpet spoken of in Matthew 24:31 is the last trumpet to sound in its *time of occurrence.* Yet, we know that this cannot be the "last trump" mentioned in I Corinthians 15:52. This is the problem. For a solution to this problem we will again consult our Word Studies.

Our Word Studies give us insight that will help us to know, without doubt, the answer to this apparent difficulty. As we look at this word, the answer becomes one of those beautiful gems reserved only for those who will honor God's Word completely.

This word "last" becomes a major clue to correct prophetic understanding. This word is used to qualify and distinguish the trumpet that sounds at the time of the Rapture. We find that this word can have two possible meanings.

1. The Greek word *eschatos,* translated "last" can mean the same as we would understand it in English. That is the last or final of something. It might be speaking of things, or people, or places or time.

2. There is another understanding, however, and it is that this word "ESCHATOS," when it is used with a noun, can mean the last of a series of things.

We know and understand that any series can be *within* the

framework of any given subject. And, there *is a series* of TRUMPETS within the framework of the TIME FRAME of prophecy. That series of trumpets will actually come BEFORE the final trumpet — the trumpet sounded at the end of the Tribulation Period.

Throughout Scripture there are many trumpets blown. But in the prophetic Scriptures there is a set series of trumpets, and they carry a special message of revelation.

They are specifically seven separate visions of occurrences that happen WITHIN the 70th week of Daniel, and BEFORE that final trumpet of Matthew 24:31. The "last trump" is the last of that series of trumpets, as we will clearly see in our study of the Book of Revelation.

There is no other possible answer without doing great harm to the Word of God. Or, as Paul says, "handling the Word of God deceitfully." Another author says, "adulterating the Word of God."

If words mean anything at all in the divine act of the communication of truth, we must understand, then, that this "last trump" has to be the last trumpet of this series. We must be willing to admit that if this is not so, the only other answer is that it is indeed that of Matthew 24:31; and that would throw the whole prophetic picture into unanswerable confusion.

I am convinced that an honest look at the Scriptures and sequence of events given to us in the Book of Revelation will show us, beyond a reasonable doubt, that the final and SEVENTH TRUMPET is in fact this "last trump" of I Corinthians 15:52.

If we cannot accept this, then words have no definite meaning at all. If so, we are all lost in a fathomless sea of nothingness, with no hope of a true and reliable understanding ever being reached. I, for one, dare not play carelessly with the Word of God.

As we continue with the sequence of events in this great moment of prophetic history given to us in I Thessalonians 4, we come to the moment of the resurrection of the "dead in Christ." As we have seen, this is the result of Christ's shout, possibly, He may call each by name, then give the command to "come forth."

Then the dead shall be raised incorruptible; and are no longer subject to the curse of death, nor the laws that govern our physical universe. Their final enemy will have been conquered in personal experience in Christ:

> *So when this corruptible shall have put on incorruption,*
> *and this mortal shall have put on immorality, then shall*

be brought to pass the saying that is written, Death is swallowed up in victory. (I Corinthians 15:54.)

This is true resurrection, just as Christ Himself was raised from the dead on that first, glorious Easter morning. This is not revival, nor is it a resuscitation, and it is certainly not reincarnation. This is real, honest-to-goodness RESURRECTION.

> *. . . it is written, The first Adam was made a living soul; the last Adam was made a quickening spirit.*
>
> *Howbeit that was not first which was spiritual, but that which is natural; and afterward that which is spiritual.*
>
> *The first man is of the earth, earthy: the second man is the Lord from heaven.*
>
> *As is the earthy, such are they also that are earthy: AND AS IS THE HEAVENLY, SUCH ARE THEY ALSO THAT ARE HEAVENLY,*
>
> *And as we have borne the image of the earthy, WE SHALL ALSO BEAR THE IMAGE OF THE HEAVENLY.* (I Corinthians 15:45-49.)
>
> *. . . There is a natural body, and there is a SPIRITUAL BODY.* (I Corinthians 15:44.)

It is not only interesting to us, but it is also important for us to have an understanding about the ORDER of the resurrection. This order is given to some degree in this book of I Corinthians where we read:

> *. . . now is Christ risen from the dead, and become the FIRSTFRUITS of them that slept.*
>
> *For since by man came death, by man also the resurrection of the dead.*
>
> *For as in Adam all Die, even so in Christ shall all be made alive.*
>
> *But EVERY MAN IN HIS OWN ORDER:*
>
> *(a) Christ the FIRSTFRUITS;*

(b) afterward they that are Christ's at His coming.

(c) Then cometh the END, when He shall have delivered up the kingdom to God, even the Father . . .
(I Corinthians 15:20-24.) [Sentence breaks into (a), (b) and (c) added for emphasis.]

There is unmistakably an ORDER of sequence given to us here concerning the resurrection of *all* mankind.

(a) First in order of resurrection was Christ. Jesus was the very first to experience true resurrection. There were others who, like Lazarus, were returned to life and raised from the dead, but always to die again. There were some who never tasted death at all because God "took" them; such were Enoch and Elijah. Still, NONE, before Christ, were ever resurrected to receive their new spiritual body. Christ was the very first, the FIRSTFRUITS of the resurrection.

(b) Secondly, in order of sequence, will be "those that are Christ's *at His coming.*" To understand this we must realize that the "coming" of Christ will actually take place in TWO PHASES:

- The first phase of Christ's coming is that when He comes FOR HIS CHURCH at the time of the RAPTURE.

- The second phase of Christ's coming is that when He comes WITH HIS SAINTS at the end of the Tribulation. Then He comes to judge the world and establish His Kingdom.

At each of these two phases of Christ's coming there will be a resurrection of the SAVED.

(a) *First*, it will be that of the Church, or all the "dead in Christ" at the sound of the last Trump.

(b) *Secondly*, it will be the resurrection of those who had died "for His name's sake." Those who died during the Tribulation Period, together with all the saved dead; from the times of the Old Testament, to the close of the terrible days of suffering known as The Great Tribulation.

It is at this time when Christ comes as pictured for us in Revelation 19. He comes then, in power and glory, to judge the lost world and to establish His Kingdom. This second phase of the resurrection of the saved is described for us:

> *And I saw thrones, and they sat upon them, and
> judgment was given unto them: and I saw the souls of
> them that were beheaded for the witness of Jesus, and for
> the word of God and which had NOT WORSHIPED THE
> BEAST, neither his image, neither had received his mark
> upon their foreheads, or in their hands; and THEY LIVED
> AND REIGNED WITH CHRIST A THOUSAND YEARS.*
> (Revelation 20:4.)

It is usually understood that this will be a general resurrection of the saved. It includes all God's people from the Old Testament ages, from Adam on. And those who will have confessed Christ during the reign of the Antichrist, and had paid the ultimate price in a martyr's death.

The one exception would be that of the Church, those that are peculiarly "in Christ" and identified as "His Body." These will already have been resurrected at the time of the Rapture.

After these two phases of the resurrection, there is not to be found in Scripture any reference to any further resurrection of SAVED people. Indeed, this is called in Scripture, "The First Resurrection." There is no resurrection of the saved following the Kingdom of Christ. Therefore we know that the saved of that Kingdom period WILL NOT DIE.

We can now see the order of the FIRST RESURRECTION. First, it was Christ. Next, it will be those of the Church at the Rapture. And then the remaining saved at the coming of Christ in glory. Then we will reign with Him WITH A ROD OF IRON.

(c) *Thirdly,* in order of sequence of the resurrection, is the resurrection of the lost. This is the resurrection of the *rest* of the dead. They, too, will be raised to life, but their "life" will be eternal death:

> *Then cometh the end . . .* (I Corinthians 15:24.)

This is the "end" of the resurrection, or the "rest" of the dead as in Revelation 20:5. These will "live not again until the thousand years were finished." This resurrection is followed by the Day of Judgment and the Great White Throne. It is described for us in graphic detail:

And death and hell were cast into the LAKE OF FIRE.
THIS IS THE SECOND DEATH.

And whosoever was not found written in the BOOK OF
LIFE was cast into the lake of fire. (Revelation 20:14-15.)

So now as we return to the Scripture under consideration, I Thessalonians 4:16-17, we have a fuller grasp of the subject of the resurrection. We know now that, at the time of the Rapture, the resurrection of the Church, the "dead in Christ," those that "sleep in Jesus," takes place.

This, then, brings us to our next event in the sequence, the SIXTH in order of sequence as related in the verse under view. They occur at the time of the Rapture. This sixth event involves:

. . . we which are alive and remain . . .
(I Thessalonians 4:17.)

This has to do with those of us, believing Christians, who are still living and have not yet experienced death, yet, when that last trump sounds. We will be taken home to glory, but will not have passed through the valley of the shadow of death.

Yet, we cannot go AS WE ARE! We must be changed and fitted for heaven and the spiritual world of the fourth dimension. We must receive our new spiritual body without dying. That is the reason the Bible says:

. . . we shall not all sleep, but we shall all be changed,

In a moment, in the twinkling of an eye . . . (I Corinthians 15:51-52.)

It will happen just that fast! As the dead are raised, we will be transformed and made like unto Christ. We will, in a micro-moment of time, have a "resurrection" body without having ever experienced death. Praise His sweet name!

Then, wonder of wonders, we, with the resurrected saints, will be taken to glory. We will go in a burst of majestic song and the brilliance of a million sunrises as we meet the Lord in the air.

. . . we . . . shall be CAUGHT UP together with them . . .
(I Thessalonians 4:17.)

This SEVENTH event, which immediately follows our transformation into the image of the Heavenly, is that of the CATCHING UP of the Church. It is that great and glorious event for which we wait. It is the occurrence that gives us HOPE in the darkness of this world.

It is Christ's promise to His Church, and it is pictured in Scripture in graphic detail. It is seen symbolically in many Old Testament figures, principally that of Enoch and Elijah:

And Enoch walked with God: and he was not: for God TOOK HIM. (Genesis 5:24.)

And it came to pass, when the Lord would TAKE UP Elijah into heaven by a whirlwind . . . (II Kings 2:1.)

And it came to pass, as they still went on, and talked, that, behold, there appeared a CHARIOT OF FIRE, and horses of fire, and PARTED THEM BOTH asunder, and ELIJAH WENT UP BY A WHIRLWIND INTO HEAVEN. (II Kings 2:11.)

You think this is far-fetched? Well, it is not. It is a type, or picture, of the Rapture of the Church in miniature. What happened to them WILL HAPPEN TO US!

An important thing to see here is that this was a divine act. Enoch was "taken" by God personally. Elijah went up in a "whirlwind." That expresses violence and force, also rapidity. God was in control, and it was a controlled situation.

This is the same idea given to us by God's use of the words "caught up" for the Rapture. It, too, will be a controlled event. It, also, will be forceful and rapid. The Greek word *Harpazo*, from which we get the English, "Rapture," is used thirteen times in the New Testament: Matthew 11:12 and 13:19; John 6:15 and 10:12, 28 and 29; Acts 8:39 and 23:10; II Corinthians 12:2 and 4; I Thessalonians 4:17; Jude 23; and Revelation 12:5. This word always expresses force and violent action. Our Word Studies are again helpful in our understanding of this word.

VINE'S: *Harpazo*, "to snatch or catch away, to carry off suddenly and by force." This verb conveys the idea of force suddenly exercised."

BULLINGER'S: "To snatch away, to carry off suddenly and by force."

This word *Harpazo* carries the meaning of snatching something out of, or away from danger or destruction. It signifies speed, or swift action and power. It is pictured in the story of Elijah and his being carried off to heaven. It is also seen in the event in the ministry of Philip after he had baptized the eunuch where: "The Spirit of the Lord caught away Philip, that the eunuch saw him no more . . ." (Acts 8:39). These events show the divine power used, as indicated by this word, in transferring a person or persons, miraculously and swiftly, from one location to another.

What a picture of the RAPTURE! Forceful, sudden departure from earth as the Lord Jesus takes us to Himself. He will deliver us from the dangers then to fall upon all that are left behind.

From our Word Studies we can see most clearly that those that are raptured, or "caught up," are acted upon. It is not something that they do themselves! It is not their action!

Like the angels took old Lot by the hand and *took him out of Sodom.* When our Lord went back to glory after His resurrection, He was NOT caught up! He was not Raptured! The Scriptures clearly state that Christ ASCENDED:

> *Wherefore he saith, when he **ascended** up on high, he led captivity captive, and gave gifts unto men.*
> (Ephesians 4:8.)

> *Jesus saith unto her, Touch me not; for I am not yet **ascended** to my Father; but go to my brethren, and say unto them, I ASCEND UNTO MY FATHER; and your Father; and to my God, and your God.*
> (John 20:17.) [Emphasis added]

This is an entirely different word, *Anabaino*, and it means to go up, to rise up like the smoke of the incense. The indication is *effortlessly*, as it was, drifting upward. Now, we must remember that these two words are used by divine choice. God knows what He is doing.

I stress this because we will find the word "caught up" *Harpazo*, further along in our study. If we miss this important point of understanding now, we will not understand it then. I say this because there are those who will and do apply this word *harpazo* to Christ, and this is impossible.

Remember this, and put it into your memory bank for instant recall. It is the CHURCH, THE BODY OF CHRIST, that is "caught up" or raptured. We will be taken up. We will be seized and carried off *forcibly*, "captive." WHY?

It will not be because we are resisting, but because there will be a great demonic, satanic force to oppose and resist our departure. You recall that Satan is the prince of the power of the air. We must pass right through his domain on our way to glory.

Thank God for MICHAEL! The war in the heavens will be a real war. The powers of the heavens will be shaken, but we will arrive safely.

If we understand all that is involved, we can comprehend better why Paul finishes Chapter Four of I Thessalonians by saying:

Wherefore COMFORT one another with these words.
(I Thessalonians 4:18.)

A THIEF IN THE NIGHT

Having now an understanding of the SEVEN events in sequence at the time of the RAPTURE, we are ready to go on. These events are for your review:

1. The Lord Himself descends.

2. Christ descends with a shout, initiating the resurrection.

3. Michael, the archangel, voices a command to his angelic army.

4. The "last" trump sounds.

5. The resurrection of the "dead in Christ" occurs.

6. We, the living saints, are "changed," transformed.

7. The Body of Christ is RAPTURED, or "caught up" and we meet the Lord Jesus in the air and go on to

glory with Him.

As we move along in our study, we will continue with a look at I Thessalonians, Chapter Five, for more important information.

Paul is teaching the Church about this glorious truth of the Rapture. He says to the believers that they have no need for him to write to them about the "times and the seasons." The believers know that the coming judgment of God would come swiftly, even as it did in the days of Noah and of Lot.

The problem is not with the believer, but with the unbeliever. THE UNBELIEVING WORLD IS IN DARKNESS. It is to the unbelieving world that Christ will come "AS A THIEF IN THE NIGHT."

> *For when they shall say, Peace and safety; then sudden destruction cometh upon **them**, as travail upon a woman with child; and **they** shall NOT ESCAPE.*
>
> *But **ye, brethren, are not in darkness, that that day should overtake you as a thief.***
> (I Thessalonians 5:3-4.) [Emphasis added]

How often have you heard preachers say that the Lord will come in the Rapture as a thief in the night, and take us home to heaven? This is usually the way it is presented from our pulpits. This statement is often taken out of its context. It does not apply to the believer, nor to the Rapture of the Church.

The idea given is one of sudden, unexpected destruction and judgment that will fall upon the unsuspecting, unbelieving world.

The world will one day wake up and find themselves alone. The hated Christians are gone; not one is to be found; they have just disappeared. Everyone will rejoice. But, their joy will only last a moment, for with the restraining influence of the Church gone, evil will envelope the world.

The spiritual darkness will be so thick that one can almost touch it. Then, God will begin to pour out His divine retribution of judgment upon this Christ rejecting world of godless people.

It will happen suddenly. As a thief comes in upon an unsuspecting sleeper. The door of grace will be closed as the door of judgment is opened. This is the subject of the Book of Revelation.

The "thief" will come, in the darkness of a spiritual night, upon all those who are in the darkness, having rejected the light. Yet, Paul says of the believers:

> *Ye are all the children of light, and the children of the day:*
> *we are NOT OF THE NIGHT, nor of darkness.*
>
> *For God hath NOT appointed us to WRATH, but to obtain*
> *salvation by our Lord Jesus Christ.*
> (I Thessalonians 5:5 and 9.)

How thankful we can be that: It is by divine appointment that the RAPTURE WILL REMOVE THOSE OF US WHOM BELONG TO THE LORD. Remove us BEFORE that great and terrible day of the wrath of the Lord God Almighty comes.

For all who believe that the Church will go through the Tribulation Period, I humbly say that: you are wrong, so very, very wrong. Your belief, if it is such, is in direct contradiction to this beautiful word of hope and comfort as given to the Church by our blessed Lord through His servant, Paul.

We are children of the LIGHT, children of the DAY. WE WILL NOT BE HERE in that awful NIGHT OF DARKNESS when the "thief" comes in the terrible, destructive wrath of Almighty God. PRAISE HIS HOLY NAME!

TAKEN OUT OF THE WAY
II Thessalonians 2:1-12

It is only natural that we follow up on this subject of the RAPTURE with a close look at II Thessalonians, Chapter Two. This is the way that the Holy Spirit led in the unity of the Bible. This chapter will give to us several more important FACTS that will help us to see the LIGHT in the confusion of prophetic teaching today.

The question that Paul is now focusing upon is the same as that that he has just taught in I Thessalonians, Chapters Four and Five: The coming of our Lord Jesus Christ, and our collection together unto Him.

Paul is now led by the Holy Spirit to give to us some interesting and important FACTS. They deal, not only with the events, but with the TIMING of those events at the time of the RAPTURE.

He is writing that believers might know these facts. And that, by adding the facts together, they might come to proper prophetic conclusions and convictions based upon the Word of God.

Why is it that so many have swallowed the Devil's lie, "You cannot know"? It is true that we cannot set dates for these events now, but there is so much that we can know. And, thus, can understand when the RAPTURE is *about* to take place.

INSTANT RECALL, remember that God is working on and according to an appointed timetable, and that He is right on schedule. GOD IS NEVER LATE! Nor is He ever early. God is never taken by surprise, or caught off guard.

Some would say, glibly, "The Rapture can occur at any moment." They, by that, hide their ignorance of prophetic truth with this and other Christian clichés. We all should know that the Rapture cannot and will not take place until God's appointed time comes.

Some, in Paul's day as in our's, were confused because of the false teaching that abounded. They were being given to understand, because of the then present persecution, that the time of trouble, of the end times, had already begun.

They were told it was the time of divine retribution upon the ungodly referred to in II Thessalonians 1:6-7. They were confused because, if the time of Tribulation had already come, then why were they still here? Why had they not been "caught up" in the Rapture?

False teaching was causing them to question their faith. Paul, therefore, is now seeking to clarify for them the TRUTH concerning that DAY OF CHRIST. Trying to help them understand the day of His glory, the day of the wrath of the Lamb; and its relation to the rapture, or "our gathering together unto Him."

Concerning that terrible time of judgment and the coming wrath of God, Paul says:

> Let no man deceive you by any means: **for that day
> shall not come,** except there come a falling away FIRST,
> and the man of sin be REVEALED. (II Thessalonians 2:3.)

In effect, we might say that Paul was saying that the Day of the Wrath of the Lamb was imminent (likely to happen soon, WEBSTER), but not immediate.

"Immediate," is to expect something to happen NOW, at once. "Imminent" clearly means "likely," or perhaps it may, a possibility, it MIGHT be soon. Not NOW but SOON, but we do not know how long it might delay.

This must be what Paul is saying. Because he was telling the believers that at least two things had to take place before that time of wrath would come:

- There would be a great "falling away," and

- The man of sin would be revealed.

Until these two things occurred, that day of divine judgment, that Tribulation Period, could not come. For confirmation, study the following:

1. "APOSTASIA": This word means to abandon, or forsake the faith. The first thing that Paul told the Christians to look for was apostasy within Christendom. It is related in time to the end time events in this chapter. This word tells us to look for a defection, a turning away from the true faith of the Word of God.

I am absolutely amazed that some, who are of the pre-tribulation Rapture belief, try to support that truth by saying that this term refers to the Rapture of the Church as the believers "fall away from the earth." How far afield from the truth can you get?

Paul is saying that this will be the spiritual condition of the professing Christian Church at the time of the end. It is this state of apostasy that is so clearly voiced by a minister of the Christian religion who would dare to say, "Who needs God?"

This is the state of Christianity pictured by the Church of Laodiceans in Revelation 3:14-22. There Christ is pictured OUTSIDE; and Christian, Biblical Truth has been exchanged for the humanistic philosophy we see so prevalent today.

2. "APOKALUPTOO" — REVEALED: The revelation of the man of sin. This is the second thing that must occur BEFORE the Day of Wrath comes. This "son of perdition" is the Antichrist.

Here we are given a most important truth. It is to be understood, and then it is to be stored in your Memory Bank for INSTANT RECALL. This is the REVELATION OF THE ANTICHRIST.

This word "revealed" signifies, "to uncover, unveil, to remove the covering, to expose to open view what was before hidden, to make manifest." These definitions are from our Word Studies by Vine and

Bullinger.

Understand this: The Antichrist, before he is *revealed* as the Antichrist, *will be present in world politics!* He will be a trusted, elected leader. He will have APPEARED on the scene BEFORE *what he is to be* is revealed!

He will *appear* on the scene of world political history as "the prince that shall come." He will, as that "prince," sign or confirm a covenant, or peace treaty, with many peoples. He will bring peace to the Middle East and give security to Israel.

This covenant will be a *seven year treaty or pact*, as we now know from our instant recall of Daniel 9:27. As the "prince," he will have the trust and confidence of the world.

What is shared here, under the close guidance of the Holy Spirit, is this FACT: It is at the time of the REVELATION of the ANTICHRIST that the Day of Wrath will come upon the unsuspecting world. This does not happen at the time of the *appearance of the "prince,"* when he confirms the covenant. It will occur at the time of the *revelation of the man of sin*, when the "prince" becomes the Antichrist, the son of perdition.

Paul next tells us just what this revelation of the Antichrist will consist of:

Who opposeth and exalteth HIMSELF ABOVE ALL THAT IS CALLED GOD, or that is worshiped; so that HE as GOD sitteth IN THE TEMPLE OF GOD, shewing HIMSELF that HE IS GOD. (II Thessalonians 2:4.)

This is nothing more, or less, than the ABOMINATION OF DESOLATION spoken of by Daniel and again by Christ. We know, by instant recall, that this will take place in *the midst of the week*.

The "prince" will have gained the world's confidence and trust. His position will have become secure as a respected world leader. He previously authorized the rebuilding of the temple in Jerusalem. Now, he will go into the temple, and he will stop the temple worship and sacrifices. Then, he will declare himself to be GOD, and demand the worship of the entire world.

The Antichrist, thus, will be *revealed*. He will be filled with satanic powers. This event starts the last three and a half years. That will be the Day of Christ, the day the Wrath of the Lamb comes!

At this point Paul introduces a great truth. He shares, with the

Church at Thessalonica, a FACT that they should now recall: Something *present* was "withholding" the revelation of the Antichrist. His appointed time had not come, and would not come, until that special entity was *removed*.

> *And now ye know what withholdeth that he might be revealed IN HIS TIME.*
>
> *For the mystery of iniquity doth already work: only he who NOW letteth **will let**, UNTIL HE BE TAKEN OUT OF THE WAY.*
>
> *And THEN shall that wicked be REVEALED . . .*
> (II Thessalonians 2:6-8.)

The "mystery of iniquity" was already at work in Paul's time. Though it is held in check by "that which withholdeth," it will increase. Finally, when that withholding entity is "taken out of the way," then it will come to full bloom.

This mystery of iniquity will culminate in the *revelation of the man of sin*, the Antichrist. This is a very important statement given to us by the Holy Spirit as He tells of "things to come."

This mystery of iniquity surely is that evil undercurrent, the course of this world, as it is directed by the "god of this world." It is the "prince of the power of the air," the "spirit that now worketh in the children of disobedience." As the apostle John wrote:

> *Every spirit that confesseth not that Jesus Christ is come in the flesh is not of God: and this is that SPIRIT OF ANTICHRIST, whereof ye have heard that it should come; and EVEN NOW ALREADY is it in the world.*
> (I John 4:3.)

We, the true believers, are the "light of the world." We, by our Christian living and proclamation of the Gospel, war against the forces of the "rulers of the darkness of this world."

This is why we must put on the whole armour of God. In this manner, we "may be able to stand against the wiles of the devil." Paul said, in his letter to Titus, that the grace of God brought salvation and teaches us that we should live: "soberly, righteously and godly in this present world."

Paul had this war-like life in mind when he was ready to depart from this life and said:

> . . . *I am now ready to be offered, and the time of my departure is at hand.*
>
> *I have **fought a good fight**, I have finished my course, I HAVE KEPT THE FAITH.* (II Timothy 4:6-7.) [Emphasis added]

It was he, this beloved defender of the faith, who said to us:

> *Preach the word; be instant in season, out of season; reprove, rebuke, exhort with all longsuffering and doctrine.*
>
> *For the time will come when THEY WILL NOT ENDURE SOUND DOCTRINE; but after their own lusts shall they heap to themselves teachers having itching ears.* (II Timothy 4:2-3.)

We can see here that it is through the preaching of the Word of God, by His Church, that the evil forces of the mystery of iniquity are being withheld, or held under. But, Scripture shows that they will increase in their corrupting influence and downward trend:

> *Jude, the servant of Jesus Christ, and brother of James, to them that are sanctified by God the Father, and **preserved** in Jesus Christ, and called:*
>
> *Mercy unto you, and peace, and love, be multiplied.*
>
> *Beloved, when I gave all diligence to write unto you of the common salvation, **it was needful** for me to write unto you, and exhort you that ye should **earnestly contend for the faith** which was once delivered unto the saints.* (Jude 1-3.)[Emphasis added]

We can see, therefore, that our fight against the "mystery of iniquity" is a very real battle. It has been engaged for many, many years. It will come to an end, suddenly. This battle will not be won by ourselves, the Church. It will not be won until Satan is cast into hell, the Lake of Fire.

But, before the man of sin can be revealed, the *withholding entity* must be removed. Remember, the verse under consideration, II Thessalonians 2:7, states that the withholding entity is *taken out of the way.*

We are in the way of the Antichrist's being revealed. He cannot be revealed while we are here. He will be on the scene before we are raptured. He will not be revealed, though, until we are gone, ZAPPED, and SNATCHED AWAY — out of the way! This is assuredly what Verses Seven and Eight are saying.

Is there any other Scriptural foundation for this statement? YES, there is! The words of our Saviour, Himself, tell us of this.

In Luke 17:28-36, our Lord refers us back to the story of Lot, just so that we might understand the sequence of this great time and event in history. In this portion of Luke 17, Christ gives us the context of Lot's day and relates it to His statement:

> . . . *there shall be two men in one bed; the one shall be taken, and the other left.*
>
> *Two women shall be grinding together; the one shall be taken and the other left.*
>
> *Two men shall be in the field; the one shall be taken and the other left.* (Luke 17: 34-36.)

We have already seen this Scripture and know, by instant recall, that it can only be referring to the Rapture. That time when Christ "takes" the Church to Himself as a man "takes" a wife. Then, Christ will *leave*, forsake, or abandon the rest to endure the sufferings and the judgment of God during the Tribulation Period.

Therefore, we KNOW that our Lord is directing our understanding about the "days of Lot," and comparing them to the days of the rapture. Here is what Christ says:

> *Likewise also as it was in the days of Lot; they did eat, they drank, they bought, they sold, they planted, they builded;*
>
> *But **the same day that Lot went out of Sodom** IT RAINED FIRE AND BRIMSTONE from heaven, and destroyed them all.*

EVEN THUS SHALL IT BE in the days when the Son of Man is revealed. (Luke 17:28-30.) [Emphasis added]

In our Lord's reference to Noah's day, he is referring to the characteristics of unbelief and indifference that the people then had right up until the flood came and took them all away. They would not believe the message Noah preached.

Please note that there is an important, different focus here, in our Lord's teaching, about the days of Lot. There is still unbelief and indifference, but now the focus is not upon these characteristics. Here He focuses on the TIMING of the event of the falling fire from heaven. It was specifically, "the same day." Then our Lord grabs our attention by saying, "even thus shall it be," THE SAME DAY!

This is underscored for us as we return to the original event in Genesis, Chapter 19. There we see the angels who had been sent by God to destroy Sodom, saying to Lot:

Haste thee, escape thither; for I cannot do anything till thou be come thither. (Genesis 19:22.) [Emphasis added]

From this Scripture it is clear that Lot's presence in Sodom prevented the judgment of God from falling. This beautiful example, given by Christ Himself, that while the Church is present in the "Sodom" of this world, God's judgment will not come.

That is, of course, the judgment of the Day of His Wrath, the Day of the Lord.

Still, just when the Church is removed in the rapture, "the same day," the day of the Wrath of the Lamb will begin. The story and example continue:

. . . Arise, take thy wife, and thy two daughters, which are here; lest thou be consumed in the iniquity of the city.

And while they lingered, the men laid hold upon his hand, and upon the hand of his wife, and upon the hand of his two daughters; THE LORD BEING MERCIFUL UNTO HIM: and they brought him forth, and set him without the city.

The sun was risen upon the earth when Lot entered into

Zoar.

*THEN the Lord rained upon Sodom and upon Gomorrah
brimstone and fire from the Lord out of heaven;*
(Genesis 19:15-16, 23-24.)

What a picture of our deliverance at the RAPTURE! That was the way it was, and that is the way it will be! This is exactly what Jesus is telling us.

We, therefore, can conclude, after looking at the FACTS, that at the very time of the rapture of the Church — just as soon as we are "taken out of the way" — the Man of sin, the Antichrist, will be REVEALED. Simultaneously, the judgment of God will begin upon the earth. We know this to be the Tribulation Period, or THE GREAT TRIBULATION.

We KNOW this to be the case; because Scripture clearly tells us that this REVELATION of the Antichrist will consist of this particular action of "the prince that shall come":

*. . . so that he AS GOD sitteth in the temple of God,
shewing himself that HE IS GOD.*

*Even him, whose coming is **after the working of Satan**
with all power and signs and lying wonders.*

*And with all deceivableness of unrighteousness **in them
that perish**; BECAUSE THEY RECEIVED NOT THE LOVE
OF THE TRUTH that they might be saved.*

*And **for this cause** God shall send them strong delusion,
that they should believe a lie:*

*THAT THEY ALL MIGHT BE DAMNED who believed not
the TRUTH, but had pleasure in unrighteousness.*
(II Thessalonians 2:4, 9-12.) [Emphasis added]

This is that terrible act of abomination that Jesus told the Jewish people to watch out for in Matthew 24:15. Christ there identifies it as the act referred to by the prophet Daniel, in Chapter Nine and Verse 27, as the "ABOMINATION OF DESOLATION."

Three times in the Scripture, in II Thessalonians Chapter Two, this act is called the REVELATION of the Man of sin, the son of perdition! Yes,

THREE TIMES! Christ gives THIS ACT as the *starting point* of the Great Tribulation in Matthew 24: 15-22.

We cannot simply ignore this FACT. It will be when the Church is "taken out of the way," that this revelation of Antichrist occurs, and The Great Tribulation begins.

This may not fit your doctrine. If that is the case, please do not try to change the Scripture by shuffling it around; CHANGE YOUR DOCTRINE!

About these great events and this unparalleled time in history, Christ says:

> *Watch ye, therefore, and pray always, that ye may be counted worthy to* **escape** *all these things that shall come to pass, and to STAND BEFORE THE SON OF MAN.* (Luke 21:36.) [Emphasis added]

We know that the only ESCAPE is like the escape of Lot, and that is to be "taken out of the way" just before the judgment falls. Thus, we can conclude from these New Testament teachings of our Lord and His apostles that there is an ORDER of EVENTS and a TIME SCHEDULE to which that order is subject:

1. The peace treaty will first be signed, and people will be rejoicing with the cry of "peace and safety." The 70th week of Daniel will, thus, have begun. (Daniel 9:27 and I Thessalonians 5:1-3.)
2. As they rejoice in the security of their "peace," sudden destruction will come upon them. This peace will be broken by the invasion from the North. (Ezekiel 38-39 and Revelation 6:3-4.)
3. Christians who are of the DAY, and of the LIGHT, will not be taken by surprise; because of their knowledge of the Word of God (I Thessalonians 5:1). They will now know that the Day of the Lord is very close; and that the rapture of the Church is truly imminent. (I Thessalonians 5:2.)
4. In the vacuum that is left with the destruction of the Northern Powers, the "prince" will become the prominent World Leader. He will move to Jerusalem to make his headquarters there. (Daniel 11:41-45; II Thessalonians 2:3.)
5. Christians who have been battling the forces of darkness (II Thessalonians 2:7; Ephesians 6:12) for many years will suddenly be removed from the world scene in the event known as the RAPTURE, at the sound of the "last trump."

(I Thessalonians 4:13-18; I Corinthians 15:51-52; Revelation 10:7; and II Thessalonians 2:7.)

6. The Church of Jesus Christ, His Body, will then stand before the throne, and be dressed in white robes as they receive their rewards. Then, they will serve the Lamb night and day. (Revelation 7:9-17; Luke 21:36; I Thessalonians 1:10 and 5:9; Revelation 3:10; and II Corinthians 5:10.)

7. At the same time, "the same day," that the Body of Christ is "taken out of the way," the "prince that shall come" will enter the temple of God in Jerusalem. It will have been newly rebuilt. This "prince" will then declare himself to be GOD. With the help and the support of the False Prophet, he will demand the worship of the whole world. (II Thessalonians 2:4, 10-12; Revelation 13 and 14.)

8. This act of the "prince" will be the revelation of the Antichrist. He will be filled with all satanic power. He will perform miracles by which he will deceive the peoples of the world. This, because they will have rejected the message of Truth, the Gospel, and believed the lie (II Thessalonians 2:10-12). The world will worship him (Revelation 13:14-18) and be forever lost. (Revelation 14:9-11.)

9. Following the departure of the Church, the Mantle of Truth will be picked up by the 144,000 who will become the Evangelists of the Tribulation Period. They will win many of their fellow Jews to faith in Christ as the Messiah.

These new believers will be slain for their testimony of faith in Christ. Their souls will be found "under the altar" until the day of their resurrection, at the close of the Tribulation Period, when Christ returns in glory and power to reign. This is the close of the First Resurrection. (I Corinthians 15:23; and Revelation 20:4-5.)

10. "The rest of the dead," the unsaved, are not resurrected until the close of the millennial Kingdom. Then, they will be judged before the Great White Judgment Throne and cast into the Lake of Fire. (I Corinthians 15:24; and Revelation 20: 11-15.)

May YOU be counted worthy to *escape* these things; to stand among the blessed at the time of the rapture. May you be there when we gather before our Lord in heaven to receive the rewards He will give each of us for our faithfulness to Him.

If you are left behind, you must understand that it will be to worship the Antichrist, and to believe the lie that he is God. You will be judged and killed in that Day of the Wrath of the Lamb, and forever lost! Why not come to Jesus now? He is calling for YOU! His invitation is directed to you personally:

> *Come unto me, all ye that labour and are heavy laden, and I WILL GIVE YOU REST.* (Matthew 11:28.)

> *Behold, I stand at the door and knock: if ANY MAN hear my voice and open the door, I WILL COME IN TO HIM, and will sup with him, and he with me.* (Revelation 3:20.)

> *And the Spirit and the bride say, COME. And let him that heareth say, COME. And let him that is athirst COME. AND WHOSOEVER WILL, **let him take of the water of life freely**.* (Revelation 22:17.) [Emphasis added]

> *. . . Believe on the Lord Jesus Christ, and THOU SHALT BE SAVED, and thy house.* (Acts 16:31.)

The Book of Revelation is unique. We turn there now to learn what Christ has to tell us in this last great book.

SIX

The Book Of Revelation

INTRODUCTION: REVELATION AT A GLANCE

Revelation is the story, foretold, of the retaking of the world and its people from the great, evil usurper, Satan, by the LAMB of God.

As we begin our study of this great Book of prophecy, it is well to recall that it is the only one of its kind in the entire New Testament. Our blessed Lord chose to bring to a close all Divine revelation with this wonderful Book. It has as its contents the fulfillment of all preceding prophecy. It is the final unfolding of all God's secrets as given to His prophets.

Christ is herein sharing with His Church the unknowable, as He does the impossible, bringing to an end all history in a manner which is unthinkable. His love and mercy, His sovereignty and authority, His righteousness and justice are all clearly and beautifully displayed in such a manner that His Holiness is everywhere magnified. God is GOOD!

So that you may develop a working knowledge of this glorious

Book and have an easy, quick view of its significant contents, I would suggest the following "look at a glance" of this wonderful revelation:

1. *Chapter One*: Here we are introduced to the Book with a vision of the GLORIFIED CHRIST in His position of absolute and eternal Sovereignty. Here is the King of Kings and the Lord of Lords. Here is the Redeemer and Lover of the Church of which He is the Head and Sanctifier.

2. *Chapters Two and Three*: These are seven distinct visions of the CHURCH AGE in prophetic pre-history, and covers this entire era. It is the picture of the Kingdom of Heaven in its struggle against the gates of Hell and the forces of darkness. It ends, finally, in a state of apostasy and judgment after the True and Faithful have been removed. These chapters give us the SPIRITUAL, or RELIGIOUS, HISTORY of this age.

3. *Chapters Four and Five*: These two chapters also make a unit, but there is a change. The scene now is in Heaven. The LION-LAMB, the resurrected and glorified Son of God, is seen to take His rightful place in heaven's economy as Sovereign and true heir. He is worshiped by the angels and saints alike, as all heaven sings His praise. He is given the SCROLL, sealed with SEVEN SEALS, that is title deed to all of creation, for He has redeemed it to Himself with His own blood. He is seen to be the only one worthy. WORTHY is the LAMB!

4. *Chapter Six*: This one chapter covers the same time period as that covered by Chapters Two and Three. They were spiritual, or religious, history; while this chapter gives to us the political, civil, or SECULAR HISTORY of these last days. This chapter is the NEW TESTAMENT continuation of the Times of the Gentiles. It includes the major characteristics of this time. It is the vision of the opening of the SEVEN SEALS of the Scroll in the hand of the Lamb of God.

5. *Chapter Seven*: This is an INTRODUCTORY chapter, and its visions cover two major events that must take place before the TRIBULATION PERIOD of Divine judgment can begin. The scene is both in Heaven and upon the earth. These two great visions are:

   (1) The sealing of the 144,000 Jewish believers upon the earth.

   (2) The saints, comprising the BODY OF CHRIST, are seen as they arrive IN HEAVEN to stand before

their Lord. This is not a vision of the Rapture, as such, but of the PRESENCE of the RAPTURED CHURCH in Heaven, after they have been removed from the trouble below.

6. *Chapters Eight and Nine*: These two chapters are about the sounding of the first SIX of the SEVEN TRUMPET visions. Chapter Eight gives to us the sounding of the first four trumpets. These are four separate visions of ONE SINGLE event. These four trumpets are related to the INVASION of ISRAEL by the Northern armies of Gog and Magog found in Ezekiel, Chapters 38 and 39. The visions of Chapter Nine are separated from those of Chapter Eight because the fifth and sixth trumpets are distinct from the first four. These two trumpets (5 and 6) are to be related, in our understanding, to the JUDGMENT of God upon the unbelieving world of godless men during the last three and a half years of Daniel's 70th week.

7. *Chapters Ten and Eleven*: These two chapters are an important INTRODUCTION to, and PREPARATION for, the sounding of the SEVENTH and "LAST TRUMP" that is referred to in I Corinthians 15:52. It is notably the LAST of this series of Seven Trumpets. We are, at this point, half way through the Book of Revelation, and also half way through the 70th week of Daniel. The greatest events of all history, other than Calvary and the resurrection, are now to take place. The Seventh and "last trump," is not actually sounded until verse 15 of Chapter Eleven.

8. *Chapter Twelve*: The Last Trump has just sounded, and this important chapter immediately follows, showing its close relationship with the sounding of the "last trump." Here the MYSTERY OF GOD is completed. Here is where and when it happens. THE MAN CHILD IS CAUGHT UP! SATAN is, at this time, defeated and CAST DOWN to earth with "great wrath." The Great Tribulation begins at this point in time, and in conjunction with these great prophetic events.

9. *Chapters Thirteen and Fourteen*: As would be expected, according to the events of Chapter Twelve, we have in these two chapters the establishment of the KINGDOM OF ANTICHRIST, and his reign, as he takes control of life upon the earth. He is worshiped by all the world, under the direction of his FALSE PROPHET. His kingdom is ripe for God's coming judgment.

10. *Chapters Fifteen and Sixteen*: These chapters introduce us to the SEVEN VIALS filled with the WRATH OF GOD. These are now POURED OUT upon the Christ rejecting, Antichrist worshiping world

of rebellious sinners. These two chapters are the heart and core of THE TRIBULATION PERIOD. They cover the time of the reign of the Antichrist, the last half of Daniel's 70th week, THREE AND A HALF YEARS.

11. *Chapters Seventeen and Eighteen*: The union of these two chapters remind you of the two legs and the ten toes of Daniel, Chapter Two. It is here that we have the vision of union of the TWO BRANCHES of the ROMAN EMPIRE and their DESTRUCTION. Here we see that union of the POLITICAL AND THE RELIGIOUS, as the WHORE rides upon the BEAST. Both are the focus of Divine wrath and judgment. The Whore is judged first because of her deception and corruption, through false religious teachings and practices, throughout the world. This UNION is called "MYSTERY BABYLON" because it is part of the entire system of idolatrous religion and political corruption represented by the IMAGE, in the dream of NEBUCHADNEZZAR, in Daniel, Chapter Two.

12. *Chapter Nineteen*: In this chapter CHRIST RETURNS in great glory and power, with His church, TO REIGN in righteousness upon the earth. The TRIBULATION PERIOD is brought to a close with the capture of the Antichrist, his False Prophet, and the destruction of his army in ARMAGEDDON. It is here, also, that the "TIMES OF THE GENTILES" comes to an end as Israel is brought back to her God and Messiah.

13. *Chapter Twenty*: Here is pictured for us the close of the 70th week of Daniel. It shows the RESURRECTION of all the MARTYRED saints of God who died at the hands of the Antichrist and his people. This brings to a close the FIRST RESURRECTION. The MILLENNIAL REIGN of Christ begins and ends in this chapter. SATAN IS BOUND for those 1000 years, loosed, and judged, all within the scope of these fifteen verses. It is here that we find the GREAT WHITE JUDGMENT THRONE; and those not found to be written in the Lamb's Book of Life are cast into the Lake of Fire, which is HELL, and is here called "THE SECOND DEATH."

14. *Chapters Twenty-One and Twenty-Two*: These are glorious chapters, because here we see the revelation of the NEW HEAVEN AND THE NEW EARTH. Here we are shown the eternal PARADISE we call HEAVEN. Here we have the eternal City of God, NEW JERUSALEM, the BRIDE OF CHRIST, where God will dwell with His people forever. It also is here we find that solemn warning and urgent admonition to guard the integrity of the Word of God. All who would dare to ADD TO, or TAKE FROM any part of the REVELA-

TIONS of this Holy Book, the BIBLE, given by God in His love, shall be judged by God Himself. It is here that the Saviour, the Holy Spirit, and the Church of the living God, make one final appeal and invitation to the lost to come to the Fountain of Living Water, JESUS, and be saved.

Let me give you a concise, easy to remember overview of the Book of Revelation:

OVERVIEW OF REVELATION

CHAPTER(S)   CONTENT

■ ■

1 – The glorified Christ, Shepherd of the Saints

2 + 3 – The 7 Letters, Ecclesiastical History

4 + 5 – Worthy is the Lamb, the Redeemer

6 – The Seven Seals, Secular History

7 – 144,000, and the Saints in Heaven

8 + 9 – The Seven Trumpets, invasion from the North

10 + 11 – The 7th Trumpet, uniquely the "last trump"

12 – The man child "caught up"; Satan cast down

13 + 14 – Kingdom of Antichrist and the False Prophet

15 + 16 – The Seven Vials of the Wrath of God

17 + 18 – Mystery Babylon, the Whore and the Beast

19 – Christ returns in glory and power, Armageddon

20 – Millennial Kingdom; Satan bound; Final Judgment

21 + 22 – New Heaven and New Earth; Heavenly Jerusalem

REVELATION — CHAPTER ONE, CONSIDERATIONS

Before we begin our detailed study of the particular prophecies of this wonderful Book, I ask you to briefly review, in your mind, through INSTANT RECALL, the major factors of the TIME FRAME of prophecy. Also, try to recall the major events that we have been given and their relation to that Time Frame. This is important, because everything that we will now see is definitely and specifically related to that Time Frame and the events already seen.

We are now to receive the final pieces of the puzzle, and the picture will be seen in great detail. Yet, if we cannot properly relate this fresh truth to those already studied and understood, we will surely be lost in the fog of forgetfulness; and the mists of misunderstanding will only grow denser.

Unless we let the Light shine through, we will miss the blessings that are promised to all who will diligently study this wonderful Book.

> *Blessed is he that readeth, and they that hear the words of*
> *this prophecy, and keep those things which are written*
> *therein: for the time is at hand.* (Revelation 1:3.)

This blessing is not for the casual reader, nor for the indifferent hearer. It is our Lord's promise to those who read with comprehension, hear with heart, and KEEP those things here shared of His secrets. The blessing is for those who possess a conviction, knowing that, herein, God is revealing how the course of all history will conclude.

A first among many important truths given to us here is found in the very first verse:

> *The Revelation of Jesus Christ, which God gave unto Him,*
> *to SHEW unto his servants things which must shortly*
> *come to pass; and he sent and SIGNIFIED it by his angel*
> *unto his servant John.* (Revelation 1:1.)

From our Word Studies we find that this word "SHEW" means: "To point out, as with a finger," "to explain, to teach." This would clearly indicate to us that this Book is for our UNDERSTANDING. It should not be, as most preachers say, hard to grasp. That is, unless we are spiritually and scripturally illiterate.

Know this, then, you can understand this Book if you will study it in conjunction with all other prophecies, as we have been doing. This Book should never be the beginning of a study on prophecy, but the very end of such a study. It is based upon those prophecies already given, and must be properly related to them.

Next, we look at the word "SIGNIFY." This word, because the first verse specifically says that this is the manner of revelation, is of utmost importance. This word is the verb form of the word "sign," and means to give a sign. The word "sign" indicates a "signal." It is a sign by which something is designated, distinguished, or known. This word is used of the miracles of our Lord. It was by these "signs" that He might be known as the Christ, the promised Messiah. Christ's miracles, or "signs," authenticated His mission and His person. The "sign" was perceived with reference to what it demonstrated. Nicodemus is seen to have comprehended this when he said:

> . . . *Rabbi, we KNOW that thou art a teacher come from*
> *God: for no man can do these miracles that thou doest,*
> *except God be with him.* (John 3:2.)

Another thing that we should understand from the start is that Revelation is not a Book of TYPES. A type has a hidden meaning; it represents something similar, as to person or event. For example, Lot: we have seen him to be a type of the Church at the time of the rapture. Lot was a real person. He had his own identity and his own experiences, but we see in him something similar to that which we ourselves will experience.

Types, in history, are arranged by God in His sovereign will for the purpose of teaching. There are a great many types in the Bible, but there is not one in the Book of Revelation. This Book is a book of "signs" and not of "types." To read this Book as though it represents types will lead to very wrong conclusions.

Every vision is the actual event and not some other. Every vision is given in such a way that it "points out," and "signals" an event; one that is so great and grand, so terrible or complex, that words are not sufficient to do it justice.

Of course the unbeliever, who is without the aid of the Holy Spirit, is in a muddle from the beginning. Thus it is important for us to know that, in this Book, John is John and Christ is Christ. Christ is seen as the LAMB; and, it signifies Christ as the Lamb of God along with His redemptive work on Calvary. Here a city is a city, a place where people live, and sometimes the people who constitute that city, depending upon context.

As John was "in the Spirit," so must we be if we would desire to comprehend and benefit from this glorious Book. Ask the Lord to help you now, before we get into its depths.

This study that I am sharing with you is not meant to be a "devotional" writing, nor is it a verse by verse commentary. I will, therefore, not linger on much that is a sure delight to the soul of every believer. I will, on the other hand, concentrate our thoughts on the particular prophetic significance of each section or vision. I would like to begin by calling your attention to an often misrepresented verse:

> *Write the things which thou has SEEN, and the things which ARE, and the things which SHALL BE hereafter.* (Revelation 1:19.)

This verse is usually seen as an outline of the Book of Revelation. It is commonly said that "the things which thou has seen" is Chapter One. The "things which are" is the Church Age consisting of Chapters Two and Three. Then, "the things which shall be hereafter" is understood to be everything AFTER THE CHURCH AGE, and consists of Chapters Four through Twenty-Two. The RAPTURE is commonly put in verses one and two of Chapter Four, using John as a TYPE of the Church. This, then, is said to be followed by the Tribulation Period, and so on.

This is purely fanciful thinking. Some Bible teachers try to "prove" this by the use of the Greek, and the unknowing swallow the bait of "scholarship." This kind of teaching is a total misuse of the word of God. It is making Scripture say what "I" want it to say so that it will fit into "my" scheme of things. It is construing Scripture to one's mold, instead of being sculpted by Scripture. Those who teach in this manner necessarily bypass, overlook, and nullify some clear statements given in this Book, as we will see.

Rather than looking at this verse as an outline of the Book, I suggest that you read it as a TABLE OF CONTENTS, similar to one in any other book. John's writing was to include:

(1) The vision then being viewed of the glorified Christ.

It is followed by:

(2) Visions covering the present dispensation. They take us to the end of the 70th week of Daniel.

(3) Visions covering the dispensation of Christ's Kingdom.

(4) Then, the Eternal Kingdom.

This is no outline of the Book, but it is clearly the CONTENT found in Revelation. What is often overlooked is that this dispensation of Grace ends with, but includes, the Great Tribulation. Every dispensation throughout history and in all of Scripture has ended in JUDGMENT. And, this present dispensation will not end with the rapture, but with judgment. Even the dispensation of the Kingdom Age will end in Judgment.

This so called "Church Age" will end with the apostate Church, as it is seen in the "sign" of the Laodicean Church, being left behind at the time of the Rapture. It will then go into the judgment of the Tribulation Period as the harlot Church — the great WHORE. The apostate Laodicean Church is spued from the mouth of the Lord. This act signifies the total rejection and abandonment of all who will believe the lie and worship the Antichrist.

THE OVERCOMER

The seven letters to the Seven Churches signify the major characteristics of the Church Age; from its inception, the beginning of its decline, and its final compromise as it struggles against the forces of evil. The Mystery of Iniquity brought upon the world the dark Ages, but the Overcomers continued the struggle against the darkness of this world. The reformation brought the Light of truth again into view. The Church period of the open door — that is symbolic of the missionary outreach of the Church — followed the reformation and the Gospel was spread throughout the world.

This, according to our Lord in Matthew 24, was to be one of the major signs that the end was near. As the end of time draws closer, we are given to understand, through Paul's letters, that apostasy, brought on by compromise, would be the latter state of the professing "church." Judgment was promised, but to the faithful there was assurance that they would be kept "from the hour" of that judgment. This is, of course, a direct reference to the Rapture of the saints of God, as they are removed from the earth before judgment falls.

This commitment is to the "overcomer." The overcomer is the true believer. Here, from the beginning of this Book, we are given an important prophetic concept to understand. It is the "body within a body" concept. The overcomers are the true Church within the visible church. This is the Body of Christ within the body of Christendom. The promise is to the "overcomer" and not to the "Christian." "Christians" comprise all of Christendom, with all of its varied divisions.

The Body of Christ consists of ONLY "overcomers," those who have been washed in the Blood and born of the Spirit. So, we see here the "Church" within the church, the wheat and the tares. Here are the ten virgins of Matthew 25, five with oil and five without. This is a clear Biblical concept. The overcomer is a person of true Biblical faith:

> *For whatsoever is BORN OF GOD overcometh the world . . .*
>
> *Who is he that overcometh the world, but he that BELIEVETH that JESUS IS THE SON OF GOD?*
> (I John 5:4-5.)

Now, of the seven promises to the "overcomers," there are three that I want you to specifically recall for our study. In these it is well to remember that they are promises given by our Lord to His Church, only to HIS PEOPLE in all the years of the Church Age.

- First, we will notice this specific promise to us as overcomers:

> *And he that overcometh, and keepeth my works unto the end, to him will I give power over the nations:*
>
> *And HE SHALL RULE THEM WITH A ROD OF IRON; as the vessels of a potter shall they be broken to shivers: even as I received of my Father.* (Revelation 2:26-27.)

It is most important that we understand that Christ is here telling us that WE WILL RULE THE NATIONS WITH A ROD OF IRON. Remember this! It will help you comprehend something of great importance in a later chapter.

• Second, we see his promise to us:

Because thou hast kept the word of my patience, I ALSO WILL KEEP THEE FROM THE HOUR OF TEMPTATION, which is to come upon all the world, to try them that dwell upon the earth. (Revelation 3:10.)

This is our assurance that our Lord will take us from this earth to Glory BEFORE that HOUR of trial. The Great Tribulation Period, in which the wrath of God is poured out upon the kingdom of Antichrist and all the Christ rejecting world that has believed the LIE, is the "hour" here spoken of by the Lord. It is the "Day of the wrath of God."

• Third, we are given this beautiful promise:

To him that overcometh will I grant to SIT WITH ME IN MY THRONE, even as I also overcame, and am set down with my father in his throne. (Revelation 3:21.)

Did you grasp the meaning of this verse? We are specifically told that we will sit with Christ in His throne! He is sitting upon the throne of His Father, even as we are told in Hebrews 1:3. Now hear this: WE WILL SIT UPON THE THRONE OF GOD ALMIGHTY! The true significance of this is that WE WILL RULE WITH CHRIST! I urge you to remember these three important promises in order to be able to relate them to truths we will see further on in our study. Be prepared for their INSTANT RECALL:

1. We will rule with Christ with a rod of iron.

2. We will be kept from that awful "hour" of trial.

3. We will sit upon the Throne of God with Christ.

WORTHY IS THE LAMB
Chapters Four and Five

In these two chapters of this glorious Book, we arrive at visions which translate us from earth to Heaven. We are not here transported by the Rapture, typified by John in the first two verses, as some would suggest — it is the scene that changes. By this vision we are conveyed from the earthly scene to the heavenly scene where we behold this glorious event. John, not the Church, is in the Spirit to receive this new revelation.

Don't allow yourself to be fooled by the shallowness of teaching that is generally given about this; read it as it is, and do not add to what is said. We must not be guilty of reading into Scripture ideas that are not there. Many preachers place the Rapture of the Church here. They do so simply because they refuse to see it anywhere else in the prophecies of this Book. Their minds are literally blinded to the truth of Scripture by tradition.

We have, in these two chapters, the glorification of the Lamb of God. Christ had now died and secured salvation through His sacrifice on Calvary. He was buried, and then arose from the dead in His divine resurrection. He went to heaven, where He presented Himself to the Father and was received with great joy. He was glorified with the same glory that was His right, as is seen in Christ's own prayer to His Father:

I have glorified thee on the earth: I have finished the work which thou gavest me to do.

And now, O Father, GLORIFY THOU ME WITH THINE OWN SELF WITH THE GLORY WHICH I HAD WITH THEE BEFORE THE WORLD WAS. (John 17:4-5.)

In these two chapters we have the answer to that prayer. It is not something that is to happen. Christ is glorified! He has been given the title deed to all creation, and the scroll. The "book written within and on the backside, sealed with seven seals," is that title deed. This "book" signifies the Divine will and purpose for the remainder of time, and the events under Christ's control that will characterize time as earth is reclaimed. Both time and events are now placed in the sovereign hand of our Saviour; because He has been victorious and is worthy.

From that moment, at the time of His ascension and presentation to the Father, Christ has been given control of all history. As He began to open the seals, at that time, and not some time in the future, He demonstrated His prerogative of sovereign control, whose alone it was in directing history. Notice the impact of the following truth:

> *For the father judgeth no man, but hath committed all judgment unto the Son:*
>
> *That all men should honour the Son, even as they honour the Father . . .*
>
> *And hath given him authority to execute judgment also, because he is the Son of man.* (John 5:22-23 and 27.)

In Chapter Four we are shown the glories of Heaven and the great congregation of God's government. All of creation is represented there. Glory, praise and honor are given to Him that sat upon the throne of the universe, to the Lord God Almighty.

As we continue into Chapter Five, the "book" is introduced. No one is found worthy to open it and to govern "history," not until the "Lamb" steps forward and takes the "book." He is worthy, and Heaven bows to Him and sings His praise. God the Father gives the book to the Son, and authority is transferred once again to Him who had shared it before He had taken upon Himself the form of a servant. The Father, thus, glorifies the Son, and the Son takes His rightful place upon the throne, controlling the destiny of all creation, because He is the Son of man.

The seals are broken one at a time and history continues to unfold under the sovereign control of the Lamb of God. It is pure error to assume that the seals are not opened until the 70th week of Daniel. No, it was at the time of His glorification, and all Heaven worshiped Him:

> *Saying with a loud voice, Worthy is the Lamb that was slain to receive power, and riches, and wisdom, and strength, and honour, and glory, and blessing.*
>
> *. . . Blessing and honour, and glory, and power, be unto*

> *him that sitteth upon the throne and unto the Lamb for ever and ever.* (Revelation 5:12-13.)

Here are two charts that might help you visualize the relationship of these visions in Revelation with the 70th week of Daniel's Time Frame:

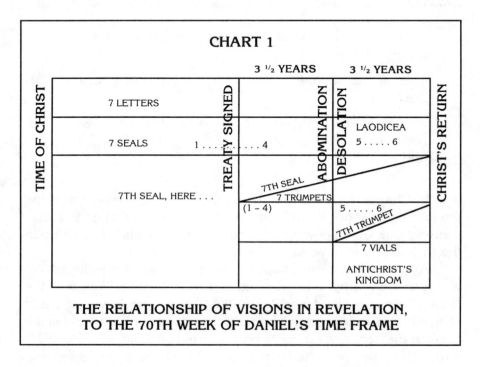

THE RELATIONSHIP OF VISIONS IN REVELATION, TO THE 70TH WEEK OF DANIEL'S TIME FRAME

In Chart 2 we have the relationship between the chapters and the visions, and the events they contain, within the Time Frame.

Notice that, in secular history, the time called the "Church Age" is actually the final part of the "Times of the Gentiles." Israel is still without her rightful King and is under the control, or supervision, of the Gentile powers, even though she is once again in her own land.

This is because this Age does not end with the Rapture of the Church, as so many teach. At the end of this dispensation the true Church will be in Heaven, and the apostate Church will become part of Antichrist's Kingdom. In the battle of Armageddon these forces will meet. The heavenly forces, under the leadership of the Lamb, will defeat the evil forces following Antichrist, his False Prophet, and Satan himself. We will be there, having returned with our Lord.

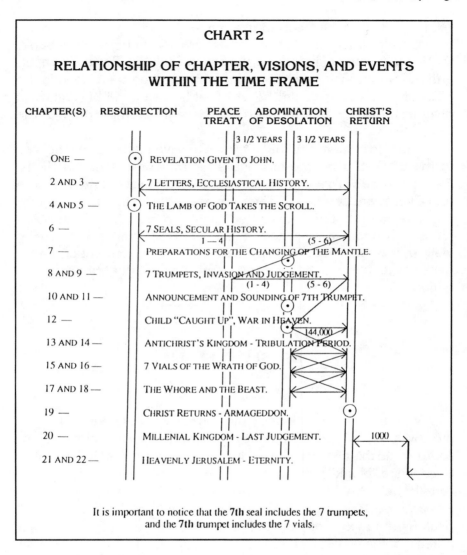

CHART 2

**RELATIONSHIP OF CHAPTER, VISIONS, AND EVENTS
WITHIN THE TIME FRAME**

CHAPTER(S)	RESURRECTION	PEACE TREATY	ABOMINATION OF DESOLATION	CHRIST'S RETURN

3 1/2 YEARS   3 1/2 YEARS

ONE — (•) REVELATION GIVEN TO JOHN.

2 AND 3 — 7 LETTERS, ECCLESIASTICAL HISTORY.

4 AND 5 — (•) THE LAMB OF GOD TAKES THE SCROLL.

6 — 7 SEALS, SECULAR HISTORY.
1 — 4   (5 - 6)

7 — PREPARATIONS FOR THE CHANGING OF THE MANTLE.

8 AND 9 — 7 TRUMPETS, INVASION AND JUDGEMENT.
(1 - 4)   (5 - 6)

10 AND 11 — ANNOUNCEMENT AND SOUNDING OF 7TH TRUMPET.

12 — CHILD "CAUGHT UP", WAR IN HEAVEN.
144,000

13 AND 14 — ANTICHRIST'S KINGDOM - TRIBULATION PERIOD.

15 AND 16 — 7 VIALS OF THE WRATH OF GOD.

17 AND 18 — THE WHORE AND THE BEAST.

19 — CHRIST RETURNS - ARMAGEDDON. (•)

20 — MILLENIAL KINGDOM - LAST JUDGEMENT.   1000

21 AND 22 — HEAVENLY JERUSALEM - ETERNITY.

It is important to notice that the 7th seal includes the 7 trumpets,
and the 7th trumpet includes the 7 vials.

Another point of interest is that the "book" of the seven seals does not begin with the start of the 70th week of Daniel, but with the glorification of our Lord; when he takes the Title Deed of creation and becomes, once again, the sovereign Ruler of the Universe. This is borne out as a comparison is made between Matthew 24 and the first four Seals. Each Seal is a vision of the development and progress of the mystery of iniquity in the world. This progress will culminate in the revelation of the Antichrist, his terrible rule, and Divine judgment. This evil empire will be destroyed as the Wrath of the Lamb is poured forth upon it, even as we saw it in the dream of Nebuchadnezzar when the "stone" fell upon the "feet" of the image.

It is also important to note, and to place in your memory bank, that in these series of judgment, the Seven Seals, the Seven Trumpet, and the Seven Vials, each following unit of seven is included in the SEVENTH of the preceding seven. That is to say, the Seventh Seal gives us the Seven Trumpets, and the Seventh Trumpet gives us the Seven Vials.

It is also noteworthy that each set of seven takes us all the way to the END, to the time of Christ's return. These series of Seals, Trumpets and Vials are not equal, but they are related and their time and Events are correlated. They are not sequels, the one following after the other, but are interrelated each with the other. Each vision focuses in upon some special event, or detail of an event already viewed, or a concept concerning the event in view. Remember, we are dealing with ideas, concepts, and events beyond our human imagination.

THE SEVEN SEALS

With the aforementioned truths firmly settled in our minds, we are now ready to proceed with the visions of Chapter Six ofRevelation. As you read this chapter in your Bible, you will find, readily, that there is a definite "break" between the fourth and fifth seal. There is also a "break" between the sixth and seventh seal. The first four seals form a clear unit of thought that is often identified as "The Four Horsemen." Seals five and six are also related visions given in verses 9-17. It is then noted that the SEVENTH SEAL is not opened until the eighth chapter and is the series of the Seven Trumpets.

There are many wrong ideas taught concerning these first four seals, or the Four Horsemen. Each is a vision containing a truth that God wants us to perceive about the PROGRESS of history. Each horseman, in union with the others, generates the progression and characteristics of our secular history. They begin at the time of Christ, continue and progressively worsen until the "mystery of iniquity" culminates in the revelation of the Antichrist, his terrible world kingdom, and the horrors of Divine judgment. This is shown in one of Paul's letters:

For the mystery of iniquity doth ALREADY work: only he who NOW letteth will let, until he be taken out of the way.

And then shall that Wicked be revealed . . .
(II Thessalonians 2:7-8.)

This undercurrent of evil would continue to flow almost un-abated throughout the course of history. The only resistance to its progress is the preaching of the Gospel and the presence of the Holy Spirit in the Church of Jesus Christ. We are the sole force holding it back. The more the Church compromises, the stronger is the kingdom of darkness. This is the "course of this world" directed by the "prince of the power of the air" spoken of by Paul in the book of Ephesians. Again, it is that which is referred to by the Apostle John:

Little children, it is the last time: and as ye have heard that antichrist shall come, even NOW are there many antichrist; whereby we KNOW that it is the last time.
(I John 2:18.)

Every spirit that confesseth not that Jesus Christ is come in the flesh is not of God: and this is the spirit of antichrist, whereof ye have heard that it should come; and EVEN NOW ALREADY IT IS IN THE WORLD. (I John 4:3.)

This undercurrent of evil, this "mystery of iniquity" is the expression of the "spirit of antichrist," and is opposed to everything godly and good. It combats God's truth. Its greatest enemy is the Word of God in the hands of the Church of Jesus Christ. Evil will continue to progress, and it will get even worse. Crime will become ever more prevalent, and always more violent. Society will continue its downward course of corruption and moral decay. Immorality and an ethical vacuum will be the order of the day. This Age will NOT end in a world wide revival, but in moral chaos as men turn their backs, more and more, upon the Lord and the Gospel message. The world will become "ripe" for judgment, as the "cup of iniquity" becomes full. Finally, it will all come together as the "man of sin" APPEARS upon the scene of history. This is that for which the world is heading. Don't let anyone fool you; it is not going to get better!

THE FOUR HORSEMEN

It is important for us to know that as long as the Church, that Body of true believers, is present on earth, the "man of sin" cannot be revealed as the Antichrist. As the Scripture says, we are simply "in the way." The rider of the first horse, the WHITE HORSE, is the "mystery of iniquity," the "spirit of antichrist," that will finally manifest itself in the actual APPEARANCE of the "man of sin." He will then be REVEALED as the Antichrist at the time of the Rapture of the Church. The Antichrist will lead the whole world on a collision course with the Lord of Glory, our blessed Saviour, as He returns to earth with the armies of Heaven at the close of the Great Tribulation. This rider on the White Horse is identified with religious teaching in the verses that we saw from I John.

This is the confirmation and correlation of that which was spoken by our Lord in answer to His disciple's questions concerning these END TIMES:

> . . . *Take heed that no man deceive you.*
>
> *For many shall come in my name, saying, I am Christ; and shall deceive many.*
>
> *And many false prophets shall rise, and shall deceive many.*
>
> *And because iniquity shall abound, the love of many shall wax cold.* (Matthew 24:4, 5, 11 and 12.)

With this evil current of iniquity flowing throughout this Age, and as a direct result of it, comes the rider of the second horse, the RED HORSE. He has galloped across the pages of history with increasing destructive force. This is the awful impact of evil producing envy, covetousness, hatred, and violence in the soul of sinful man that is evidenced by wars and bloodshed of every kind.

Because of the moral decay in the souls of men, nourished by the godless teaching of false prophets, the world has experienced a continuous flow of bloodshed, man against man, neighbor against neighbor, family against family, race against race, government against government, and nation against nation. This is the rider on the Red Horse. It is seen in the turmoil, the riots, insurrections, rebellions, civil wars, terrorist killings, murders, and every form of man's inhumanity to man, both in our cities' streets and in the international arena. It is the absence of peace among men and the constant unrest that is seen the world over.

Oh, the evil heart of the son's of Adam, caught up in the course of this world, and directed in the fight against all that is holy by the "spirit of the Antichrist." Where will it all end? It will not end in the sought after world peace, but in the awful battle of Armageddon. This rider on the Red Horse is what our Lord spoke of when He said:

> *And ye shall hear of wars and rumors of wars: see that ye not be troubled: for all these things MUST COME TO PASS, but the end is not yet.*

> *For nation shall rise against nation, and kingdom against kingdom: and there shall be famines, and pestilence, and earthquakes, in diverse places.*

> *ALL THESE THINGS ARE THE BEGINNING OF SORROWS.* (Matthew 24:6-8.)

The rider on the third, the BLACK HORSE, represents the awful results of all the above as he rides across the pages of history in the wake of the White and the Red horses. As seen in the verses given by our Lord and quoted above. The rider of the Black Horse rides side by side with the rider on the PALE HORSE, and they are BOTH IN VIEW as our Lord speaks in Matthew 24:6-8. This is clearly seen when one compares the two verses of Scripture:

> *And when he had opened the third seal, I heard the third beast say, Come and see. And I beheld, and lo a BLACK HORSE; and he that sat on him had a pair of BALANCES in his hand.*

> *And I heard a voice in the midst of the four beasts say, A measure of wheat for a penny, and three measures of barley for a penny; and see thou hurt not the oil and the wine.*

> *And when he had opened the fourth seal, I heard the voice of the fourth beast say, Come and see.*

*And I looked, and behold a PALE HORSE: and his name
that sat on him was Death, and Hell followed with him.
And the power was given unto them . . . to KILL with the
SWORD, and with HUNGER, and with DEATH, and with
the BEASTS of the earth. (Revelation 6:5-8.)*

Here is the results of the wars and constant fighting among men.
Hunger due to famine, starvation, suffering, sickness, and despair,
death and hell. All of these are the direct results of man's rejection of
God and His laws, the rejection of Christ the Saviour. The homeless,
the street people, the dope shooting, the drinking, the deaths due to
AIDS and related sicknesses, alcoholism, tobacco, cancer in its many
forms; all are the results of a world gone wild. Greed, sin, covetousness and lust direct our every motive in this godless world system.
This is the course of history predicted by our Saviour, and prophesied
in Revelation with the vision of the Four Horsemen.

As these Horsemen ride from year to year, these characteristics
will increase and grow in intensity, until Jesus comes to end it all in
final judgment upon the godless. This is exactly what our Lord was
saying when He told His disciples:

All these things are the BEGINNING OF SORROWS.
(Matthew 24:8.)

History itself is the best witness to the truth of this understanding.
It is only the believer who can look at such an awful historical record
and still know that the "book" is in the hands of the Lamb of God. How
we praise the Lord for that truth! Yes, there will be more war, and more
unrest and suffering, and the "man of sin" is soon to appear on the
stage, and the final scenes of this drama in real life will be played out
just as it is recorded in the Bible. Make sure that YOU are on the Lord's
side. Get down before Him and surrender your heart and life to the
Lord of Glory now. Jesus is Lord!

Recalling from your memory bank the statement of our Lord,
given above, about the BEGINNING OF SORROWS, you will
remember that this term literally carries the significance of "birth
pangs." It may help to underscore the truth related here concerning
the development of the "mystery of iniquity," and the running of the
Four Horsemen throughout history. Birth pangs come finally after
months of progress and the development of the fetus. Birth pangs

begin rather suddenly, but with less intensity and are well spaced. When the moment of birth draws near the pains become much more intense and much more frequent. This is what our Lord is telling us about history. There would be a gradual development of the "mystery of iniquity," but as the end draws near all of these properties will grow worse and worse, both in intensity and frequency. Christ compares the suffering of humanity with the suffering of birth contractions.

We have witnessed such an increase in the "pains" of suffering humanity in this century, especially in these past few years, that we cannot help but know that the end is near. The human race simply cannot endure much more without completely destroying itself. Jesus is coming!

A few years ago we never thought possible things that today are every day occurrences. Without question, the Middle East is the focus of our attention. The need for a peace treaty to settle the boiling cauldron of enmity among the nations there has been brought out so clearly. For the first time, even our politicians, some may know nothing of Bible Prophecy, have seen the absolute necessity of a multinational peace-keeping force in that region. The need for a peace treaty, a peace accord, is so truly urgent that it is seen as the only solution in that troubled area.

Of course the real problem in the Middle East, the core of the hatred, is that small nation of Israel. All of the furor of activity, and the swelling hatred in the Middle East has its origin, ultimately, in Satan's hatred for the Nation of Israel. There is so much enmity between the Arab States and Israel that almost any action there will erupt into an all-out "holy war" against Israel and her allies. The Middle East is ready to explode.

I digress, back to the peace treaty. When such an accord is confirmed, it will be for a period of SEVEN YEARS; and it is THE SIGN, given by God Himself, for us to know that the 70th week of Daniel has begun. The prophetic clock will have begun to tick. When this takes place the countdown to Armageddon will have begun. It will be only seven years away! Jesus is coming!

We can understand, then, that the first four Seals bring us right up to the time of the signing of this peace treaty. As this peace is secured among the nations, it will be, almost immediately, shattered by an earth shaking war as Israel is invaded from the North.

This invasion of Israel — it follows the signing of the peace treaty — is that related for us in Ezekiel, Chapters 38 and 39. This invasion, and the resulting chaos, will bring about the necessity to restore world order. The "man of sin" will move to accomplish this, gaining control of the world situation.

He will then act according to our Lord's words, and perform what is called the "abomination of desolation," Matthew 24:15. This is where he declares himself to be divine, the God-man. Perhaps he will be seen as the reincarnation of the spirit of Christ and/or of Mohammed. This will instantly unite the apostate Christian Church and the followers of Islam. He will demand the worship of the entire world. It is at this time that the truly Biblical TRIBULATION PERIOD begins. Now begins the HOUR that is to come upon the world, to try them that dwell upon the earth.

The suffering of these next three and a half years is going to be so GREAT, beyond anything the world has ever seen, that it is, THEREFORE, called GREAT TRIBULATION and is referred to by our Lord in Matthew 24:21. This correlates perfectly with the REVELATION OF THE ANTICHRIST, which we know takes place in the middle of Daniel's 70th week.

GREAT TRIBULATION

It is a Biblical fact that there is nowhere in Scripture a "seven year tribulation period." The Scriptures do not speak of such a period. There is clearly, however, a "tribulation" that has occurred concurrently with the progressive development of the "mystery of iniquity." This TRIBULATION will continue as one of the predominate characteristics of this Age: see I Thessalonians 3:3-4, II Thessalonians 1:4-5, Acts 14:22, John 15:18-21, John 16:33, and Matthew 5:10-12.

This world wide suffering of God's people will continue until, under the rule of the Antichrist, it will become so intense that many lose their lives at his hands. God's judgment will then be poured forth upon the Evil Empire of the Beast. This time will be called or classified as "the days of vengeance," Luke 21:22. In verse 23 it also says that "there shall be great distress in the land, and wrath upon this people."

Remember that national Israel will be under judgment, and it is through her suffering, at this time, that many of the Jewish people will turn to Christ as their Messiah in true repentance. Our Lord characterized those last days of suffering in this manner:

> *For in those days shall be affliction, such as was not from the beginning of the creation which God created unto this time, neither shall be.* (Mark 13:19.)

It is this change in the intensity and character of world suffering taking place following the abomination of desolation that qualifies that final three and a half year period as the "Tribulation Period." It is from this awful time of vengeance, wrath, and suffering that we, the Church, have been promised by our Lord an escape. We must be ready and have the "oil" in our "lamps" NOW. To have a dry lamp then will be to be without grace, Matthew 25:1-13. It is for this reason that Jesus says:

> *And take heed to yourselves, lest at any time your hearts be overcharged with surfeiting, and drunkenness, and cares of this life, and so THAT DAY come upon you unawares.*
>
> *For as a snare shall it come on all them that dwell on the face of the whole earth.*
>
> *WATCH ye therefore, and pray always, that ye may be accounted worthy to ESCAPE all these things that shall come to pass, and to stand before the Son of man.*
> (Luke 21:34-36.)

The FIFTH AND SIXTH SEALS are visions that depict specific things connected with this awful time of suffering, the "Great Tribulation." Everything involved with the first four seals has a natural, or earthly, tone to it. Now we are confronted by that which goes beyond the natural and is "otherworldly," or supernatural. This gives us a clear break in the visions of the Seals. Notice the difference:

THE FIFTH SEAL

> *. . . I saw UNDER THE ALTAR the souls of them that were SLAIN for the word of God, and for the testimony which they held:*
>
> *And they cried with a loud voice, saying, HOW LONG, O Lord, holy and true, dost thou not judge and avenge our blood on them that dwell on the earth?*
> (Revelation 6:9-10.)

Here is a vision of souls saved by faith in the Redeemer, Jesus Christ. These souls are those who have been killed because they have trusted in Christ and the Word of God. They are martyred saints who have been killed during this time of the "Great Tribulation." They have been pursued and murdered by the followers of Antichrist, and at his command. They would not receive his mark, nor would they worship him. This is confirmed by these verses:

> *. . . and cause that as many as would not worship the image of the beast should be killed.* (Revelation 13:15.)
>
> *. . . and I saw the souls of them that were beheaded for the witness of Jesus, and for the word of God, and which had not worshiped the beast, neither his image, neither had received his mark . . .* (Revelation 20:4.)

This tells us that upon taking charge of world affairs, and with the abomination of desolation, the Antichrist is going to call for global "war" against all who will dare to stand against him. He will act upon the Biblical axiom that all who are not for him are against him, The only ones who will dare to take such a stand will be those who have now accepted the truth of Scripture and believed in Jesus Christ as the true Messiah. These will be basically from among the Jewish peoples, because the Gentiles will have forsaken the Gospel to believe the "lie" of the Antichrist. This is clearly shown to us in II Thessalonians 2:9-12. It is ISRAEL who will now be the focus of God's grace, and the target of Antichrist's hatred and destructive force.

And the dragon was wroth with the woman, and went to make war with the remnant of her seed, which keep the commandments of God, and have the testimony of Jesus Christ. (Revelation 12:17.)

It is certainly clear that all of this takes place during the latter half of the 70th week of Daniel's prophecy, for the time is plainly stated as being:

. . . for a time, and times, and half a time, from the face of the serpent. (Revelation 12:14.)

We, therefore, have in the Fifth Seal a vision of the souls of those who have been killed for their faith in the Lord Jesus Christ, and for refusing to worship the Antichrist during the time of his reign. These souls are seen to be "UNDER THE ALTAR." This is important because we can differentiate between them and those of Chapter Seven of Revelation who are seen to be "standing" before the Lord. The fact that these are seen to be "under the altar" shows that they have not been resurrected as yet. They are, then, killed AFTER the Rapture of the Church; that takes place prior to the REVELATION of the Antichrist.

This is simply adding the facts of Scripture, and coming to the only logical conclusion that can be reached. Two plus five is seven, and if you come to another answer you are wrong. So it is with the Word of God. We must be able to add up the facts given in order to come to a proper conclusion. We know, from II Thessalonians, Chapter Two, that the REVELATION of the Antichrist occurs at the time of the abomination of desolation. These souls under the altar cry out to God, "How long?" The answer comes to them:

. . . that they should REST yet for a little season, UNTIL their fellow servants also and their brethren, that SHOULD BE KILLED AS THEY WERE, should be fulfilled. (Revelation 6:11.)

We now comprehend that the Fifth Seal spans the time of the three and a half years of the GREAT TRIBULATION. This Seal thus identifies the suffering of God's people, at the hands of the Antichrist, with that time. They are told that they must wait for the resurrection that is to take place at the end of that TRIBULATION PERIOD, when Christ would return in glory and power. These souls will be resurrected then and rule with Christ for one thousand years. This is positively stated for us:

> And I saw thrones, and they sat upon them, and
> judgment was given unto them: and I saw THE SOULS
> OF THEM THAT WERE BEHEADED FOR THE WITNESS OF
> JESUS, AND FOR THE WORD OF GOD, and had not
> worshiped the beast, neither his image, neither had
> received his mark upon their foreheads, or in their hands;
> AND THEY LIVED and reigned with Christ a thousand
> years.   (Revelation 20:4.)

THE SIXTH SEAL

As a direct result of the cry of these souls under the altar for God to "avenge our blood," and in accord with God's eternal purpose, the WRATH OF GOD is poured forth upon the kingdom of the Antichrist. This WRATH is supernatural in nature; but it will include the entire natural world. It will involve a great earthquake, one final great quake that will destroy cities all over the world. Mountains will fall, and the islands of the world's oceans will disappear. This astronomical event will include all of creation:

> And the heaven departed as a scroll when it is rolled
> together; and every mountain and island were moved out
> of their places. (Revelation 6:14.)

Fear will grip the whole world, and men, wicked as they are, will recognize the Day of the Wrath of God. They will not repent, but will seek to escape, hiding in the caves and dens of the earth, as they cry to the mountains:

> Fall on us, and hide us from the face of him that sitteth on

the throne, and from the WRATH OF THE LAMB:

For the great day of his wrath is come; and who shall be able to stand? (Revelation 6:16-17.)

We now perceive that it is these two elements that will make this three and a half year period so totally different from all other tribulations. This is why it is called by our Lord a time of "GREAT TRIBULATION."

FIRST, it is because of the intense, global effort of the Antichrist to destroy every soul who dares to name the Name of Christ, and to stand against him.

SECOND, it is because of the great suffering, world wide, as the wrath of the Lamb of God is poured upon the world. A world of Christ rejecting unbelievers who chose to follow the Antichrist.

Both the FIFTH AND THE SIXTH SEALS depict for us this awful time of unequaled suffering; from which the Church of Jesus Christ has been delivered by the RAPTURE. It is interesting to note that the Fifth and Sixth Trumpets depict this same time period as we shall see.

PREPARATION

The next vision that John was given was not that of the Seventh Seal as one would normally expect. Chapter Seven of Revelation is seen to be a parenthetic vision of preparation for the opening of the Seventh Seal. It is given to help us see the relation of the two parts of this preparation, and so that we can relate them to the time of the Great Tribulation. This Great Tribulation is the time of the "HURTING" of the earth under the great suffering of that time period. Before the earth can be "hurt" God gives to us, in the vision of Chapter Seven, His purpose of keeping safe under His care TWO GROUPS of saints from this "hurting." The group, the 144,000, sealed with the seal of God would be kept DURING AND THROUGH the "hurting," and the other group, the "great multitude," would be kept FROM AND OUT OF this time of "hurting," as they are seen to be standing before the throne. The one group is on the earth, and the other is in Heaven.

EXCHANGE OF THE MANTLE

In this chapter we have a beautiful picture of what will actually take place at the time of the Rapture of the Church. Here we are introduced to a CONCEPT OF SPIRITUAL TRUTH that is most important for our correct comprehension of prophecy in general and the Book of Revelation in particular. This great event, for it is an actual event that will take place, is pictured for us IN TYPE in the book of II Kings, in the story of Elijah. All these things are earthly events that show a heavenly truth. The type is physical and seen, while the reality is spiritual and apprehended by faith — but nonetheless real.

The story of Elijah and the prophets of Baal in I Kings, 18, shows us that Elijah was a prophet of God. He stood before God! He was a personal representative of God, and God's POWER and PRESENCE was with him. This PRESENCE and POWER of God was associated with THE MANTLE Elijah wore. That is, Elijah was the WEARER OF THE MANTLE of God's PRESENCE and POWER. It is Scripturally correct to say this without fear of contradiction.

We first begin to see this as God told him to sanctify, or anoint, Elisha to take his own place. This was because God was about to TAKE ELIJAH HOME. We read:

So he departed thence, and found Elisha . . . who was plowing . . . and Elijah passed by him, and CAST HIS MANTLE UPON HIM. (I Kings 19:19.)

Remember, God is teaching us a wonderful, spiritual concept of truth. We read in verse 21 that from time to time the two of them were together. Then, as we continue into the story in II Kings, Chapter Two, we come to the time when God would take Elijah to Heaven. This entire incident is a picture of, or TYPE of, the RAPTURE. It all emphasizes one important thing, and that is THE EXCHANGE OF THE MANTLE of God's PRESENCE and POWER. The Lord told Elijah what He was going to do. It is an elaborate, beautiful, suspenseful story of what God will do at the time of the Rapture. One thing was obvious: Elijah knew that he was going to be taken out of the world scene. He did not know just how soon, but he knew that it was imminent, or as the dictionary says, "Likely to happen soon." As they were to cross the river Jordan, Elijah took his MANTLE and parted the waters:

> *And Elijah took his mantle, and wrapped it together, and*
> *smote the waters, and they were divided hither and*
> *thither, so that they two went over on dry ground.*
> (II Kings 2:8.)

This act of the supernatural had no other purpose than to demonstrate the fact that the PRESENCE and POWER of God was with His prophet, and they were uniquely seen to be in THE MANTLE. Elisha was duly impressed by this PRESENCE and POWER of God with Elijah. When he was asked what he would like Elijah to do for him before leaving, Elisha's answer came quickly:

> *. . . I pray thee, let a double portion of thy SPIRIT be upon*
> *me.* (II Kings 2:9.)

Elisha had understood what was taking place when Elijah had put his mantle upon him. He knew that God was separating him to be His prophet. He knew that God was going to take Elijah. Elisha wanted to do the will of God, but only if the Power and Presence of God would be with him as God was with Elijah. He wanted, with all his heart, to serve the Living God. HE WANTED TO BE THE WEARER OF GOD'S MANTLE! He wanted to do it for the glory of God. It was not self ambition, but the call of God. Therefore, Elisha answered Elijah's question as we have it in the verse above. Then Elijah remarked:

> *. . . Thou hast asked me a hard thing: nevertheless, if thou*
> *see me when I am TAKEN from thee, it shall be so unto*
> *thee.* (II Kings 2:10.)

Glorious truth, we have here the divine TRANSFER of God's ministry, of His POWER and PRESENCE, of the supernatural working of the Spirit of God from one servant to another. This is the concept that God wants us to understand, for we will see it in Revelation.

This breathtaking story continues. Elisha is standing there

when, suddenly, he sees Elijah taken up from him in a fiery chariot, and by a whirlwind. These both represented divine action, suddenly and forcefully accomplished — JUST AS IT IS DESCRIBED FOR US CONCERNING THE RAPTURE OF THE CHURCH in I Thessalonians, Chapter Four, and in I Corinthians, Chapter 15. Then, in our story we read:

> *He took up also the MANTLE of Elijah that FELL FROM HIM, and went back and stood by the bank of Jordan;*
>
> *And he took the MANTLE of Elijah that fell from him, and smote the waters, and said, Where is the Lord God of Elijah? And when HE ALSO had smitten the waters, they parted hither and thither: and Elisha went over.*
> (II Kings 2:13-14.)

Beyond question, the PRESENCE AND POWER of God was now with Elisha. As God had been with Elijah, so was He now with Elisha. Elisha was now the WEARER OF THE MANTLE! This is borne out by the Word of God, for it says:

> *And when the sons of the prophets which were to view at Jericho saw him, they said, THE SPIRIT OF ELIJAH DOTH REST ON ELISHA. And they came to meet him, and bowed themselves to the ground before him.*
> (II Kings 2:15.)

Elisha had now become the "wearer of the mantle" that represented the fact that the POWER and the PRESENCE of God was with him in his ministry as God's servant. It is this TRANSFER OF THE MANTLE that we have pictured for us in Revelation, Chapter Seven.

There is so much confusion about this important chapter. Satan has tried for many years to hide its truth from the People of God. Consequently, this truth is basically overlooked completely, and much of the point of the visions of Revelation is missed. Before the Great Tribulation can get under way, before the wrath of God is poured out upon the earth, there must be a transfer of this "mantle" of the Presence and Power of God, simply because God will not leave Himself without a "servant" to be His witness among the lost of this world. This "Presence and Power" of God, at this present time, rests with the CHURCH, the Body of Christ. This truth is witnessed to in Scripture:

> . . . *All power is given unto me in heaven and in earth.*
>
> *Go ye THEREFORE . . . AND LO, I AM WITH YOU ALWAYS, even unto the end of the world.*
> (Matthew 28:18-20.)
>
> *But ye shall receive POWER, after the Holy Ghost is come upon you: and ye shall be WITNESS UNTO ME . . . unto the uttermost part of the earth.* (Acts 1:8.)
>
> . . . *He hath said, I WILL NEVER LEAVE THEE, nor forsake thee.*
>
> *So that we can boldly say, THE LORD IS MY HELPER . . .*
> (Hebrews 13:5-6.)

When our Saviour came to this earth, he was the POWER and the PRESENCE of God among men, sent by the Father, and the Father was with Him. When He was to leave this world, he told the disciples that He and the Father would send the Holy Spirit, and He would abide, not just upon, but WITHIN the believer. Together, we believers constitute the Body of Christ. Our Lord told His disciples, who were representative of the Body:

> *Then said Jesus to them again, Peace be unto you: as my Father hath sent me, EVEN SO SEND I YOU.*
>
> *And when he had said this , he breathed on them, and saith unto them, RECEIVE YE THE HOLY GHOST:*
>
> *Whose soever sins ye remit, they are remitted unto them; and whose soever sins ye retain, they are retained.*
> (John 20:21-23.)

If you are able to discern this, you now know that this is the actual AUTHORIZATION for the transfer of God's MANTLE from our Lord to His Church. THIS TRANSFER TOOK PLACE AT PENTECOST! We are the wearer of the "Mantle" of the Power and the Presence of God. This is why the Lord could say:

> *. . . upon this rock I will build my church; and the gates*
> *of hell SHALL NOT PREVAIL AGAINST IT*
> (Matthew 16:18.)

Now that we see this concept as a valid, Scriptural concept, let us get back to our study in Revelation, Chapter Seven. In this chapter we have two happenings that are really one! The FIRST EVENT recorded for us here is that of the SEALING of the 144,000 with the SEAL of God. God is with these Jewish believers whose eyes have opened. They have witnessed the marvelous, glorious truth of the RAPTURE, just as Elisha witnessed the "rapture" of Elijah. By God's infinite grace and awesome power, the Church, a great multitude of people from all over the world, is "caught up" like Elijah in his "fiery chariot" and the "whirlwind" of His Spirit (Acts 2:2). This Rapture is the SECOND EVENT recorded in this chapter, although it is not the incident itself that is here in view, rather the results of that milestone. In this vision these two occurrences form ONE GRAND PHENOM-ENON.

As the Church is Raptured, taken up, the MANTLE of God will FALL FROM US! This Mantle is then to be picked up by these 144,000 as God begins again to deal with national Israel. These now become the "Wearer of the Mantle" of God's Presence and Power in this wicked world. They will wear this "Mantle" throughout the reign of the Antichrist. This chapter is the AUTHORIZATION for the TRANSFER of the "Mantle," and it will actually be transferred at the time of the rapture. This great occurrence is pictured with clarity and in beautiful harmony with the context of its surrounding circumstances a little later in our study.

THE GREAT MULTITUDE

It may be helpful, here, for me to assist you through some of the jumbled teachings that are very misleading concerning this multitude. It simply cannot be, as is generally taught, that this multitude, whose number defies counting, consists of those people saved during the TRIBULATION PERIOD. That is impossible for two Scriptural reasons:

- First, we are clearly told that those saved during that time of TRIBULATION will die for their faith, and their souls have already been pictured for us as being "under the altar." They are not resurrected, nor will they be, until the end of the Tribulation Period, as we have seen in Revelation 20:4. These, therefore, are clearly two different groups. It is the resurrected, transformed CHURCH that is here in view. We see them STANDING BEFORE THE THRONE.

- Second, we know that there will not be a "great multitude" who are saved during that awful time of suffering. We have already been told by Paul, in II Thessalonians 2:9-12, that those left after the rapture of the Church and the revelation of the Antichrist would "believe a lie." This, because God will send them "strong delusion" since they WILL NOT believe the truth. How can we believe, then, that a great multitude, beyond number, will be saved after the Rapture of the Church.

That is contradictory. But, there is further proof from the Word of God that tells us that during that terrible time of judgment people WILL NOT REPENT in spite of everything:

NEITHER REPENTED THEY of their murders, nor of their sorceries, nor of their fornication, nor of their thefts. (Revelation 9:21.)

. . . and they REPENTED NOT to give him glory. (Revelation 16:9.)

. . . and they gnawed their tongues for pain.

And BLASPHEMED the God of heaven because of their pains and their sores, and REPENTED NOT of their deeds. (Revelation 16: 10-11.)

I cannot comprehend how some people read REVIVAL in these verses. The opposite is surely true. There will be no great multitude saved during that time. If these Scriptures are not enough to convince you, then consider the following:

> *And he caused ALL, both small and great, rich and poor, free and bond, to receive a mark in their right hand, or in their forehead.* (Revelation 13:16.)

> *If any man worship the beast and his image, and receive his mark in their forehead, or in his hand,*

> *. . . The same shall drink of the wine of the wrath of God . . .* (Revelation 14:9-10.)

How can these Scriptures be true and there still be a great multitude, which no man can number, saved during that time? The multitude spoken of is, it must be, the Church of the Living God. It is the Body of Believers, the Body of Christ, which have come "out of great tribulation," mentioned in Revelation 7:14.

This has to do with "point of origin," for it is at their departure from the earthly scene that the Abomination of Desolation occurs, and the Great Tribulation Period begins. This word "OUT OF" is the exact same word used by Our Lord in His promise to the Church and translated "FROM" in I Thessalonians 1:10, and in the following verse:

> *. . . I also will keep thee FROM the HOUR of temptation, which shall come upon all the world.* (Revelation 3:10.)

I pray our blessed Lord will help you to see clearly this beautiful truth He has given to us in Revelation, Chapter Seven. And, may your sight not be blurred or muddied with the shallow teaching so commonly heard, due to a lack of Scriptural understanding. Remember that the important truth of prophecy to be seen in this chapter is that of TRANSFER OF THE MANTLE! We will identify this "Mantle" further along in our study.

THE SEVENTH SEAL

Chapters Eight and Nine of Revelation cover the opening of the Seventh Seal. We soon see that it consists of the SEVEN TRUMPETS. As we study this, it is well for us to have before us the TIME FRAME, as we have learned it, so that we can see each of these prophecies in their proper relation to that Time Frame. It is of note and interest to find that these visions are prefaced by the offering up of the prayers of all the saints upon the golden altar. This is to help us understand that we have before us God's answer to the prayers of His people, from generation to generation, as we pray, "Lord, How long? Even so, come Lord Jesus."

It seems clear that now, after centuries of prolonged waiting, God's time clock begins to tick again. The End Time has come. The Last Week is now to begin, and our prayers are now going to be answered. "Lord, Thy will be done; Thy Kingdom come."

THE SEVEN TRUMPETS

These Trumpets encompass the 70th week of Daniel. It is interesting to find that they are divided, as were the Seals, into two marked groups:

- The FIRST group is that of the first four Trumpets.

- The SECOND group is that of the fifth and sixth Trumpets.

There is a definite distinction between these two groups because they fall into the two halves of the 70th week of Daniel's prophecy.

Many see in these two groups the supernatural working of God, as He strikes the earth in His judgment and wrath, happening throughout the entire seven year period. Thus, they call it the TRIBULATION PERIOD. This designation, however, is without Scriptural foundation, and is based upon human assumption. It is true that all of God's working is supernatural because He is a supernatural Being. But we must never forget that God commonly uses nature, and natural means, to accomplish His purpose among men through His supernatural control of all history. Another reason that these Trumpets are misrepresented by many is that it is viewed as humanly impossible to accomplish what they describe.

There is a degree of truth in the supernatural element of these Trumpets. The supernatural is clearly and indisputably brought forth in the Fifth and Sixth Trumpets. These two visions, without question, represent things beyond man's capability. This distinction is brought before us as a clear warning:

> . . . *Woe, woe, woe, to the inhabiters of the earth by*
> *reason of the other voices of the trumpet of the three*
> *angels, which are yet to be sounded!* (Revelation 8:13.)

You will note that although the writer of Revelation includes Trumpets Five, Six and SEVEN in this warning, I mention only the Fifth and Sixth Trumpets in the second group. This, because the Seventh Trumpet is treated separately in the prophetic writings of Revelation. The Seventh Trumpet consists of the Seven Vials of the Wrath of God.

THE FIRST FOUR TRUMPETS

Looking at these first four trumpets, we find that they do, indeed, appear to be beyond man's capabilities. Yet, with the dawn of the Nuclear Age, this has all changed. How many times have we heard that man now has the ability to destroy the whole world? The truth of the matter is that if God wanted to use supernatural power to accomplish the results shown to us of the first four trumpets, He could do so. He is sovereign. We must still recognize that God commonly uses, as He has throughout history, men and nations, as well as nature, to accomplish His purpose. Everyone familiar with God's dealings in the Old Testament knows that this it true. Another consideration that we must deal with is Ezekiel, Chapters 38 and 39.

When does the great invasion of Israel come into the picture? We know, from our study of those chapters, that it cannot be Armageddon that is described there; because that is to take place at the very end of this Age. It does not, cannot, fit the picture given in those two chapters of Ezekiel. Reviewing, by means of our "Instant Recall," we are reminded of the seven years during which Israel will be burning those abandoned weapons of war. Fitting this fact into the computer of prophetic Scripture, an immediate identification is seen with the seven years of the covenant to be confirmed.

Considering all the evidence, it is easy to come to the conclusion, then, that these first Four Trumpets are visions of that war where the armies of the great Northern invader are destroyed upon the mountains of Israel. As we examine each of these four trumpets we find that they describe perfectly the actual results we may expect from a nuclear exchange between World Powers. Just what everyone is afraid WILL HAPPEN. Each trumpet of this first group is a vision of a particular result of atomic warfare. Note the combined destruction given:

First Trumpet: Hail, fire, blood, fall upon the earth. One-third of the trees are burned up. All green grass is burned. (Revelation 8:7.)

Second Trumpet: A great mountain, burning with fire, is cast into the sea. One-third of the sea becomes blood. One-third of sea life dies. One-third of the ships are destroyed. (Revelation 8:8-9.)

Third Trumpet: A great star falls from heaven, burning, as if it were a lamp. It falls upon one-third of the rivers and springs of fresh water. It is called "Wormwood," which signifies bitterness, or poisonous. Many die from the use of these waters. (Revelation 8:10-11.)

Fourth Trumpet: The light of the sun, moon and the stars are

affected. Only one-third of their light reaches
the earth. (Revelation 8:12.)

These are the words of a man who lived some 1900 years ago,
about seventy years after Christ's crucifixion. He describes what he
sees in the visions given to him. He knew nothing of atomic power.
Our fathers knew nothing of atomic power just a few short years past.
We, however, are living in the atomic age, and such things as
satellites, rockets, missiles, and even nuclear explosions are common
sights to us. We all remember the first sputniks and how they looked
just like a star except that they were moving faster. It does not require
a strong imagination to see that what we have here, in these first four
trumpets, could easily be the description of the results of a nuclear
exchange. Certainly, it says that one-third of the earth is going to be
affected. Fire, blood, smoke, fallout, and radioactivity on a massive
scale might bring death to multitudes of the inhabitants of the earth.

It also indicates that this will be a limited nuclear exchange, for
only a part of the earth will be affected. God is in control. Man is not
going to destroy the world! Which part of the world may be affected
we cannot surely say. It is easy for me to believe, though, that when
the Northern Bear does go South, "to take a spoil and prey," it will
naturally seek to neutralize any Western opposition. This, then, would
not only include America, but TARGET America, these United
Stated, the leader of the Western World. We can see how Western
Europe is, even now, being disarmed.

If one reviews our study of Daniel and Ezekiel, he will find out that
it is out of the ashes of world chaos that the Antichrist will arise and
take control. He will then bring order to the disorder of the destruction
caused by this exchange between the warring Powers. He will have,
as a political leader in the West, confirmed the treaty bringing a
peaceful solution to the Middle East turmoil. This peace will have been
shattered by the invasion of Israel from the North, and then this
invading army is itself destroyed on the mountains of Israel.

From all this, the "prince," this Western Leader who will survive
a NATIONAL WOUND, will regain control of the chaotic situation. He
will then move in upon the Middle Eastern scene and into Jerusalem
as the new Messiah, the saviour of the world, and perform the
ABOMINATION OF DESOLATION spoken of by Daniel in 9:27.

This act of his is confirmed by our Lord in His prophecy of
Matthew 24:15. In order for Ezekiel 39:9 to be literally fulfilled, if it is
to coincide with the Time Frame, Israel will have to be invaded within

the year of the signing of the peace treaty. Where else can seven, plus seven, equal seven but here? This treaty will, in effect, remove the "walls" of defense from Israel, making her a tempting "prey" to the Bear.

Her "walls" are thick and strong today. They have been attacked and stormed many times since they were built in 1948, but they have never been breached. After the signing of this treaty, and at the time of the invasion, the Scriptures tell us that Israel will be "cities without walls."

THE FIFTH AND SIXTH TRUMPETS

As the Antichrist establishes his control and rule over the world from Jerusalem, the Lord God will then bring to pass the judgments recorded for us in the Fifth and Sixth Trumpets. These judgments describe the unlocking of demonic and satanic powers that will then cover the earth with their evil designs, and bring such suffering upon all the earth that men will seek death as a way of escape:

> *And in those days shall men seek death, and shall not find it; and shall desire to die, and death shall flee from them.* (Revelation 9:6.)

This is the true TRIBULATION PERIOD! These various judgments extend for just three and a half years, and it will not be prolonged. These judgments are unimaginably horrible, and indescribably terrible. It is a unique time of suffering. We cannot truly comprehend the magnitude of anguish, nor can we explain all that will take place. God alone knows. It will be His doing. Believe it, and make certain NOW that you will not be there THEN! The only ones safe will be those who are sealed with the seal of the living God, as is told in Revelation 9:4, and they are all identified as Israelites, Revelation 7:4.

Preparations for Armageddon are seen as the Sixth angel

sounds his trumpet and the Euphrates River is dried up. This makes a way for the forward progress of an army of 200,000,000 from the combined Eastern Nations, the Far East. We are told of this as part of the world wide gathering of armies in Revelation 16:12-16. As they march toward Jerusalem, they will destroy and kill everything in their path. They march to the beat of Satan's drums to fight against the Lord of Glory as he returns in power and great glory with the armies of heaven. We, the Body of Christ, will be in the Lord's army on that great occasion. Chapter Nine of Revelation tells us twice, in its closing verses, that men upon the earth will not repent of their evil. Their rebellion and hatred of the Lord God is unbroken. There will be no revival among the gentiles!

SEVEN THUNDERS

Here we find the Lord, even in wrath, showing mercy. It is here in Chapter Ten that we find the answer to the riddle of one of our Lord's statements:

> And except those days should be shortened, there should
> be no flesh be saved: but for the elect's sake those days
> shall be SHORTENED. (Matthew 24:22.)

It was not that Jesus was saying that time would not be the same. NO, God's Time Frame would remain exactly as He had given it to Daniel. A day would still be a day, and a week a week, although the nights will seem eternal due to the horrible suffering. Even those who are sealed with the seal of God and protected from death are affected by the unthinkable evil of that time. It is for their sakes, therefore, that God says that he will "shorten" those days. He would, in mercy for His Own, limit the awfulness of it all. So, as we come to Chapter Ten, we find John in a spectacular vision of Seven Thunders, seven more horrible judgments. He was about to write them in this Book, as he had the other visions, when he was told:

*. . . Seal up those things which the seven thunders
uttered, and write them not.* (Revelation 10:4.)

God, in His mercy and out of concern for His elect, had canceled the judgments of the Seven Thunders. I have had people tell me that they won't read the Book of Revelation because it scares them too much. Better it is to be frightened now and flee to Jesus than to be willingly ignorant and be caught up in the judgment of that day with nowhere to hide and no Saviour. God is here seen to change the script, to drop the "thunders" from the drama of history, for His elect's sake. O, what love! What grace, as God, in pity for His Own, says, that's enough, and stays the hand of the destroying angels.

THE MYSTERY FINISHED

With gracious cancellation of the Seven Thunders, John hears the mighty angel proclaim another significant message:

. . . that there should be time no longer:

*But in the days of the voice of the SEVENTH ANGEL,
when he shall BEGIN TO SOUND, the MYSTERY OF GOD
should be FINISHED, as he hath declared to his servants
the prophets.* (Revelation 10:6-7.)

All of Scripture is important, of course, but this is a pivotal statement. Everything about it speaks of a special message, an important meaning. This is the beginning of the end of the drama of man's history. The literal meaning of these words is that there was to be no longer any delay. Something is drawn to a conclusion, something beyond the "play" itself. Something is now to be "finished," it is to be a major part of the last "act."

What caused this delay, according to the Scriptures?

> *The Lord is not slack concerning his promises, as some*
> *men count slackness; but is longsuffering to us-ward, not*
> *willing that any should perish, but that all should come to*
> *repentance.* (II Peter 3:9.)

What has been the delay? Why has God been waiting so long to judge the evil on this earth? It is true that people are always saying, "Why doesn't God do something?" Well, the answer to every question like this is that God has been waiting, holding back judgment. He gives every lost sinner many opportunities to be saved, to repent and believe the Gospel, to confess Christ as Saviour and Lord.

Now, though, at long last, the door of opportunity is to close, and the day of grace will be forever past to the gentile peoples of the world. It is like that day in the time of the Flood, when God told Noah to go into the ark with his family, and then GOD CLOSED THE DOOR. It is now that the "restrainer," the Body of Christ, is removed from the scene. The last gentile to be saved has entered the Body, is in Christ, and the door is now to close. It is time for the REVELATION of the Antichrist, and the One who was "in the way," is mtaken "out of the way," as shown in II Thessalonians 2:7. It is time for the Day of the Lord to Begin. It is time for the Divine visitation upon planet earth when "time shall be no more."

We are, accordingly, informed about the sounding of the Seventh Trumpet: It is when it "begins to sound" that all this starts to happen. It is abundantly clear that the Seventh Trumpet sounds throughout the last three and a half years, in the forms of the Seven Vials of the wrath of God. It is, as it were, one long blast of judgment!

We do not actually encounter these Vials filled with the wrath of God, the Seventh Trumpet Judgment, until Chapters Fifteen and Sixteen. There still remain the great events that are preparatory for that final judgment as the Seventh Trumpet BEGINS to sound, and they are found in Chapters Ten and Eleven.

This Seventh and LAST TRUMP is seen to be sounded in Chapter 11, verse 15. The sounding of the LAST TRUMP brings on the remarkable events of Chapter 12; and it is followed immediately by the occurrences of Chapters 13 and 14. It is in these two chapters that one finds the establishment of the Empire of Antichrist and his evil, cruel reign over the souls of men. This sequence of events, all related to the sounding of the LAST TRUMP, is of great importance to a proper understanding of prophecy. It is chiefly here that total confusion enters into all traditional teaching. These few chapters are the heart and core of the Book of Revelation.

Ergo, with all this in mind, we are forced to conclude that this Seventh and LAST TRUMP is sounded in the middle of the 70th week of Daniel's prophecy; and that it extends throughout the following three and a half years in the form of the Seven Vials of the Wrath of God. It is here at the Last Trump that the Abomination of Desolation occurs. It is here that he (the "prince," the "little horn") goes into the temple in Jerusalem and declares himself to be God, or Divine. At this time he begins his world rule and demands the worship of the entire world. This is the "last trump" of I Corinthians 15:52, and the "trump of God" in I Thessalonians 4:16. This is the time of the Rapture of the Church, the Body of Christ. This is when the "restrainer" of II Thessalonians 2:7-9, is "taken out of the way." It is also the time of the TRANSFER OF THE MANTLE OF THE PRESENCE AND POWER OF GOD; as it is "picked" up by the 144,000 when it "falls" from the Raptured Church, the Body of Christ. This transfer of the mantle is graphically pictured in the context of the sounding of this Seventh Trump. For complete comprehension of a significant clue to these prophecies, look at the specific words that God chose to use:

"THE MYSTERY OF GOD . . . FINISHED"
Revelation 10:7

These are common words in Scripture. The word "mystery" is used twenty-two times, I believe, directly or indirectly, in connection with the Church. This word refers to New Testament truth that had not previously been revealed. It involves the union of believing Jews and Gentiles into ONE BODY with the Saviour, Jesus Christ. This union of one body is called THE BODY OF CHRIST.

. . . by revelation he made known unto me the MYSTERY . . .

. . . as it is now revealed . . .

That the Gentiles should be FELLOWHEIRS, and of the

same BODY, and PARTAKERS of this promise IN CHRIST by the Gospel. (Ephesians 3:3, 5 and 6.)

And to make all men see what is the FELLOWSHIP of the MYSTERY . . .

To the intent that now . . . might be known by the CHURCH the manifold wisdom of God. (Ephesians 3:9-10.)

This is a great MYSTERY: but I speak concerning Christ and the Church. (Ephesians 5:32.)

. . . Christ is the head of the CHURCH: and he is the saviour of the Body. (Ephesians 5:23.)

He is the head of the BODY, THE CHURCH . . . (Colossians 1:24.)

. . . for HIS BODY'S sake, which is the CHURCH. (Colossians 1:24.)

Even the MYSTERY which hath been hid . . . but now is made manifest to his saints:

To whom God would make known what is the riches of the glory of this MYSTERY among the Gentiles; which is CHRIST IN YOU, the HOPE of glory. (Colossians 1:26-27.)

That their hearts . . . being KNIT TOGETHER in love . . . to the acknowledgment of the MYSTERY of God. (Colossians 2:2.)

It is easy to see that these Scriptures are absolutely relating the MYSTERY OF GOD with the CHURCH, the Body of Christ, that consists of all true believers. When John said, in Revelation 10:7, that the Mystery of God would be FINISHED as the LAST TRUMP begins to sound, he is using a word that does not mean to terminate. It means to COMPLETE. It is like a man who makes a table in his shop, when he has completed his work, the table is finished. So it is here, at the sounding of the Seventh and LAST TRUMP, the MYSTERY OF GOD, the Church, the Body of Christ is complete. When it is finished, it is removed from the "shop."

Behold, I shew you a MYSTERY; we shall not all sleep,

but we shall all be changed,

In a moment, in the twinkling of an eye, at the LAST TRUMP: for the TRUMPET SHALL SOUND and the dead shall be raised incorruptible, and we shall be changed. (I Corinthians 15:51-52.)

For the Lord himself shall descend from heaven with a shout, with the voice of the archangel, and with the TRUMP OF GOD: and the dead in Christ shall rise first:

Then we which are alive and remain shall be CAUGHT UP TOGETHER WITH THEM. (I Thessalonians 4:16-17.)

What more can we say? That is the way it is in the word of God, and that is the way it will be in actual experience in time and space history. The big question is: Are you ready? There will come a time when there will be no more delay. The Trumpet will sound, and, if you are not saved then, may God have mercy upon your soul! Jesus is coming!

THE LITTLE BOOK

This latter part of Chapter Ten stands out because it underscores the continuing progress of time and events. John is given this "little book," and is told to "eat" the book. This is to symbolize for us his digestion of God's prophetic Word concerning these important last chapters. He was told that he must prophecy again, and that these prophecies would involve the peoples of the whole world. It is, thus, to be understood that the "little book" contained revelations of the last three and a half years of Daniel's prophecy, of the Millennial Kingdom of Christ, and of the New Heaven and the New Earth. All of these were to be revealed in symbolic form and are pictured for us in the eating of the "little book."

As John eats the "little book" we find that it symbolized two different aspects of those last years. The book was found to be sweet in his mouth, "sweet as honey." This indicated the blessedness and the joy of those who, like John, belong to the Lord. It would include the joyousness of the rapture as the saved are "caught up" and gathered home. It shows the holiness of those who, through the teaching of the Two Witnesses, and the ministry of the 144,000, come to a saving faith in the Messiah, Jesus Christ, and lay down their lives as martyrs. It embraces the greatness of that glorious day when our Lord returns in power and glory with the armies of heaven to defeat the Antichrist and his powers of darkness. It encompasses the Millennial Kingdom, when the earth will again be like the garden of Eden, and Christ rules with love and righteousness. Finally, it contains that glorious time when we, throughout all eternity, live with our Lord in the New Jerusalem, the New Heaven and the New Earth. Yes, these prophecies are, in truth, "sweet as honey" to all of us who love the Lord and look for His coming.

Yet, we also read that after John had eaten the "little book" it was "bitter" in his "belly." This BITTERNESS that John experienced was the truth of the awful affliction and suffering that will engulf the entire world after the Rapture has taken place and Antichrist has begun his rule. This "bitterness" emphasizes the fact of the unprecedented "tribulation" of those days. It is for this reason that these three and a half years are the true Scriptural TRIBULATION PERIOD, and is called the GREAT TRIBULATION. There are to be two basic causes of the unparalleled affliction of the days of the last half of Daniel's vision.

- First, is the affliction caused by the Antichrist and his evil forces of darkness, the cruelness of his reign, and his pursuit of the saints of God. He will have a demonic hatred for every Jew and will seek to kill all the Jewish people and destroy the Nation of Israel.

- Second, we need to comprehend that the suffering of those days will be primarily due to the righteous judgments of God, as His holy wrath is poured out upon the kingdom of the Antichrist and his Christ rejecting followers. The world will be in the grip of an angry God.

The "bitterness" that John experienced also consists of the horrors of the battle of Armageddon, as the earth is "reaped," and the Antichrist, along with his False Prophet, are captured and cast into hell. Finally, it incorporates the Judgment of the Great White Throne, where the "books are opened," and those who are not found in the "Lamb's book of life" are cast into the Lake of Fire.

It is no wonder that these prophecies were "bitter" in John's belly. They should be in ours as well, driving us to reach out to the lost while there is yet hope.

GOD'S TWO WITNESSES
Revelation, Chapter 11

Chapter 11 of the Book of Revelation begins in such a manner that it helps us know that we are, in our study, right in the middle of the Last Week of Daniel's prophecy of the Seventy Weeks. Here we are told that the court of the temple is "given unto the Gentiles: and the holy city shall be tread underfoot forty and two months." This is the LAST HALF of the LAST WEEK of seven years. This is the "hour" of the GREAT TRIBULATION. This is the length of time, the duration, of the affliction such as the world has never known. This is THE TRIBULATION PERIOD. This forty and two months is identical to the time of the reign of the Antichrist:

> . . . *and power was given unto him to continue FORTY AND TWO MONTHS.* (Revelation 13:5.)

It is here, in the context of the last three and a half years, that God's two witnesses minister as God's special servants. The time of their ministry is given as "a thousand two hundred and threescore days." This is 1,260 days, or 42 months, or 3 $1/2$ years, or a time, times and a half of time. We know that this period will begin with the Abomination of Desolation that occurs immediately following the RAPTURE of the Church, as the Body of Christ, the "restrainer" is "taken out of the way."

These two witnesses will probably be Elijah and Enoch, or possible Moses. They will walk the earth again. They will have miraculous powers and do mighty wonders as they trouble the

Kingdom of Antichrist. It may be that they will lead the 144,000, and perhaps defend them as they reach out to every Jew with the Gospel of God's grace in Christ.

As the Great Tribulation approaches its final hours, God will allow these two Witnesses to be killed. The world will rejoice and celebrate. Encouraged by this seeming victory, Antichrist and his massive army will converge upon Jerusalem to confront Christ upon His return to the earth. To the great surprise of everyone, these two witnesses, after three days, will rise from the dead and ascend to heaven in the sight of all their enemies. At this time the earth is shaken. The cities of the earth fall, as this one last great earthquake, also mentioned elsewhere in Revelation, shakes the earth, striking fear into the hearts of every unbeliever; but still they do not repent.

The battle of Armageddon becomes a reality as the Lord returns and the armies of heaven are with Him. Great destruction covers the earth with few left alive, and the birds of the air are called in to devour the dead.

We will return with Christ if we are His and love Him now. I'll be there! Will you? Which side will you be on in that last great battle? Today is the accepted time. NOW is the day of salvation. Believe on the Lord Jesus Christ and thou shalt be saved. To wait is to be LOST!

THE SEVENTH AND LAST TRUMP

Please take careful note that it is here, in the context of all this that we have been seeing and experiencing with John, that we read:

And the SEVENTH ANGEL SOUNDED . . .
(Revelation 11:15.)

NOW there is no longer delay! The time has come! The RESTRAINER is to be removed and taken out of the way. With the removal of "he who now letteth," the Antichrist is to be REVEALED, and the Abomination of Desolation takes place. The Great Tribulation is now to begin. This is the Day of Christ, and of the Lamb. In His control of all things, He pours forth His WRATH upon this evil empire of "the god of this world." At long last, the prayers of all the saints are to be answered, as they have cried out to God for justice and:

> . . . *The kingdoms of this world are become the kingdoms of our Lord, and of his Christ; and he shall reign for ever and ever.* (Revelation 11:15.)

> . . . *We give thee thanks, O Lord God Almighty, which are, and wast, and art to come; because thou hast taken to thee thy great power, and hast reigned.*
> (Revelation 11:17.)

In the context of the sounding of the Seventh and Last Trump, verses 18 and 19 give to us an overview of what will be explained in more detail in Chapters 12 through 20. We find several items listed here of great interest:

1. "The nations are angry." Under Antichrist the nations of the world rise up in anger against God and His people.

2. "Thy wrath is come." This is the time of the wrath of God from which we, the Church have been rescued by the Rapture. See I Thessalonians 1:10 and 5:9.

3. "The time of the dead."
   a. It is at this time that the resurrection occurs of those who "sleep in Jesus."
   b. It is at this time that the dead, the unsaved spiritually dead, will be judged with the wrath of God.

4. "Thou shouldst give reward unto thy servants the prophets, and to the saints, and them that fear thy name." This is when we stand before the Judgment Seat of Christ.

5. "And shouldst destroy them which destroy the earth." The awful judgment of God upon the kingdom of Antichrist and the False Prophet.

6. "The temple of God was opened in heaven." In this we see the welcome home celebration given to the Raptured Church, the Body of Believers.

7. While there is glory in heaven, there is "lightening, and voices, and thunders, and an earthquake, and great hail" on earth. This is THE TRIBULATION PERIOD.

Christians have been absolutely blinded by tradition! We have been guilty of giving Scripture a "private interpretation" that we have no right to do. If we cannot see the connection and the continuity of these events and facts in Revelation, Chapters 10 and 11, it is because we are willingly blind. Our own pride can so blind us and close our eyes to truth that we will not even allow ourselves to honestly examine the Scriptures. These prophecies speak clearly. So don't let tradition keep you in the dark and from the wisdom that God wants you to have. God has spoken plainly.

Remember just where we are NOW in the Time Frame. The last Seven Years begins with the signing of the peace accord among many nations. This is followed by the first Four Trumpets that describe a nuclear exchange, of limited scope, but it will destroy one-third of the world. Then we have, in the Fifth and Sixth Trumpets, an overview of the last half of the 70th Week of Daniel, now known as the Tribulation Period. Next is the vision of the Seventh Trumpet that sounds at the middle of that last week; and, at that time, the Rapture of the Church occurs, as well as the Abomination of Desolation, and the revelation of the Antichrist.

You might ask: How can you have the sequence of Trumpets One, Two, Three, Four, Five and Six, and then place the Seventh Trumpet BETWEEN the Fifth and the Sixth? This is because they are NOT consecutive *events*, but continuous visions, or revelations of events. Trumpets Five and Six cover that time of the Wrath of God. The Seventh Trumpet covers that same time period, for the wrath of God is contained in the Seven Vials, which are introduced by the vision of the Seventh Trumpet.

Preparations for the sounding of the Seventh Trumpet are included in Revelation 10 and 11, and the events of the Seventh Trumpet actually cover all of Revelation 12 through 20. Remember that the SEVENTH SEAL included the SEVEN TRUMPETS, and the SEVENTH TRUMPET INCLUDED the SEVEN VIALS of the Wrath of

God.

Think on this until the pattern of REVELATION becomes clear to you. The point to remember is that these are not consecutive EVENTS, but VISIONS of events that are not sequential in their fulfillment; though there is a definite progression of fulfillment.

Please reexamine again Charts 2 and 3 until you grasp and comprehend this reality.

A GREAT WONDER
Revelation, Chapter 12

God is revealing to John, and to us, the development of the events in these visions of the "Last Days." We have come up to the sounding of the Seventh Trumpet at the middle of the 70th week of Daniel. This next vision is referred to as a "great wonder," and this implies a vision, or revelation, of GREAT IMPORTANCE. It depicts an eminent prophetic truth, the significance of which God wants us to discover and comprehend. Chapter 12 is the center of the Book of Revelation. And, in the New Testament, this chapter is, perhaps, the most important for correct comprehension of the entire book.

As Satan would have it, it is the least understood. Tradition glosses over and effectively destroys this exquisite truth by relegating it to the manger scene at the birth of our Saviour in Bethlehem. Tradition removes this chapter from prophecy and places it in history, thereby robbing it of all relevance. Christians have been so deceived by "scholarship" that almost the total Church has lost the glory of this "great wonder" of revelation. The birth of Christ has nothing to do with the prophecies of this book of revelation. It is out of place here. It is out of context, and the very words of Scripture prove it to be so.

Please allow yourself the blessing of seeing the beauty of the truth God gives to us in this chapter.

As the Seventh Trumpet sounds, the next revelation of events is symbolized for us ever so beautifully:

> *. . . a woman clothed with the sun, and the moon under*

her feet, and upon her head a crown of twelve stars . . .
(Revelation 12:1.)

Discernment of this symbol is extremely important. It is best for us to identify this woman, not with a person, or a group of people, but with a TRUTH, A SPIRITUAL CONCEPT. We have many spiritual concepts in the Word of God, such as "The Kingdom of Heaven"; this is the concept of the rule of God within the human heart. Then there is the "mystery of iniquity," that is the rule of Satan, the god of this world, "the spirit that now worketh in the children of disobedience." Scripture is full of spiritual concepts because we are dealing with spiritual things.

The spiritual CONCEPT now viewed in this WOMAN is seen in TYPE in the Old Testament. Let us examine her. She is seen to be "clothed with the sun." This is clearly to indicate the "light" of truth of the Word of God. The sun is best noted for its LIGHT and its warmth. We all know that the LIGHT of God WARMS the heart of the believer. We talk about people growing COLD when they grow away from God's truth. This Light of the sun is the Gospel of our blessed Saviour, the central message of all Scripture. This WOMAN is CLOTHED with the sun. This word indicates a wrap-around. It is our word MANTLE. This WOMAN is the wearer of the MANTLE of the PRESENCE AND POWER OF GOD. This is what she SIGNIFIES. This same CONCEPT we have seen clearly TYPIFIED for us in the story of Elijah. Pause and use your instant recall, then notice these Scriptures:

O send out thy LIGHT and thy TRUTH . . . (Psalms 43:3.)

Thy WORD is a LAMP unto my feet, and a LIGHT UNTO MY PATH. (Psalms 119:105.)

The Gentiles shall come to thy LIGHT . . . (Isaiah 60:3.)

. . . I am the LIGHT of the world.; he that followeth me shall not walk in darkness, but shall have the LIGHT OF LIFE. (John 8:12.)

AS long as I am in the world, I am the LIGHT of the world. (John 9:5.)

YE ARE THE LIGHT OF THE WORLD . . . (Matthew 5:14.)

Let your LIGHT so shine before men . . . (Matthew 5:16.)

> . . . *this is the condemnation, that LIGHT IS COME INTO THE WORLD, and men loved DARKNESS rather than LIGHT, because their deeds were evil.* (John 3:19.)

It is easy for us to know that Christ wore the MANTLE of the power and the presence of the Father as He walked among men. All that He did demonstrated this fact, and it is witnessed to by Nicodemus when he said to Jesus that night as he talked with the Saviour:

> . . . *Rabbi, we KNOW that thou art a teacher COME FROM GOD: for no man can do these miracles that thou doest, except GOD BE WITH HIM.* (John 3:2.)

We know that the Father sent His Son into the world, and while Jesus was upon the earth He also testified that the works that He did were actually those of the Father:

> *For the Father loveth the Son, and sheweth him all things that himself doeth: and he will shew greater works than these, that ye may marvel.* (John 5:20.)

> . . . *the works which the Father hath given me to finish, the same works that I do, bear witness of me, that the Father hath sent me.* (John 5:36.)

> *I must work the works of him that sent me, while it is day . . .* (John 9:4.)

> . . . . *the works that I do in my Father's name, they bear witness of me.*

> . . . *I am the Son of God?*

> *If I do not the works of my Father, believe me not.*

> *But, if I do, though ye believe not me, BELIEVE THE WORKS: that ye may know, and believe, THAT THE FATHER IS IN ME, AND I IN HIM.* (John 10:25, 36-38.)

It is unquestionable that Jesus was testifying to the fact that the Power and Presence of God the Father was with Him. HE WORE THE MANTLE! But then, Jesus was soon to leave and return to Heaven.

He, therefore, made provision for those who would "wear the Mantle" after Him. He told the disciples that He would ask the Father to send to them the Holy Spirit, and that the Holy Spirit of God would abide in them. In fact, the Lord told them:

> . . . *If a man love me, he will keep my words: and my Father will love him, and WE WILL COME UNTO HIM, AND MAKE OUR ABODE WITH HIM.* (John 14:23.)

We remember our Lord saying to His disciples that He would be with them even unto the end of the world. We can see Christ's authorization for the transfer of this MANTLE in His words:

> . . . *Peace be unto you: as my Father hath sent me, even so I send you.*
>
> . . . *RECEIVE YE THE HOLY GHOST:*
>
> *Whose soever sins ye remit, they are remitted unto them; and whose soever sins ye retain, they are retained* (John 20:21-23.)

This is not where it took place. The MANTLE was not here transferred, for the Lord was yet with them. They did not, at this moment, receive the Holy Spirit. Then, what do we have here but the AUTHORIZATION for the transfer of the MANTLE of the PRESENCE AND POWER OF GOD. This is evidenced by those last words of "remitting sin," for, "Who can forgive sin but God only?" This is why the Lord told them to wait in Jerusalem for the PROMISE OF THE FATHER. He told them:

> . . . *ye shall RECEIVE POWER, after that the Holy Ghost is come upon you: and ye shall be witnesses unto me* . . . (Acts 1:8.)

So, clearly, we have the promise that the PRESENCE and the POWER of God would come upon the DISCIPLES. This was to happen to them as a BODY. Yes, individually, too; but we are well aware of the New Testament doctrine that we, as individual Christians, are members of ONE BODY with Christ as its Head. We belong to the Body of Christ, and this Body of Christ is the Church that He is building. The Church is the MANTLE WEARER in this present age. The TRANSFER OF THIS MANTLE actually took place at PENTE-COST.

> *And when the day of Pentecost was fully come, they were all together with one accord in one place.*
>
> *And suddenly THERE CAME a sound from heaven as of a rushing mighty WIND, and it filled all the house where they were sitting.*
>
> *And there appeared unto them cloven tongues like as of fire, and it sat upon each of them.*
>
> *And they were ALL FILLED WITH THE HOLY GHOST, and began to speak with other tongues, as the Spirit gave them utterance.* (Acts 2:1-4.)

Here is the amazing reality of the TRANSFER OF THE MANTLE OF POWER AND THE PRESENCE OF GOD. Remember that this Mantle wearing is a SPIRITUAL CONCEPT, but it is just as real as the physical Mantle that Elijah wore. We are the Wearer of this Mantle in this present time. We will wear this Mantle until it falls from us at the Rapture. Then, it will be picked up by the 144,000 of the Nation of Israel. It is critical that you fathom this truth. As we grasp this concept and the reality of it, we will be able to see it in the symbol God gives to us in Revelation, Chapter 12. Thus, we identify this WOMAN, in the vision of the wonder that John saw. THE WOMAN SYMBOLIZES THE WEARER OF THE MANTLE! We should not identify her as a person, or a group of people as such, because the Wearer of the Mantle can CHANGE from person to person, and from a body of people to another body of people. The Wearer of the Mantle is a spiritual CONCEPT that we identify WITH a person, or a body of people. If you will examine the following Scriptures with this CON-CEPT IN VIEW, I am sure that the Lord will give you new insight to the reality of this truth: John 20:21-23; Matthew 28:18-20; Mark 16:4-21; Luke 24:44-49; and Acts 1:2-12 and 2:1-47. The fact of this CONCEPT OF THE MANTLE WEARER is indisputably witnessed to in the Word of God.

Viewing the Church, then, as the Mantle Wearer at this time, we would recognize this as symbolized by the Woman clothed with the sun. The Church, being the "restrainer" of evil and wickedness in the world, is therefore seen to have the moon, the "ruler of the night," (Genesis 1:16) under her feet. Remember Paul's words:

> *For we wrestle not against flesh and blood, but against principalities, against powers, against THE RULERS OF THE DARKNESS OF THIS WORLD, against spiritual wickedness in high places.* (Ephesians 6:12.)

The MOON symbolizes these RULERS OF DARKNESS. This gives meaning to this GREAT WONDER that John saw. As we continue to look at the Woman, we see that she wears a crown of TWELVE STARS. It takes no great imaginative exploration to relate these to the TWELVE APOSTLES, who, as it were, formed the foundation for the Church of our Lord, Jesus Christ, through their writings. They were the first leaders of the Church. They had the preeminent role in the Church, for it was to them that the Lord gave, by revelation, all New Testament truth.

They were taught personally, by our Lord, and in turn teach us, even today, through their inspired written works. They were guided and directed in all that they did by the Holy Spirit. It is well to remember that Judas was replaced by the Apostle Paul, as is confirmed in these Scriptures: I Corinthians 15:7-10; Galatians 1:14-16 and 2:7-9; also I Corinthians 3:10-11.

There were always only TWELVE APOSTLES appointed by our Lord. Needless to say, we do the Lord and His Word a great injustice to say that this woman symbolizes Israel as bringing Christ into the world, and it is a horrible miscarriage of truth to even suggest that she is Mary giving birth to Jesus. That kind of teaching is nothing more than sloppy, and the handling of the Word of God deceitfully.

THE MAN CHILD

Continuing in our study of this GREAT WONDER, we now see

a realistic picture of what is a present actuality. This Woman clothed with the sun is with child. She is about to give birth:

> *And she being with child cried, travailing in birth, and*
> *pained to be delivered.* (Revelation 12:2.)

Here, again, we are given another great truth. It is one with which we are familiar, but it is again the CONCEPT that is symbolized in contemplation of this Child and the Woman. This is one of those "mysteries of the Kingdom of Heaven," and our Lord illustrated this concept many times.

What we are to see, in this mother-child relation, is not the idea of origin, as a child comes from its mother. In this Wonder we see something else that is real-to-life, and it is the CONCEPT of something being formed within something else. It is the concept of a BODY WITHIN A BODY.

We have here an absolutely true picture of the real experience of the Church. There is the BODY that is seen and observed by all, and is identified as the CHRISTIAN CHURCH. It is equally called CHRISTENDOM, and consists of all churches and all peoples who claim to be, in any manner, associated with Jesus Christ and His teachings. It includes all denominations and branches of Christianity world wide.

The second BODY, but just as real, is the BODY OF TRUE BELIEVERS that is found WITHIN CHRISTENDOM, but is UNSEEN. It is being formed within the body of the "mother" that is seen in everyday experience. The one, being formed within the other, is a part of the whole.

The Body of Believers is "invisible" only in the sense that we cannot surely identify them. Only the Lord knows those that are His, and we are not to so judge. We are told by our Lord that we are not to try to separate the two, as is seen in the parable of the Tares in Matthew 13:30. Jesus tells us there:

> *Let both grow together until the harvest . . .*
> (Matthew 13:30.)

Again this concept is seen in the parable of the Ten Virgins. There were ten of them and they were apparently indistinguishable the one from the other; but five had a missing ingredient, the oil representing the Holy Spirit — that completely separated them from the others. We cannot surely tell who has the Holy Spirit, but God knows.

As you read this parable in Matthew 25:1-13, you will find that the five without the oil were left out when the door was shut. Together they picture CHRISTENDOM, but the five with the Holy Spirit pictures the true BODY OF BELIEVERS. The Lord said to those without the Holy Spirit," I know you not."

That is what is symbolized for us in the vision of the woman with child. There is the whole body of the VISIBLE CHURCH, but within her is being formed the INVISIBLE BODY OF CHRIST. This vision is not meant to show that Christendom gives birth to the true Church; that would be to misunderstand the symbol. Its purpose is to show the formation of a Body within a body. In the vision, as John saw it, the BIRTH of the child symbolizes for us the time and event when, in actual experience, the BODY within will be separated and removed from the body wherein it grew.

This, of course, happens to each of us at death, but it will happen to *this* BODY only at the time of the Rapture. This Woman should, therefore, not be viewed as the Church, but as the WEARER OF THE MANTLE of God's PRESENCE AND POWER. Christianity appears to wear that Mantle now, but ONLY because of the presence of the Body of Christ. There is no other place where the Presence and Power of God is manifested other than within the Christian Church.

THE GREAT RED DRAGON

The next part of this great wonder is that of this Dragon, and here we are not left to ourselves for the Scriptures plainly state for us who he is:

> *The great dragon . . . that old serpent, called the Devil,*
> *and Satan, which deceiveth the whole world . . .*
> (Revelation 12:9.)

Satan is here identified with the serpent in reference to the Fall of man in the Garden of Eden. He is seen to have SEVEN HEADS, and these symbolize for us the SEVEN GREAT WORLD POWERS, or EMPIRES that have been under his control throughout human history. They are Egypt, Assyria, Babylon, Media-Persia, Greece, Rome, and Antichrist. This is in concert with what is written in Revelation 17:7-10, where these "heads" are called "mountains." This word mountain, in Scripture, is a symbolic word for a political power. It is further stated in the same chapter that these are Seven "kings," or kingdoms, and that "five are fallen," or passed on into history. The Sixth was then in power, which was Rome, and the Seventh was yet to come.

The Seventh world Empire will be that of the Antichrist, and it will be the revived, or renewed, Roman Empire, the confederation of Western Nations. This teaches that SATAN is the sure ruler behind every earthly Empire. He is the "god of this world."

The TEN HORNS, mentioned in Revelation 12:3 as belonging to Satan, are the same as the TEN TOES of Daniel 2:41-42, and the TEN HORNS of Daniel 7:7. They are also the same TEN HORNS of Revelation 13:1, and 17:7-12. These TEN HORNS are the Ten united Powers of the Western World that will unite under the leadership of Antichrist and become the core of his kingdom.

This identifies for us the reality of Satanic control of all our political systems. Is it any wonder that our world today is in such chaos? Thank God for His supernatural powers and overruling sovereign control. God is in charge.

In our study of Revelation, Chapter 12, Satan is seen to have drawn one-third of all "stars of heaven, and cast them to earth." This is a reference, in symbolic form, to the true event recorded for us in Isaiah 14:12-16, and in Ezekiel 28: 1-19, where Lucifer became Satan the great deceiver. He, at that time, drew with him, in his rebellion, one-third of God's angelic beings. These became Satan's spiritual army of demons with whom we do battle. Then we are told concerning the WOMAN:

> And she brought forth a MAN CHILD, who was to rule all nations with a rod of iron: and her child was CAUGHT UP UNTO GOD, AND TO HIS THRONE. (Revelation 12:5.)

John is telling us what he saw, and what he saw was symbolic of some eminent truth. This is not the manger scene! This is a MAN CHILD. Christ was such, of course, and so is HIS BODY. The child is then "CAUGHT UP UNTO GOD, AND TO HIS THRONE." Almost every teacher will say that this is Christ, and that it could be none else. There are, however, some critical clues given to us here that are almost always overlooked.

You will recall from our study of the Seven Letters to the Seven Churches in Revelation, Chapters Two and Three, that it is there promised to the "overcomers" that:

1. "He shall rule them with a rod of iron . . . even as I received of my Father." (Revelation 2:27.)

2. "To him . . . will I grant to sit with me on my throne, even as I . . . am sat down with my Father on his throne." (Revelation 3:21.)

We can, thus, see assuredly that this statement about the MAN CHILD truly does apply to the BODY OF CHRIST. Furthermore, and even more conclusively, this verse in Revelation 12:5 CANNOT refer to Christ, not if we believe in the verbal inspiration of the Word of God. The reason is because the Child is here said to be "CAUGHT UP UNTO GOD." It happens, in the context of verse four, "as soon as it was born." This word "caught up" is exactly the same word used in I Thessalonians 4:17, and that we know to be the RAPTURE OF THE CHURCH. It is the word chosen by God to teach us that we, the Church, will be "taken away by force." This word is never used of Christ.

Jesus was never Raptured! Even when He returned to Heaven after His resurrection, the Bible clearly tells us that He ascended, and that is a totally different concept from Rapture. Too, Christ's ascension took place about 33 years after His birth, while *this* MAN CHILD is Raptured AS SOON AS IT WAS BORN.

To say that this verse applies to Christ abuses this verse in Revelation so that it does great harm to God's prophetic truth. It is to impose upon the Word of God an opinion, and to discredit the Truth given by the Holy Spirit.

The true Church, the Body of Christ, though, just as soon as it is separated from the Body of Christendom, WILL BE CAUGHT UP UNTO GOD AND TO HIS THRONE. This truth absolutely applies to the Church of Jesus Christ. Yes, we will rule with Him with a rod of iron even as He has promised us. We will return with Him, Revelation 19:14; and we will rule with Him, Revelation 20:4.

THE FLIGHT OF THE WOMAN

Follow the amazing continuity of this chapter. Immediately upon the Rapture of the "child," we find the "woman" fleeing into the wilderness. Here is a clear transition. Unless you have understood the CONCEPT of the first verse of this chapter, you will not understand what is happening now. The thing to remember is that the WOMAN is the WEARER OF THE MANTLE. Now, like Elijah of old, when he was caught up, his mantle fell from him. It was picked up by another, Elisha. At that moment, Elisha became the WEARER OF THE MANTLE. Even so here, when the BODY OF CHRIST is Raptured the MANTLE OF GOD'S POWER AND PRESENCE will fall away from us. It will then be picked up by ISRAEL, or the 144,000, and Israel will become the WEARER OF THE MANTLE. This is symbolized by the Woman fleeing from the Antichrist. This, then, is the TRANSFER of the Mantle from the Church to Israel, and Israel will wear God's Mantle throughout the TRIBULATION PERIOD. It is for this reason that Satan seeks to destroy her, and he pursues her endlessly:

> And the dragon was wroth with the woman, and went to make war with the remnants of her seed, which keep the commandments of God, and have the testimony of Jesus Christ. (Revelation 12:17.)
>
> And to the woman were given two wings of a great eagle, that she might fly into the wilderness, into her place, where she is nourished for a time, and times, and half a time, from the face of the serpent. (Revelation 12:14.)

We see here that her flight into the wilderness is for three and a half years, the whole time of the rule of Antichrist. She flees because Satan, through Antichrist, wants to destroy her, the Nation of Israel.

This may help you to understand the indescribable hatred on the part of many for Israel even today. We find that they are protected by God's sovereign grace and power to fulfill His divine purpose and promise.

Here is a thought for you, if you are able to spiritually digest it: What happens to the Body of Christendom when once the body of Christ is Caught Up? When there are no true believers within her, what will she be then? When once the Rapture has occurred, the VISIBLE Church will be TOTALLY VOID OF ALL TRUTH. She will be APOSTATE. She will no longer be the Wearer of the Mantle, and will have believed the Lie of II Thessalonians 2:10-12. Christendom is, in that state, symbolized by the woman of Revelation 17:1-6, and is there called by the Lord "THE GREAT WHORE." This will be the true state of Christendom without the Body of Christ within her. It is only the presence of true believers that give any validity to Christianity at all.

WAR IN HEAVEN

There is a final, momentous account we must look at in our present chapter. It will round out the whole teaching of this important vision of Chapter 12 and give it meaning. It is also here that we find the reason why we are going to be Raptured at all.

There was war in heaven: Michael and his angels fought against the dragon; and the dragon fought and his angels,

And prevailed not; neither was their place found any more in heaven. (Revelation 12:7-8.)

When Lucifer fell, back in the beginning of time, he took one-third of God's angelic beings with him in his rebellion, as he was cast out of heaven. He then became the "prince of the power of the air." He was then confined to the FIRST and SECOND HEAVENS, having been cast from the THIRD HEAVEN, that is God's dwelling place.

Lucifer, who is the Devil and Satan, now resides in space, and in our atmosphere. He has access to the earth, and controls the godless population of our planet as "the god of this world." He is "the spirit that now worketh in the children of disobedience," and governs the "course of this world." He is, in spite of this, subject to God's sovereign control.

Now, though, in our vision we see another development of this ongoing saga of the confrontation of good and evil. We have before us two great spiritual armies that come together in a battle to the finish. This is not a battle on the earth using regular military might. But a battle that is fought in the heavenlies, and with gigantic spiritual forces. What has precipitated this confrontation? The context of this battle shows us that it is the RAPTURE OF THE SAINTS, the Body of Christ, that is the immediate cause of this spiritual encounter of supernatural forces. The logic of this is that upon our transformation and/or resurrection, at the sounding of the LAST TRUMP, and our being CAUGHT UP, we must pass through Satan's territory. Satan stands, with all of his forces, between Heaven and Earth. We have to pass through his front yard! He is not about to let us pass easily. We are told that:

> . . . the dragon stood before the woman which was ready
> to be delivered, for to DEVOUR HER CHILD AS SOON AS
> IT WAS BORN. (Revelation 12:4.)

His purpose is stated plainly. He is there waiting to destroy the Church in one gigantic effort as we are caught up, "as soon as it was born." This is why "the Lord Himself will descend." This is why we must be RAPTURED! We will be taken BY FORCE to heaven. Michael, the Archangel, takes his great band of Holy Angels (²/₃ against ¹/₃) and engages the Dragon and his angels in open battle. We have read about the lightenings and thunders in heaven, and the very earth shakes as the battle rages. Who can describe such a battle? The Trumpet blows; the angels march; there is a shout from the Lord as the dead are raised, and the voice of the archangel gives command to his troops. We, the saints, under armed guard and accompanied by our Lord Himself, get through, and the "saints go marching in," as all heaven breaks forth in the Hallelujah Chorus. Satan and his army are defeated, but not destroyed. They are now banished to the earth.

*And the great dragon was cast out, that old serpent, called
the Devil, and Satan, which deceiveth the whole world:
he was CAST OUT INTO THE EARTH, and his angels were
cast out with him.* (Revelation 12:9.)

Remember, all of this happens in the MIDDLE of the Last Week
of Daniel's prophecy. This happens at the LAST TRUMP, when the
Man Child is CAUGHT UP TO GOD. This happens at the time of the
Abomination of Desolation that immediately follows the Devil's
coming to the earth. He comes in "great wrath, because he knoweth
that he hath but a short time." It will be just three and a half years! It
is then that he gives his power to the Antichrist. It is at this time that
the kingdom of Antichrist is set up and he begins to rule the earth in
satanic power.

It is now that the Antichrist, inspired by Satan, attempts to
destroy the new WEARER OF THE MANTLE, Israel. Many will die at
his hand for their faith in the Lord, having heard the testimony of the
Two Witnesses and the Hundred and Forty Four Thousand. They will
have believed the Messiah, Jesus, the Son of God. Oh, how it all
comes together in time and space, and in perfect accord with the
TIME FRAME given by our Lord through His prophet! All of these
tremendous events could actually happen within the next few years.
ARE YOU READY TO FACE THE FUTURE? What will YOUR future
be? I am thankful for our Lord's promise:

. . . I go to prepare a place for you.

*And if I go and prepare a place for you, I WILL COME
AGAIN, and receive you unto myself. That where I am
there ye may be also.* (John 14:2-3.)

Even so, come, Lord Jesus!

THE BEAST
Revelation, Chapters 13 and 14

We have just come through Chapters 10, 11 and 12. We have seen where the Seventh and LAST TRUMP was sounded, and tremendous events immediately followed. Let us review them before going on into the next chapters, so that THEIR CONTEXT is firmly in mind. Remember that, in Chapter 12, John was given an extraordinary revelation as is seen in the words, "a great wonder." In this special revelation we are introduced to the following concepts and events:

1. The Wearer of the Mantle of God's Presence and Power.

2. This Mantle Wearer has the "moon" under her feet, and it signifies her work as the "restrainer."

3. This Mantle Wearer is seen as a woman about to give birth. This introduces us to the spiritual concept of a "Body within a Body."

4. Before this woman, awaits the dragon who is Satan and the Devil. He is there to "devour" the child at the very time of its birth. This separation of the body within, from the external body, signifies the separation of the Body of Christ from Christendom at the time of the resurrection and the Rapture.

5. The Seventh and LAST TRUMPET sounds and the time of "birth," or separation, arrives. The child, a man child, is "caught up" (RAPTURED) "unto God and to His throne." The child is a "man child" because Christ is a MAN, and HE is the Head of the Body.

6. At once there is the outbreak of war in heaven. Michael and his angels fight the Devil in his evil design to devour the "child."

7. Satan is defeated and cast out into the earth. He comes with great wrath. He has a short time. He gives his power to the Antichrist who persecutes Israel, who now has picked up the Mantle of God. Many die for their faith.

8. It is now that the Antichrist reigns in satanic power. His reign will last for three and a half years. During this time God's two special witnesses, together with the 144,000 will wear the Mantle of God's Power and Presence.

This is the CONTEXT of Chapter 13, and this chapter continues the same story and gives to us many details of the kingdom of the Antichrist. In this chapter we are back upon the earth in our study. Recall that Antichrist was the political leader of the Western World. He has led the world to peace through the signing of the peace accord for a period of seven years. This began the last week of Daniel's vision found in Daniel 9:27. Still, it is not until the "restrainer," the Body of Christ, is taken out of the way and the "man child" is CAUGHT UP, that this Western leader will be REVEALED as the Antichrist. He, then, will be possessed by Satan who gives to him his power. So the evil trinity is finally formed with Satan, the Antichrist, and the False Prophet. This chapter identifies the characteristics of his evil, cruel reign upon the earth. The fact that he is seen to have Seven Heads identifies Antichrist and his kingdom with the dream of Daniel Two, and the vision of Daniel Seven. As we have noted, these Seven Heads represent the Seven World Empires of history as they are seen to be under Satanic control. These are Egypt, Assyria, Babylon, Media-Persia, Greece, Rome and the renewed Roman Empire that is Antichrist's kingdom. The reunited Roman Empire is signified by the TEN TOES and the TEN HORNS. Notice that this is clearly a satanically empowered rule upon earth:

> . . . and the dragon gave him his power, and his seat, and great authority. (Revelation 13:2.)

We are told, in the next verse, that a "wound" was received by this Beast. It was a "deadly wound," or a wound that could be classified as fatal, but he does not die. His wound is healed. It is not certainly clear, as yet, just what this may mean. In that these visions are given in symbolic form, it may well have a significance other than what is apparent. It appears that the Beast, the Antichrist, receives a wound in the head. For this reason the common understanding is that there is an attempt upon his life and that he is shot in the head. But, because this is a symbolic revelation, we must consider that some other meanings may be intended.

Yes, there will be some kind of a literal "wound." We find in the Scriptures that the word "head" often speaks of government, or even empire, such as the Seven Heads of the Beast that represent the seven world empires of world history. Another point of confirmation of this thought is found in the following verse:

> . . . *The seven heads ARE seven mountains, on which the woman sitteth.*
>
> *AND THERE ARE SEVEN KINGS: five are fallen, and one is, and the other is not yet come; and when he cometh, he must continue a short space.* (Revelation 17:9-10.)

These "seven Heads," or "seven mountains," are the seven world kingdoms under direct satanic control as we have already said. The One that "IS" was the Roman Empire that was at that time ruling the world. The One that "IS NOT YET COME" is the reunited Roman Rule under the Antichrist. It is the kingdom of Antichrist.

The "Head of State" is most often seen as representing the State itself. Our President is the official representative of the United States of America. So, a "wound" in the head can symbolically be understood to signify a wound to the State itself. With this understanding we can conclude that most likely some "deadly" thing is going to "wound," or happen to, either the Kingdom of the Antichrist, or possibly the Country from which he comes, and in which he arises.

This possibility is further borne out with this Scriptural fact: The "wound" was that of a "sword," Revelation 13:14. This word "sword," in Scripture, is a term that almost always is used to signify WAR. Remember that the First Four Trumpets give us a clear indication of a limited nuclear exchange taking place. This fact, together with the prophecies of Ezekiel 38 and 39, leads to a conclusion that this exchange of nuclear war would take place within the year of the signing of the Peace Accord. It is easy to imagine that such a nuclear exchange could be the cause of the "deadly wound" upon the Beast.

Everyone says that no one nation can win a nuclear war.

Because, a nuclear war may be expected to terminate life upon the earth. Man has the power to destroy the entire world. Still, don't ever lose sight of the fact that God is in control. Man can only do what God allows. The Western World, and the United States in particular, will be "wounded" in this exchange, but, in God's grace neither is destroyed. The "wound" is "healed."

From the chaos of this exchange, a magnificent Leader will emerge to pull the world together during the remainder of those first three and a half years. Then, at the mid-point, Satan, after being cast out of the heavens, takes control of him. So, rising out of the rubble of nuclear war that by all rights should have caused total annihilation, the kingdom of the Antichrist comes. There is left no effective opposition. He rules the world as the Seventh World Power.

As we consider these thoughts, we must always remember that our Lord is in sovereign control. He has told us what will be, and it shall be as He has said. Nothing can happen other than what He allows to happen. God will ensure that the West is not destroyed. The Antichrist must have a seat of governmental power from which to begin his evil work.

We are now informed, with absolute Biblical clarity, about the length, or duration, of the rule of the Antichrist. Many think that he will rule for seven years, and they support their belief in a "seven year tribulation period" with that assumption. That is not the case. Many equate the 70th week of Daniel with the reign of Antichrist and the Tribulation Period, but it is a mistaken thesis. It is not only un-Biblical, it is anti-Biblical, for the Scripture plainly says:

> . . . *and the power was given unto him to continue*
> *FORTY AND TWO MONTHS.* (Revelation 13:5.)

This is plain speech! "Forty and two months" is exactly three and a half years. It is one thousand, two hundred and sixty days. IT IS NOT, AND NEVER CAN BE, SEVEN YEARS. Antichrist will rule the world ONLY during the LAST HALF of the 70th week of Daniel. He will be "revealed" for what he is, the "man of sin," the "son of perdition," empowered by Satan, at the Abomination of Desolation immediately after the "restrainer" is "taken out of the way." He begins his reign at that time. Biblically speaking, there is no such thing as "The Seven Year Tribulation Period." That is an unsound expression, and extremely misleading. Also, it throws prophetic understanding askew.

The Scriptural method of identifying this time is: "The Seventieth Week of Daniel." This time period will begin, not with the rapture as is taught, but with the signing of the peace accord, Daniel 9:27. It is the middle of this 70th week when the Abomination of Desolation occurs, and the Antichrist, now empowered by Satan, begins his evil rule. His rule extends through those last three and a half years, terminating with the return of Christ and the Battle of Armageddon. It is this last half of the 70th week that is referred to by Christ as the Great Tribulation, and this is because it is a time of unprecedented suffering. Antichrist will rule the world as is seen in the following Scripture:

> . . . and they worshiped the beast, saying, Who is like unto the beast? Who is able to make war with him?

> . . . and power was given unto him over all kindreds, tongues, and nations.

> And all that dwell upon the earth shall worship him.
> (Revelation 13:4, 7 and 8.)

THE FALSE PROPHET

Remember the TWO LEGS of the image in the dream of King Nebuchadnezzar? Here, now, in this vision of John's in Revelation, Chapter 13, we see those Two Legs. These Two Legs represent the Two Parts, or Powers, of the kingdom of the Antichrist. They have existed all through the Roman Empire, and it will be so in the renewed, or reunited, or revived, Roman Empire. The First Leg is that of the POLITICAL POWER, and is fulfilled in the person of the Antichrist. The Second Leg is now revealed to us in this vision:

> And I beheld ANOTHER BEAST coming up out of the earth; he had two horns like a lamb, and he spake as a

dragon.

And he exerciseth all the power of the first beast before
him, and causeth the earth and them which dwell therein
to worship the first beast, whose deadly wound was
healed. (Revelation 13:11 and 12.)

This Second Beast is clearly RELIGIOUS in nature. He is said to have TWO HORNS like those of a LAMB. This symbol identifies his apparent "Christian" aspect. He is supposed to be a representative of Christ, who is THE LAMB in Scripture. Yet, we are told that he does not actually speak for Christ, but for Satan. He is a FALSE PROPHET, and a deceiver. As the "spokesman" for Satan, he leads the world in the worship of the First Beast, Antichrist. This brings the entire world under satanic control through RELIGION AND POLITICS. The Word of God so identifies this Second Beast as the False Prophet:

And the beast was taken, and with him the FALSE
PROPHET that wrought miracles before him, with which
he deceived them that had received the mark of the beast,
and them that worshiped his image. These both were cast
alive into a lake of fire burning with brimstone.
(Revelation 19:20.)

This Second Beast is a RELIGIOUS LIAR! He deceives people into thinking that the First Beast is the Messiah and Divine. He leads the total population of the world in idolatrous worship, and condemns to death all who will not bow the knee to his will and give him, the Antichrist, their total loyalty. This Second Beast, under satanic control, has supernatural power to perform real miracles:

And he had power to give life unto the image of the beast,
that the image of the beast should both speak, and cause
that as many as would not worship the image of the beast
should be killed. (Revelation 13:15.)

THE MARK OF THE BEAST

In order to control the world's population, we can presume, now, that a computer number, or symbol, will be assigned to every individual. Thus, personal information, about all people, will be instantly available to anyone needing it. Then, every act of normal living will be controlled. Nothing can be bought or sold; absolutely no transaction of any kind can be carried out lacking this MARK. No business, no banking, and nothing that is necessary to every day living will be permitted those who refuse this mark.

Additionally, those who refuse to submit to this authority will have to run and hide from those who will seek their lives because of their refusal to submit to Antichrist's authority. NO ONE WILL REFUSE, except those few of the people of Israel, who will have rejected this evil Empire. For, through the preaching of the Two Witnesses and the 144,000 who were sealed with the seal of God, they see in all of this the fulfillment of the Word of God, and turn to the Saviour.

Most, if not all, of these "converts" will be hunted down and put to death by Antichrist and his followers. Alternatively, we see that the Scripture places a calamitous fate upon all who worship the Beast and receive his Mark. They will be eternally damned:

> . . . *If any man worship the beast and his image, and receive his mark in his forehead, or in his hand,*
>
> *The same shall drink of the wine of the wrath of God, which is poured out without mixture into the cup of his indignation; and he shall be tormented with FIRE and BRIMSTONE in the presence of the holy angels, and in the presence of the Lamb:*
>
> *And the smoke of their torment ascendeth up FOR EVER AND EVER.* (Revelation 14: 9-11.)

Always remember that the Church will have been raptured BEFORE this reign of evil begins. The Body of Christ will have been "caught up" unto God. We will not be here, but are seen to be in

Heaven, standing before our Lord, serving Him. This is why it is important for us to have the correct sequence of events clearly in mind, or else we will miss the blessing and the comfort of it all.

Use your INSTANT RECALL, and go over the facts of Scripture as related to the TIME FRAME. Try not to allow your understanding to be clouded by the unscriptural tradition that is mouthed so glibly. Know the facts!

During this time of rule of the Antichrist, when his mark is given to the unbelieving world, we see the presence of the 144,000 who had been sealed by God. These have picked up the Mantle. They are now the "Wearer of the Mantle of the Power and Presence of God" in the earth; having picked it up as it fell from the raptured Church. The Woman of Chapter 12 is still symbolic of the MANTLE WEARER, and this is why we see her, now symbolic of this new Mantle Wearer, (like Elisha) fleeing into the wilderness. This WOMAN remains the same, as the Mantle Wearer, but changes from the Church to Israel symbolically depicting the transfer of the Mantle from the Body of Christ to the 144,000. She does not symbolize the Church or Israel, but the MANTLE WEARER. This Mantle Wearer flees, pursued by the Antichrist and his followers. Many believers are found and killed, but they are not defeated. They actually are pictured as gaining victory over the Devil and his crowd in their death:

And they overcame him by the blood of the Lamb, and by the word of their testimony; and they loved not their lives unto the death. (Revelation 12:11.)

To die is not to lose; it is not to be defeated. Those "loved not their lives," but chose martyrdom rather than the denial of their Lord. They chose Christ instead of Antichrist, and died for Him who had died for them.

Why is it that people think that because I am a believer, a child of God, that God won't let anything "bad" happen to me? It is in times of suffering that God is nearest to us, and we lean upon Him and trust in His love and grace. It is in times when death is near that we have the opportunity to give a clear witness for our Lord. The fact that the Antichrist is going to make the believers suffer horrible affliction is documented in the Word of God, but God's grace is prominently visible, also:

And it was given unto him to make war with the saints, and TO OVERCOME THEM. (Revelation 13:7.)

Blessed are the dead which die IN THE LORD from henceforth: Yea, saith the Spirit, that they may rest from their labours; and their works do follow them. (Revelation 14:13.)

They are to REST, awaiting their fellow sufferers, before they receive their rewards. They will be rewarded together. We have seen these before. These are the ones we saw "under the altar" — INSTANT RECALL:

. . . that they should rest yet for a little season, until their fellow servants also and their brethren should be killed as they were, should be fulfilled. (Revelation 6:11.)

Isn't it wonderful how Scripture confirms itself. We are not left in the dark unless we do not use the "light." The fact that their "works do follow them" is another indication of that which has been said. These are not part of those who were resurrected at the time of the sounding of the Seventh Trumpet. These are not yet standing before the throne, the Judgment Seat of Christ, to receive their rewards. They will be rewarded at the close of that terrible time of suffering when all those who will have been killed will be resurrected at the time of Christ's return in power and great glory (Revelation 20:4).

In Chapters 13 and 14 we have been looking at the activity of the Antichrist in his kingdom, but the end is not yet. We are next introduced to the terrible judgment of God which will greatly intensify the suffering of a condemned humanity. Chapter 14 closes in verses 14-20 with a graphic scene of the wrath of God contained in the vision of the Winepress of the Wrath of God.

THE GRAPES OF WRATH

We have looked at satanic activity, and now we are to view Divine activity. This takes place in, or covers, the same time period as that of Chapters 13 and 14. This vision of the winepress can also be understood to be the ultimate results of the contents of the Judgments of the Seven Vials. It is all a vivid illustration depicting the horribleness of the wrath of our Holy God upon a world that has spurned His grace. This winepress is plainly stated to be the "winepress of the wrath of God," Revelation 14:19. The earth is God's vineyard, and it is harvest time. The grapes represent PEOPLE, unbelievers, who have rejected the truth of the Gospel. They are unsaved, lost and condemned. They are gathered and cast into the winepress:

> . . . *Thrust in thy sharp sickle, and gather the clusters of the vine of the earth; for her grapes are fully ripe.*

> *And the angel thrust in his sickle into the earth, and gathered the vine of the earth, and cast it into the great winepress of the wrath of God.*

> *And the winepress was TRODDEN without the city, and BLOOD came out of the winepress, even to the horsebridles, by a space of a thousand and six hundred furlongs.* (Revelation 14:18-20.)

Now, that is gross! Yes, it is very gruesome, but it is real. It depicts the appalling results of the judgments of God. This is a vision and a sign signifying the awful wrath of God in all its destructive, all-inclusive fullness. Remember the verse before seen, in which we saw the unsaved who were MADE TO DRINK:

> . . . *of the wine of the wrath of God, which is poured out WITHOUT MIXTURE into the cup of his indignation.* (Revelation 14:10.)

The significance of this statement is that God's wrath will be PURE, and of full strength. It will have NO GRACE in it. The time of MERCY AND GRACE will have passed. We may not like this, and it may not fit the picture that we have of God, but this is the picture that God gives of Himself. Then remember that FAITH is BELIEVING GOD.

It is also important for us to comprehend that the Bible pictures for us the One who is in the winepress treading upon the grapes. It is as quoted of Him in the *Battle Hymn of the Republic.* One is there, as was the custom, tramping the grapes under foot. The juice is seen to come up around His ankles, and splattering upon His garments. This One is none other than our Lord Jesus Christ!

> *And he was clothed with a vesture dipped in BLOOD:*
> *and his name is called the WORD OF GOD.*
> (Revelation 19:13.)

> *Wherefore art thou red in thine apparel, and thy garments*
> *like him that treadeth in the winefat?*

> *I have trodden the winepress ALONE: and of the people*
> *there was none with me: for I will tread them in mine*
> *anger, and trample them in my fury; and their blood shall*
> *be sprinkled upon my garments, and I will stain all my*
> *raiment.* (Isaiah 63:2 and 3.)

We see, then, that this is the fulfillment of that spoken by the prophet many years before Christ came in His first coming. We cannot correctly give an itemized, chronological account of the terrible events of those last three and a half years. The Bible simply does not give us that information. It seems that all that is descriptive, in Chapter 16, of the pouring out of the Seven Golden Vials of the wrath of God, is that seen here, pictorially, as the treading of the winepress of the wrath of God. They are both differing views of the same horrible truth.

It is the Day of the Wrath of the Lamb, and continues throughout the entire three and a half year period, perhaps growing ever more intense with each passing day until, finally, the earth is "reaped." This outpouring of the wrath of God covers and includes the events of Chapters 17 and 18 as well. It is there where our Lord speaks specifically of the Beast and the Whore; both will be judged by Him. This judgment will only come to an end upon the return of our Lord in great glory as is seen in Chapter 19.

During this awful time of the GREAT TRIBULATION there will be putrefying sores, stinking, running, open sores that will break out upon the bodies of the unsaved. The seas and oceans will turn to "blood," as will the rivers of fresh water. Men will die, or want to die, of thirst and hunger. The heat from the sun will become intense, and men will be burned with the heat and the ultraviolet rays. The earth will be scorched and dried. Yet, the Bible tells us that in spite of all this, men still will not repent. Their hearts are hardened against God. The day of grace has come and gone!

There will be no great revival during those awful days. Don't let any preacher deceive you into thinking that your loved ones will have an opportunity to be saved after they have seen the reality of the Rapture, and the rise of the Antichrist. It simply is not in the Book.

There will be a supernatural DARKNESS that will cover the land, a darkness that causes pain so intense that men will chew on their tongues in hopeless confusion and agony. Still, the Bible says, THREE TIMES OVER, men will not repent. Read it, and read it again, until you understand that TODAY is the day of Salvation. It is NOW that the door is open. In the pouring out of the Sixth Vial, preparations for Armageddon are given, and so the end of that terrible TRIBULA-TION PERIOD comes, and Christ returns on His "white horse."

BABYLON

As with the Seventh Seal, so with the Seventh Trumpet, even so it is with the Seventh Vial. The seventh of each introduces and includes the next series of judgments, or prophetic events. The Seventh Vial of Revelation, Chapters 17 and 18, gives to us the vision of the Spiritual Babylon that consists of the Great Whore riding upon the Beast. It is the ungodly union of RELIGIOUS and POLITICAL ROME under Antichrist. The Religious rides upon the Political, or is carried along by it. It would seem that for a time the Religious actually directs the Beast, but then is, in the plan of God, destroyed by the Beast. The economies of all the world are involved in this unholy union, and every soul is affected.

Over the years many writers have believed that the real Babylon would be rebuilt, and that it would become, once again, the religious, economic and political center of the world. This, it seems, is erroneous thinking that stems from not realizing that this Babylon is symbolic. The fact that it is called "MYSTERY BABYLON" should tell us that it is not the actual city of Babylon, but that it is the mystical center of idolatry, and the heart and core of the Roman Empire.

THE GREAT WHORE

In our treatment of this portion of the prophetic Scriptures we are going to offend some people. It cannot be otherwise. We do not want to hurt any, but we must tell the truth as God has given it to us in His Word. We are simply relating that which is prophetic history, its relation to actual history, and the affairs of the world as they really are in our day as foretold by the prophets. This is God's Word! Who ever you are, and whatever your background may be, you had better listen to God. He forewarns us. This is the way God said IT WOULD BE. It was so written by the Apostle over 1900 years ago. Today, as we look out upon our world, we can actually see the very things that John wrote about. The angel said to John:

> . . . *Come higher; I will shew unto thee the judgment of the great whore that sitteth upon MANY WATERS:*
>
> *With whom the kings of the earth have committed FORNICATION, and the inhabitants of the earth have made drunk with the wine of her fornication.*
> (Revelation 17:1-2.)

This "WHORE" is seen to be seated upon "many waters." This, in Scripture, symbolizes "peoples," or "nations" of peoples. Here we are not guessing, but simply understanding the interpretation given to us by the Spirit of God in His inspired Word:

> . . . *The waters which thou sawest, where the whore sitteth, ARE PEOPLES, multitudes, and nations, and tongues.* (Revelation 17:15.)

Thus, the SYMBOL is identified for us. This is speaking of the mastery, the influence, and the power that this "whore" has over the peoples of the world. She holds them in SPIRITUAL BONDAGE and physical subjection. Even "kings," or political leaders give her homage, and honor her with ambassadors, and seek her counsel and blessing. She is called a "whore" because of her illicit, idolatrous, religious unbiblical teachings and practices while claiming to represent God.

Her illicit spiritual relations with the human race proves that, in truth, she is not the lover of our souls. She leads the world away from God and not to God. She is the enemy of the Lamb, while claiming to represent Him. She is not the BRIDE, but a WHORE, and an abomination in the sight of God. FALSE RELIGION is always depicted in Scripture as SPIRITUAL ADULTERY and WHOREDOM. This whorish woman stands in stark contrast to the Woman of Chapter 12, who, as we have seen, wears the Mantle of the Power and Presence of God in this evil world of darkness. This whore is to be judged by God. She clothes herself in PURPLE, and SCARLET, and decks herself with GOLD and precious JEWELS, and PEARLS. This woman is often seen on television, and you read about her in the newspapers of the world. You can often see her lovely pictures in many magazines, and you see her:

> *. . . having a golden cup in her hand full of abominations and filthiness of her fornications.* (Revelation 17:4.)

> *. . . the inhabitants of the earth have been made DRUNK with the wine of her fornication.* (Revelation 17:2.)

I was a missionary in South America for 22 years. I KNOW, in a personal way, the power she has over her people, and even GOVERNMENTS. In her name they will rob, and even kill. She will seek to destroy all who stand in her way. She hates the TRUTH. This whore is guilty of the deaths of thousands upon thousands of the saints of our Lord. She hates the Word of God, and the Lord Himself only knows how many she has tortured to death. Houses of inquisition STILL STAND as a living memorial to those who have died at her hands behind closed doors. In anguish and pain, on the rack, or at the stake, they died for their Lord at the hands of this whore. There is no other religious system in all the world, or in all of history, to which these words of Revelation 17 could better and more fittingly apply. You know who she is. ALL THE WORLD KNOWS, but few dare to even whisper the name, Rome.

> *And I saw the woman drunken with the blood of the saints, and with the blood of the martyrs of Jesus.* (Revelation 17:6.)

She rides upon the Beast. He, Antichrist, and his kingdom supports her and carries her, and she in turn promotes him and his evil design. It is in every way an UNHOLY UNION of RELIGION and POLITICS. Here are the TWO LEGS of the ROMAN EMPIRE, as was seen in Daniel, Chapter Two. This woman is not just religious Rome, but the whole idolatrous system that began back in the time of Nimrod just after the Flood. It was perfected in Babylon, and adopted and applied with satanic leadership in each succeeding world empire, as is indicated by the "heads" of the Beast upon which she rides. She has ridden throughout history, and today is seen in the full strength of her evil power and corrupting influence. This evil, false, corrupt form of "Christianity" is the great whore. At the end, just before the battle of Armageddon, the Beast will destroy the Whore and the seat of the False Prophet.

> *And the ten horns which thou sawest upon the beast, these shall HATE THE WHORE, and shall make her DESOLATE and NAKED, and shall eat her flesh, and burn her with fire.*
>
> *For GOD hath put it in their heart to FULFILL HIS WILL . . .*
> (Revelation 17:16-17.)

As we have indicated, God is SOVEREIGN. God's will shall be accomplished, and Rome, Mystery Babylon, the great WHORE, will be destroyed. We are given a clear statement of fact to confirm our comprehension of this lest some of you think that this is too harsh and judgmental or prejudiced. Please read carefully these following verses:

> *And here is the mind which hath wisdom. The seven heads are seven mountains, on which the woman sitteth.*
> (Revelation 17:9.)
>
> *And the woman which thou sawest IS THAT GREAT CITY, which reigneth over the kings of the earth.*
> (Revelation 17:18.)

There is no other CITY in all the world that can thus be identified, in almost any encyclopedia, as the city of SEVEN HILLS, or "mountains." It is ROME, AND ONLY ROME. The heart and core of

Rome is Vatican City. Without her, Rome would be nothing. It is from the Vatican that the Holy Roman Empire controls the hearts and minds and lives of multitudes, and millions upon millions of souls who are "drunk" with the wine of her fornication, and who will defend her to the death. As for "kings," remember this the next time you see on your television our world's political leaders going before this False Prophet for his blessing and advice. The leader of almost every nation goes there to pay him homage. Yes, this Whore is a city, and there is only one city in all the world that can fill the words of this prophecy. If this is not true, then the Bible is false. If this is not true, then God is a liar, but then, we KNOW that God cannot lie. We would, therefore, with great love and concern for the souls of men, encourage all to heed the Scriptural admonition:

> *Wherefore come out from among them, and be ye*
> *separate, saith the Lord, and touch not the unclean thing:*
> *and I WILL RECEIVE YOU,*
>
> *And will be a Father unto you, and ye shall be my sons*
> *and daughters, saith the Lord Almighty*
> (II Corinthians 6:17-18.)

In Chapter 18 of Revelation we have the death of the City and the System of Satan by Divine judgment. Like God destroyed Sodom of old, Rome will come under His wrath as well. His love for the individual continues, and we see God calling, even today, to those who have been deceived with the "wine" of religion, and are "drunk" with her fornication. Perhaps the Lord is calling to you:

> *. . . Come out of her, my people, that ye be not partakers*
> *of her sins, and that ye receive not of her plagues.*
>
> *For her sins have reached unto heaven, and God hath*
> *remembered her iniquities.* (Revelation 18:4-5.)

Because I am not writing a commentary on this Book, there is much that could be said concerning these two great chapters that I have left unsaid. My purpose, as I have indicated, is to relate the prophetic events of history to the TIME FRAME that God has given to us. This I have tried to do in all honesty. My desire has been to help you see the sequence of the events given to us in these important prophecies.

We have now come to the close of the 70th week of Daniel. The wrath of God has been poured out upon an unrepentant world. The godless armies of the world, under the leadership of the Antichrist and the False Prophet, now gather to fight the conflict of the ages in one last attempt to destroy the Kingdom of Heaven as her King returns in the fullness of His glory.

CHRIST'S RETURN
Revelation, Chapter 19

The return of our Lord is the subject of this exquisite chapter that begins with the Alleluia Chorus. God's righteousness has been vindicated, and the union of the Lamb with His people has fully come. The resurrection of all remaining saints of God occurs at this time. The saints are now all clothed in the righteousness of the Lord, and there is great joy among the ranks of the saved and in the heavens.

Christ is seen to descend from Heaven upon a white horse, signifying His glorious majesty and great power. The armies of heaven follow Him. This army consists of both the angelic and the saved of all ages. We come to reign with Christ. First, however, the earth must be purged of all corruption and evil. As in the days of Noah, God will remove every unsaved person in this last judgment at the Battle of Armageddon. Christ is seen to smite the enemy with the "sword of His mouth." Just as He created, even so now He destroys, with the Word of His mouth. From this we see that this long feared battle is short lived.

The earth will be covered with the bodies of the dead, and the fowls of the air are called together to eat the flesh of all the dead.

Remember the 144,000? They will have survived by the grace and protection of God. Perhaps there will be a few other Jewish believers with them, and maybe some children, but this would be pure speculation. The Divine record simply indicates that the earth will be "reaped," and that those who have believed will have been killed by the Antichrist. As in the Flood of Noah's time, EIGHT SOULS were delivered, so it would seem that in this judgment also few will be delivered to enter the Kingdom of our Lord. It will in all truth be a new beginning once again.

CHRIST'S KINGDOM
Chapter 20

The Antichrist and the False Prophet are now taken prisoner, and then cast ALIVE into the Lake of Fire that we know to be eternal hell. They are not killed, but will live and suffer eternal damnation, as will every lost soul. It is at this time that we read concerning Satan:

And He laid on the dragon, that old serpent, which is the Devil, and Satan, and bound him a thousand years,

And cast him into a bottomless pit, and set a seal upon him, that he should deceive the nations no more, till the thousand years should be fulfilled: and after that he must be loosed a little season. (Revelation 20:2-3.)

This is plain speech and we are to take it for what it says. There are those who think that we are actually in that time now, when Satan is bound. How blind can one be? We must be very careful not to nullify the Word of God by simplistic, humanistic thinking.

With the binding of Satan, the one thousand years of the Kingdom Age begins. The earth will be repopulated during these wonderful years of the reign of Christ. Evil will be banished and quickly judged as it raises its ugly head. The earth will again become like the Garden of Eden. The only difference is that man is not now innocent. Man still has his sinful nature, and until each individual surrenders to the Lordship of the Saviour, sin will remain enclosed in his heart. The possibility of this sin surfacing is always there, and it is for this reason that Christ will rule with a "rod of iron." This indicates swift judgment. When rebellion arises it is at once put down and the perpetrator judged.

Many will be saved during this time. All will have the need of salvation, except for those few who entered the kingdom at its inception, for they had already believed. However, as strange as it may seem to us, there will be many who will be submissive to the will of the Lord only because of the fear of judgment, but their hearts have never been cleansed by the Blood through faith. Their hearts harbor sin hidden deep within. The seed of rebellion is there, waiting.

Consequently, when Satan is loosed from his bonds at the close of the thousand year reign of righteousness, he finds many hearts ripe for his deception and evil desire. These will follow him in one last great rebellion against God and His Son, against all that is holy. Evil in the hearts of many, that has been silently awaiting the opportunity for expression, will quickly respond to the Devil's call. They will follow him to their own doom. They will be defeated in their attempt to wrest control from the Saviour, and are slain. The Devil is, at this time, taken and cast into the Lake of Fire where the Antichrist and the False Prophet have been for the past one thousand years. Only these three, and probably their demonic army of fallen angels, are there in hell. Hell was made for them.

THE GREAT WHITE THRONE

When the devil has been cast into the Lake of Fire, we next find the event of this great day of the judgment involving the lost souls of mankind. It is at this time, after the Kingdom of Christ has closed, that all the lost of all ages will be resurrected. The resurrection of the SAVED ended at the beginning of the Kingdom: that was the "First Resurrection."

From this we sense that those saved during the Kingdom Age will not die, but will live the entire length of the Kingdom Age. They would, of necessity, have to be transformed, or "changed," like the living at the time of the Rapture.

Here, though, we find the resurrection of the LOST, as the DEAD stand before Him that sits upon the Throne. That this throne is "white," would indicate absolute righteous judgment of the Lord God. Time has passed. History is over, and the Divine record books are opened. The Lamb's Book of Life is also opened, and all who are not found to be written in the Book of Life are cast into the Lake of Fire and judged by those things written in the other books.

There is no possibility of salvation here. There is no grace or mercy here. The only recourse is HELL. There is no escape. Some may foolishly say, "Well, I'll have a lot of friends in hell." You may have a lot of your friends here now that will be in hell also, but they will not be friends there. There will be no "partying" in hell. There will be no card games, gambling parties, drinking parties, or "get togethers" there. There will be only suffering and eternal torment, alone, in the darkness of everlasting blackness and despair, forever separated from the love and light of the Lord. You don't want to go to HELL! Evil is now forevermore banished to hell. It will never reappear.

The saints of the Lord, those who have been "washed in his own blood," and born of the Spirit will dwell with God and with the Lamb in the New Heaven and the New Earth. This is the subject of the final two chapters of this wonderful Book.

THE LAMB'S BRIDE

It is most interesting to see the Scriptural identification of the Lamb's Bride. We use a lot of clichés, and preachers and teachers make a lot of statements that are not necessarily Scripturally correct. We should want to be correct, in all that we say and teach, Scripturally. Here is an interesting Scriptural statement. It is what the angel told John:

> . . . *Come hither, I will shew thee THE BRIDE, THE LAMB'S WIFE.*
>
> *And he carried me away in the spirit to a great mountain and shewed me the GREAT CITY, THE HOLY JERUSALEM, descending out of heaven from God.* (Revelation 21:9-10.)

We know that this "city," as shown to John, was not just a city of buildings and streets. It was a city of PEOPLE! It was where PEOPLE were and lived. A closer look at this "city" will give us some indication of the make up of its people. Remember, that this "city" is identified by the angel as the BRIDE OF CHRIST. We find that this "city":

> ... had a wall great and high, and had TWELVE gates, and at the gates twelve angels, and names written thereon, which are the names of the TWELVE TRIBES of the CHILDREN OF ISRAEL. (Revelation 21:12.)

> And the wall of the city had TWELVE foundations, and in them the names of THE TWELVE APOSTLES OF THE LAMB. (Revelation 21:14.)

This is the dwelling place of God as he now dwells with His people forevermore, as is told to us in Revelation 21:3. This New Jerusalem, this heavenly city, will be the center of all activity throughout eternity, and this CITY is identified as the Lamb's Bride.

From the verses seen above there is no way that this can be understood to be only believers of the New Testament times. It appears from these statements of Scripture that believers under both the Old Covenant and the New Covenant are, together, the Bride of the Lamb. We, together, are the "city," and the "city" is the Bride. I see no other way of understanding this. If this is a problem for you then I would suggest that you carefully examine all the Scriptures dealing with the subject, but be careful not to read into any Scripture your own preconceived thoughts. Let Scripture shape your thinking. How beautiful heaven must be! What a joy to be His forever!

> And there shall in no wise enter into it any thing that defileth, neither whatsoever worketh abomination, or maketh a lie: but THEY WHICH ARE WRITTEN IN THE LAMB'S BOOK OF LIFE. (Revelation 21:27.)

If you have never surrendered your life and heart to the Saviour, I beg you to do so now. Just stop where you are, whatever you are doing, and give your heart to Jesus while the door of grace is yet open to you. The Lord loves YOU! Christ died for you, and He is coming again. When He comes, will He come as your Lord and Saviour, or will He come as your Lord and Judge? Remember that He is Sovereign Lord, and His will SHALL be done. May His grace, mercy, love and peace be with you.

Seek ye the Lord while he may be found, call ye upon him while he is near:

Let the wicked forsake his way, and the unrighteous man his thoughts: and let him return unto the Lord, and he will have mercy upon him: and to our God, for he will abundantly pardon.

For my thoughts are not your thoughts, neither are your ways my ways, saith the Lord.

For as the heavens are higher than the earth, so are my ways higher than your ways, and my thoughts than your thoughts.

For rain cometh down, and the snow from heaven, and returneth not thither, but watereth the earth, and maketh it bring forth and bud, that it may give seed to the sower, and bread to the eater:

SO SHALL MY WORD BE THAT GOETH FORTH OUT OF MY MOUTH: IT SHALL NOT RETURN UNTO ME VOID, BUT IT SHALL ACCOMPLISH THAT WHICH I PLEASE, AND IT SHALL PROSPER IN THE THING WHERE TO I SEND IT. (Isaiah 55:6-11.)

COME, LORD JESUS

We shall walk the streets of gold,
And the beauty of our Lord behold.
We shall sing His praise forever,
Leave His side again, no, never.
We shall live within His light,
Enjoy forever the beauty of His sight.
We shall live within the blessed City,

Never know again, for sin, His pity.
   All shall be pure Joy and delight,
Always day, and never night.
   The sunshine of his smiling face,
Singing, always, Amazing Grace.
   Jesus, O Jesus, come for us soon;
Split the skies at midnight, or at noon.
   Let us hear your blessed voice;
The trumpet call is our clear choice.
   We long to be with You forever;
Heaven's our home, the darkness, never.

Pastor, Harry Powell

GOD'S TIME FRAME: The Essence of Prophecy

would make an ideal gift. Birthday . . . anniversary . . . Christmas. Also, a perfect gift for the serious Bible student.

To order, fill in the appropriate space and send check or money order. We accept VISA and MASTERCARD orders.
(404) 518-1890

Name:_____

Address:_____

_____

I would like to purchase _____ copies of *God's Time Frame*. Enclosed is my payment of_____ .

OLD RUGGED CROSS PRESS
1160 Alpharetta Street, Suite H
Roswell, GA 30075
(404) 518-1890
We accept VISA or MASTERCARD.

OTHER BOOKS BY OLD RUGGED CROSS PRESS

☐ SAY YOU'RE NOT LEAVING, DADDY
Will Lester / Paperback / $4.95 / 136 pages.
A young father is contemplating divorce. The breakup of his family seems inevitable. Only his young son is willing to fight to save his family. *SAY YOU'RE NOT LEAVING, DADDY* is a book about the power of prayer that you will remember long after you've read the last page.

☐ THE GOSPEL OF MARK IN VERSE
Paul Buchheit / Paperback / $5.95 / 81 pages.
THE GOSPEL OF MARK IN VERSE is one of the most creative books about the Book of Mark published in years. Mr. Buchheit writes with great passion. His book will prove helpful to people who have yet to experience the healing power of God's love.

☐ A BANGED UP ANGEL
Joyce Price / Paperback / $6.95 / 192 pages.
"We will not give the child up," the young woman exclaimed.
"Tracy, you're not being practical," the old man replied in a stern voice.
Tracy reached down and picked the five-year-old boy up. As she gazed into Ted's angelic face, another small boy's face flashed before her, the same face she had seen so many times in her nightmares. "I'll never let you take Ted from me," she screamed. "Never!"

☐ HE CALLED HIMSELF THE SON OF MAN
Norman MacLeod / Paperback / $12.95 / 358 pages.
HE CALLED HIMSELF THE SON OF MAN will shatter any complacency you may have about being a Christian. Compelling . . . honest . . . provocative.
A book that should be read by serious Bible students. Whether or not you agree with Mr. MacLeod's point of view, his book will provoke you into re-examining your views on the Trinity.

☐ SOLDIER – PRIEST
John J. Morrett / Paperback / $12.95 / 332 pages / 22 photos.
SOLDIER – PRIEST is a moving testimony to the power of faith in a young soldier's darkest hours.
Captured by the Japanese during the Battle of Bataan, it was his faith in God that sustained him, giving him the strength and courage to help his fellow prisoners-of-war.

These books may be purchased by sending check or money order to:
OLD RUGGED CROSS PRESS
1160 Alpharetta Street, Suite H
Roswell, GA 30075
(404) 518 - 1890
We accept VISA and MASTERCARD.

OTHER BOOKS BY OLD RUGGED CROSS PRESS

☐ FAR JOURNEY: A Psychiatrist's Chronicle
   Dr. Yitzhak Hanu / Hardcover / $21.95 / 298 pages.
FAR JOURNEY is the story of therapy, of mythic symbol . . . of the psychic dance between patient and healer . . . and healer to his soul. *FAR JOURNEY* begins and ends at the interface between psychiatry and religion, dissolving the boundary which has for too long separated the two.

☐ MESSIAH MAN
   Dr. Russell L. Jaberg / Paperback / $12.95 / 338 pages.
Among these countless stories are men and women who live in uncertainty, who struggle against staggering odds, who die in obscurity. The glory of many of them is that the dignity of man is in them an unquenched flame. This is the story of one such man . . . Rev. Daniel Witt Clark.

☐ EYES THAT SEE
   Bertha Ives Petersen / Paperback / $5.95 / 122 pages.
EYES THAT SEE focuses on the great prophet, Isaiah. Ms. Petersen breathes life into Isaiah, allowing the reader to understand both the man and the society in which he lived. *EYES THAT SEE* is a remarkable book.

☐ PERSPECTIVES FROM THE PASSENGER SEAT
   David Overson / Paperback / $8.95 / 112 pages.
Feeling low? Down in the dumps? If so, begin reading this delightful collection of anecdotes about how joyful life can be. Some will inspire you . . . others will motivate you to take a fresh look at your life . . . while others will cause you to laugh out loud!

☐ THE LONG ROAD
   A. E. Morris / Paperback / $12.95 / 153 pages.
THE LONG ROAD is a marvelous book about life in rural Indiana in the 1880's. It is a nostalgic look back at a time when sleepy little hamlets like Little Pigeon Creek Valley held annual parades down narrow main streets.

These books may be purchased by sending check or money order to:
OLD RUGGED CROSS PRESS
1160 Alpharetta Street, Suite H
Roswell, GA 30075
(404) 518 - 1890
We accept VISA and MASTERCARD.